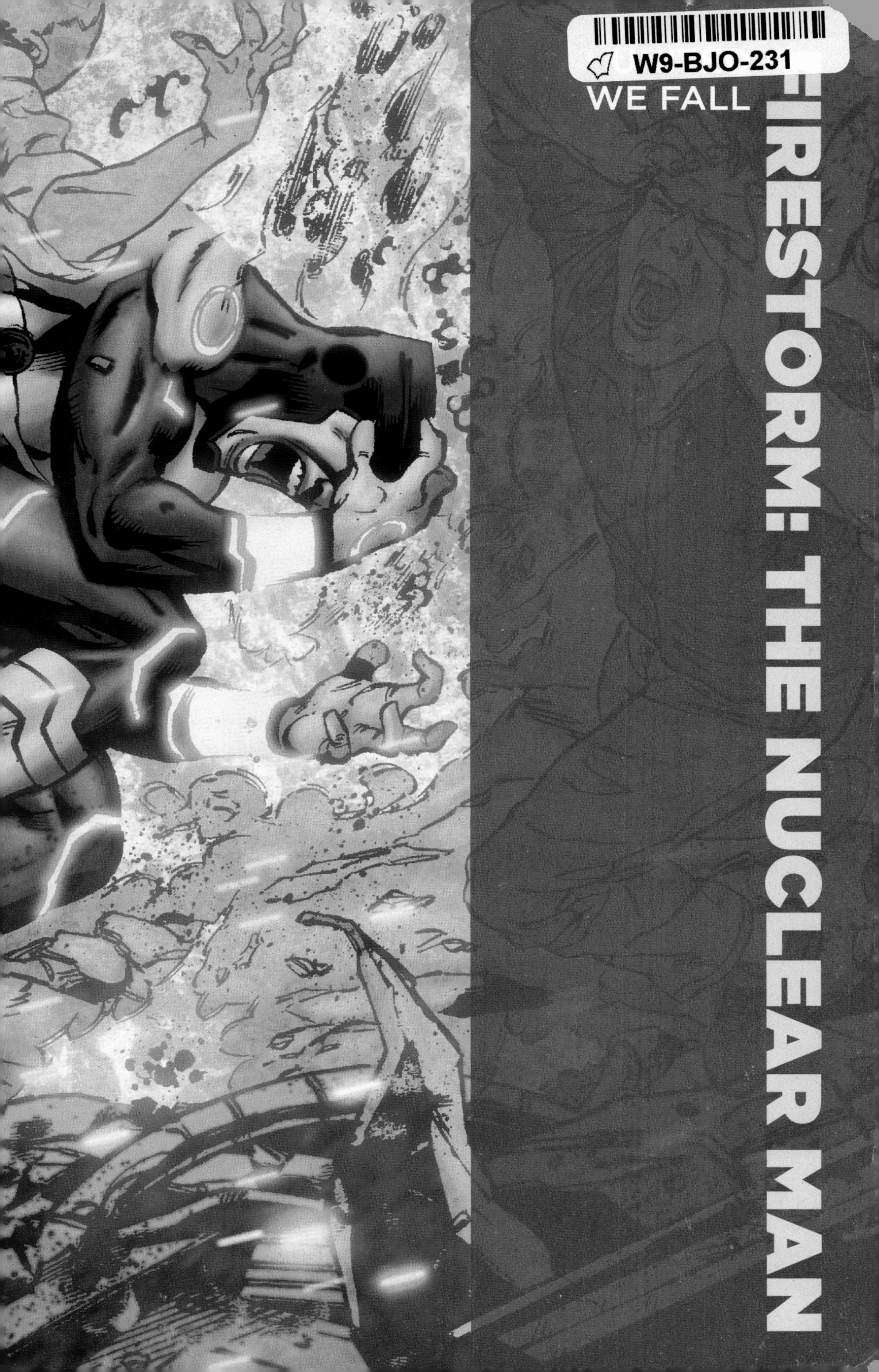
WE FALL
FIRESTORM: THE NUCLEAR MAN

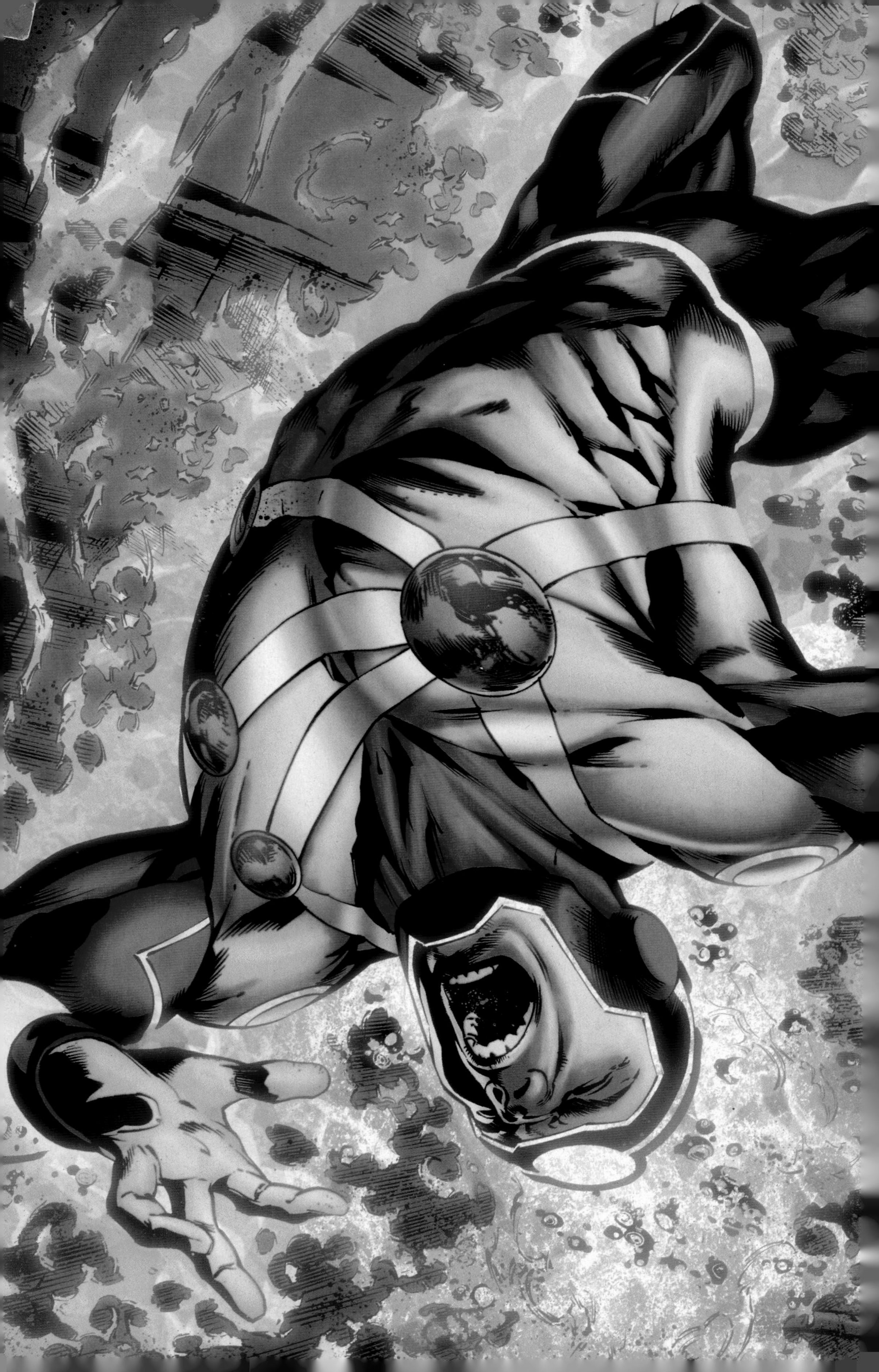

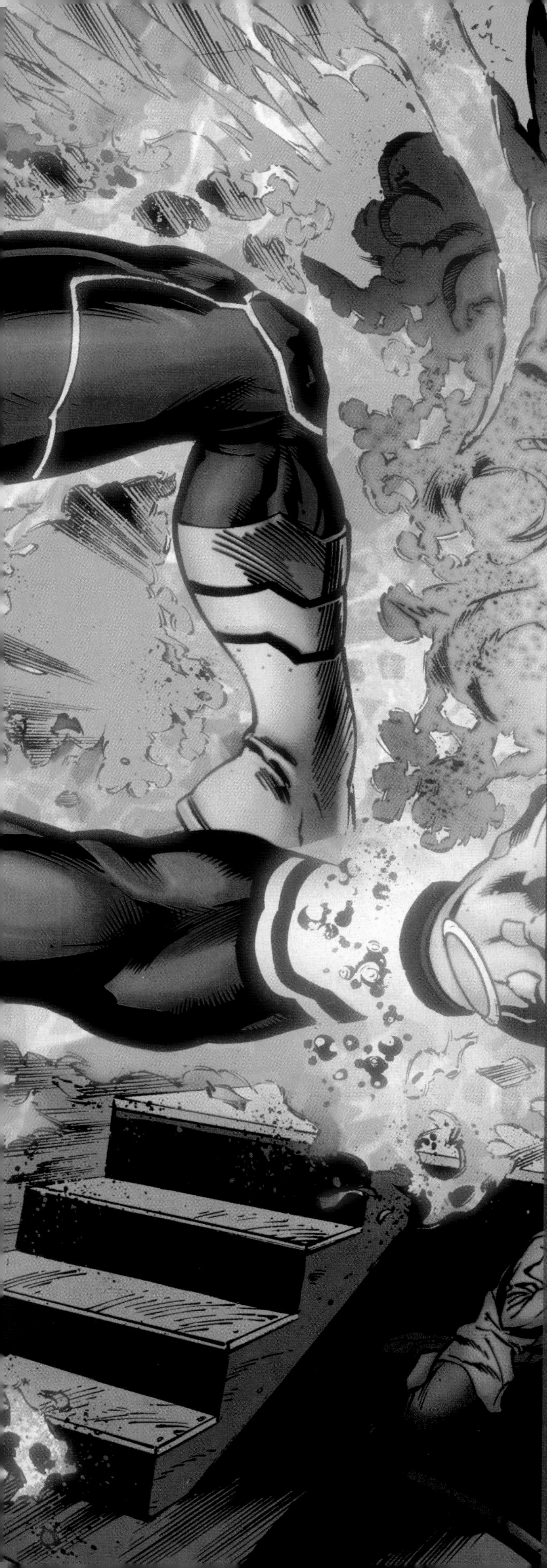

FIRESTORM: THE NUCLEAR MAN

UNITED WE FALL

WRITTEN BY
GERRY CONWAY

PENCILS BY
EDUARDO PANSICA

INKS BY
ROB HUNTER

COLOR BY
ANDREW DALHOUSE

LETTERS BY
COREY BREEN

COLLECTION COVER ART BY
CARY NORD
GABRIEL ELTAEB

FIRESTORM
CREATED BY
GERRY CONWAY
AND **ALLEN MILGROM**

JESSICA CHEN Editor – Original Series
JEB WOODARD Group Editor – Collected Editions
SUZANNAH ROWNTREE Editor – Collected Edition
STEVE COOK Design Director – Books
DAMIAN RYLAND Publication Design

BOB HARRAS Senior VP – Editor-in-Chief, DC Comics

DIANE NELSON President
DAN DIDIO Publisher
JIM LEE Publisher
GEOFF JOHNS President & Chief Creative Officer
AMIT DESAI Executive VP – Business & Marketing Strategy, Direct to Consumer & Global Franchise Management
SAM ADES Senior VP – Direct to Consumer
BOBBIE CHASE VP – Talent Development
MARK CHIARELLO Senior VP – Art, Design & Collected Editions
JOHN CUNNINGHAM Senior VP – Sales & Trade Marketing
ANNE DEPIES Senior VP – Business Strategy, Finance & Administration
DON FALLETTI VP – Manufacturing Operations
LAWRENCE GANEM VP – Editorial Administration & Talent Relations
ALISON GILL Senior VP – Manufacturing & Operations
HANK KANALZ Senior VP – Editorial Strategy & Administration
JAY KOGAN VP – Legal Affairs
THOMAS LOFTUS VP – Business Affairs
JACK MAHAN VP – Business Affairs
NICK J. NAPOLITANO VP – Manufacturing Administration
EDDIE SCANNELL VP – Consumer Marketing
COURTNEY SIMMONS Senior VP – Publicity & Communications
JIM (SKI) SOKOLOWSKI VP – Comic Book Specialty Sales & Trade Marketing
NANCY SPEARS VP – Mass, Book, Digital Sales & Trade Marketing

FIRESTORM: THE NUCLEAR MAN – UNITED WE FALL

Published by DC Comics. Compilation and all new material Copyright © 2016 DC Comics. All Rights Reserved.

Originally published in single magazine form in LEGENDS OF TOMORROW 1-6. Copyright © 2016 DC Comics. All Rights Reserved. All characters, their distinctive likenesses and related elements featured in this publication are trademarks of DC Comics. The stories, characters and incidents featured in this publication are entirely fictional. DC Comics does not read or accept unsolicited submissions of ideas, stories or artwork.

DC Comics, 2900 West Alameda Ave., Burbank, CA 91505
Printed by Solisco Printers, Scott, QC, Canada. 11/4/16. First Printing.
ISBN: 978-1-4012-6578-6

Library of Congress Cataloging-in-Publication Data is available.

PEFC Certified

This product is from
sustainably managed
forests, recycled and
controlled sources

PEFC/26-31-02   www.pefc.org

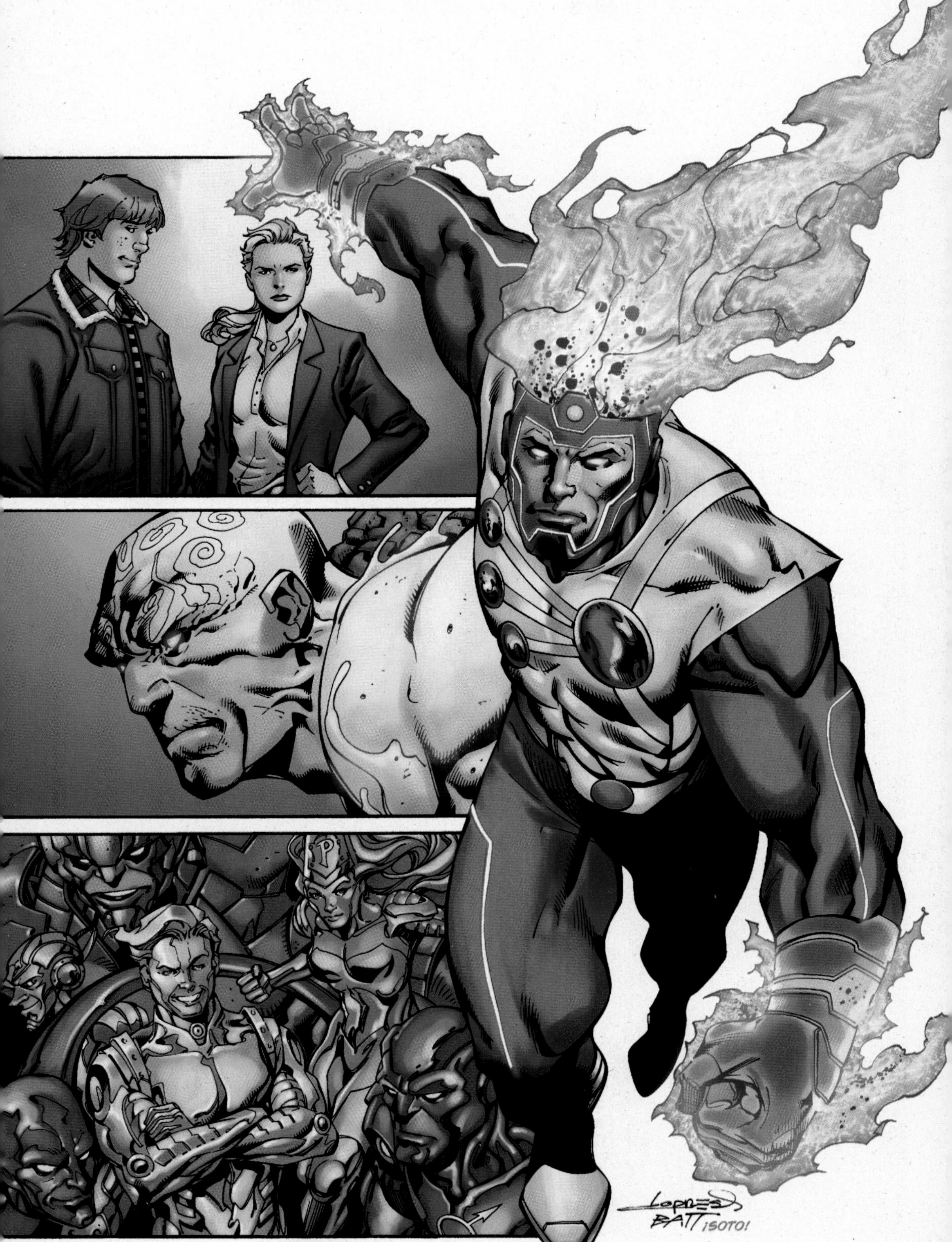

GERRY CONWAY writer **EDUARDO PANSICA** penciller **ROB HUNTER** inker **ANDREW DALHOUSE** colorist **COREY BREEN** letterer
AARON LOPRESTI and **MATT BANNING** with **CHRIS SOTOMAYOR** cover

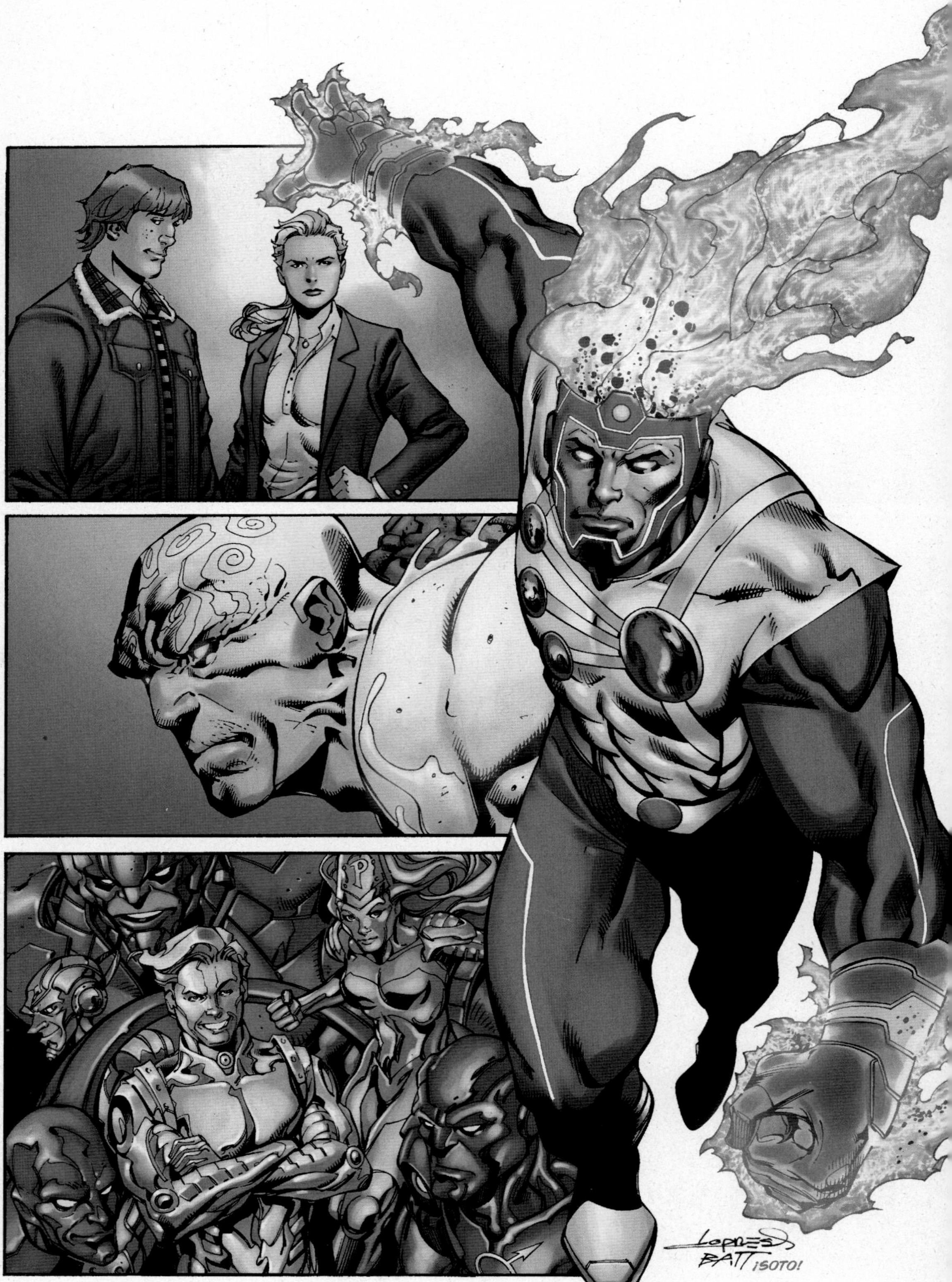
¡SOTO!

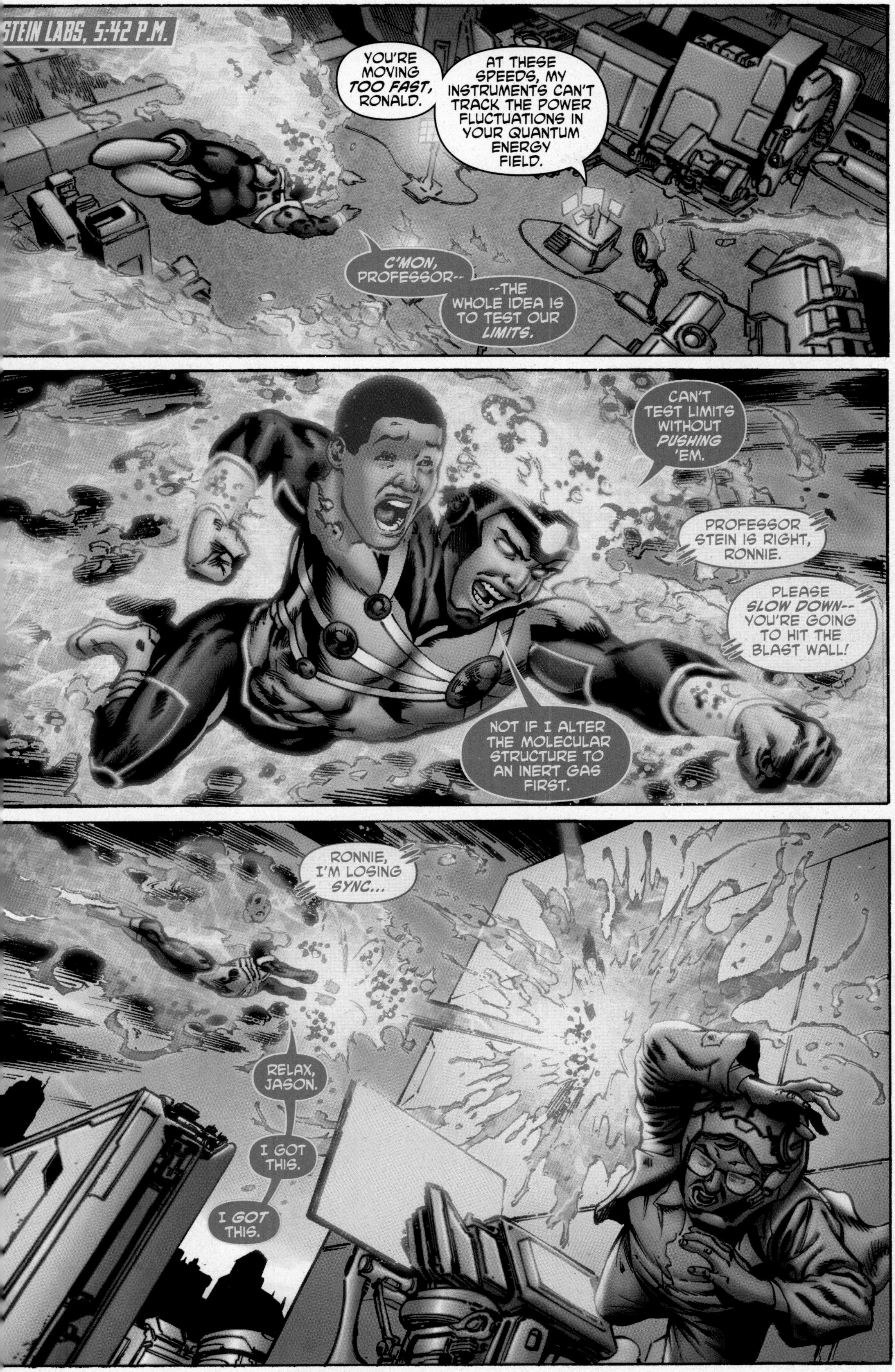
STEIN LABS, 5:42 P.M.
YOU'RE MOVING TOO FAST, RONALD.
AT THESE SPEEDS, MY INSTRUMENTS CAN'T TRACK THE POWER FLUCTUATIONS IN YOUR QUANTUM ENERGY FIELD.
C'MON, PROFESSOR--
--THE WHOLE IDEA IS TO TEST OUR LIMITS.
CAN'T TEST LIMITS WITHOUT PUSHING 'EM.
PROFESSOR STEIN IS RIGHT, RONNIE.
PLEASE SLOW DOWN--YOU'RE GOING TO HIT THE BLAST WALL!
NOT IF I ALTER THE MOLECULAR STRUCTURE TO AN INERT GAS FIRST.
RONNIE, I'M LOSING SYNC...
RELAX, JASON.
I GOT THIS.
I GOT THIS.

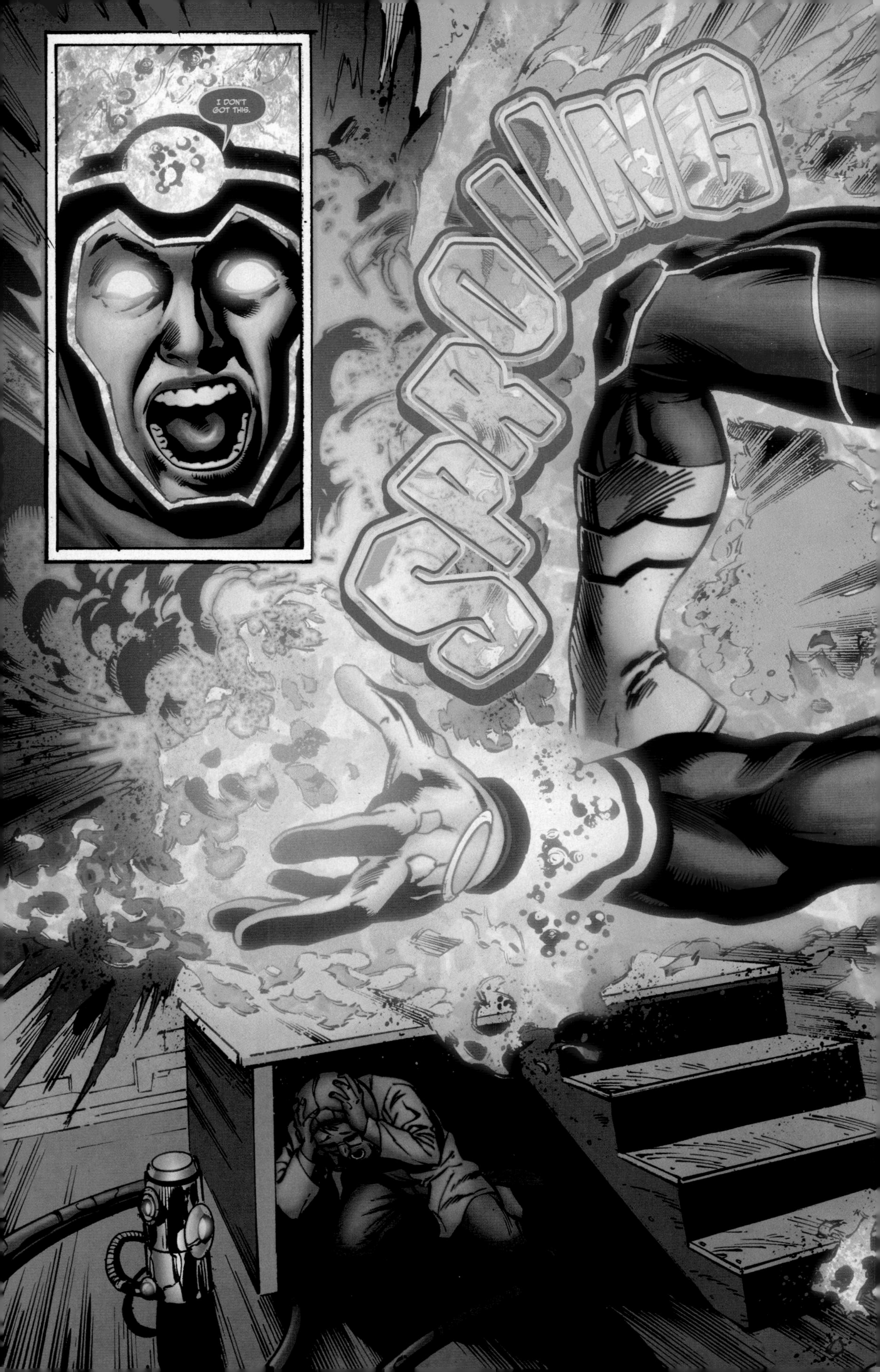
I DON'T GOT THIS.
SPROING

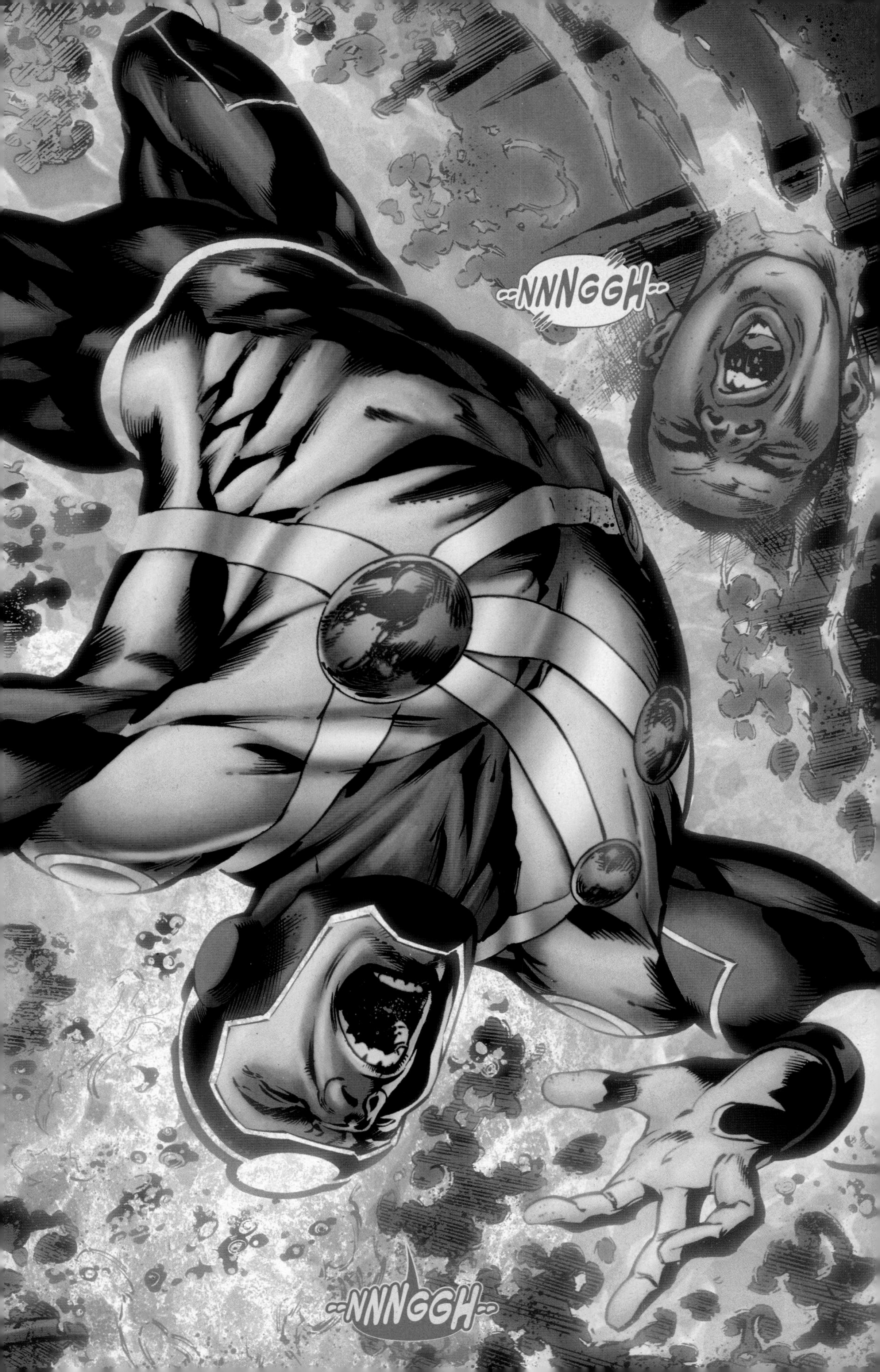
--NNNGGH--
--NNNGGH--

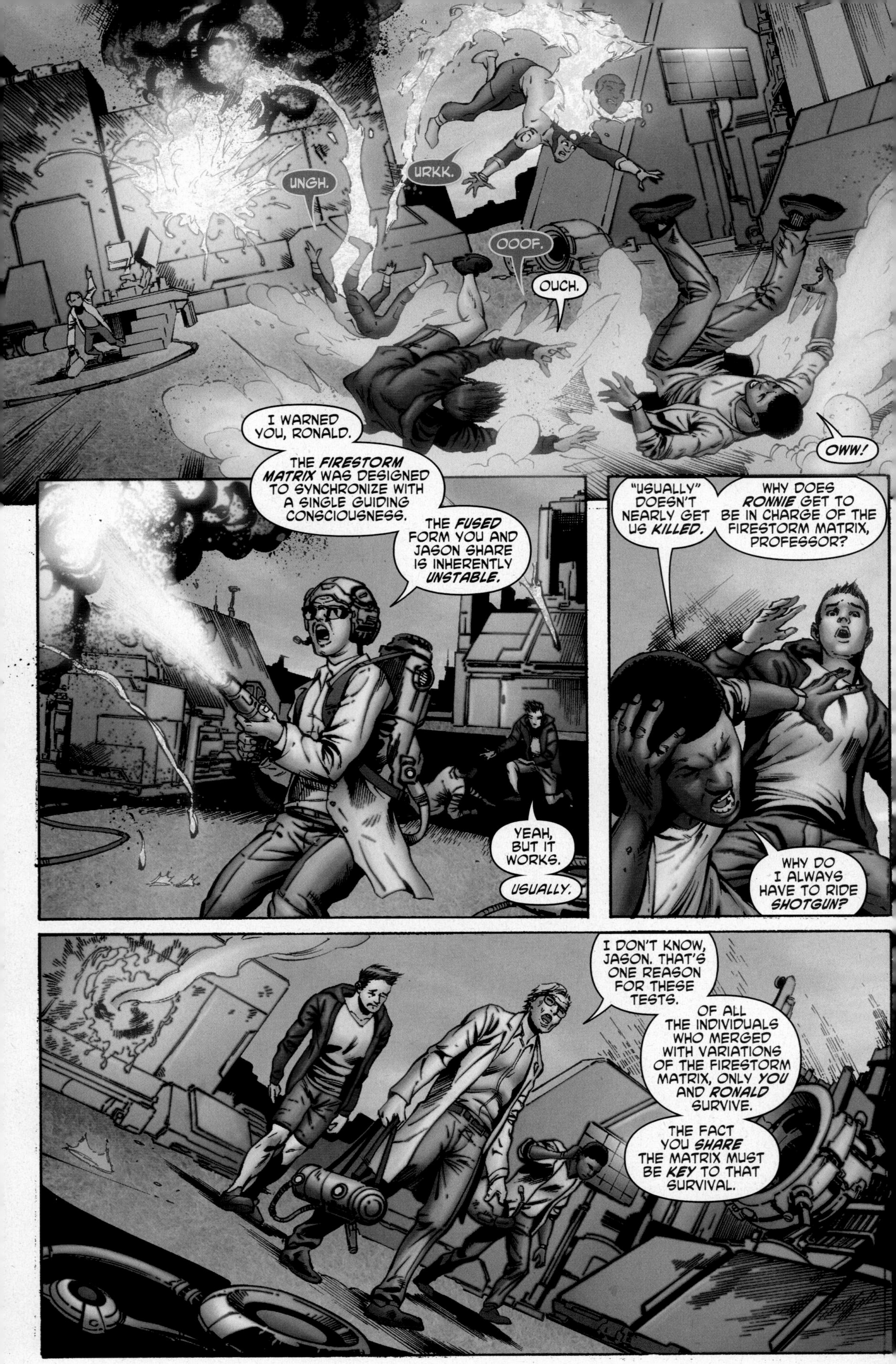
UNGH.
URKK.
OOOF.
OUCH.
OWW!
I WARNED YOU, RONALD.
THE FIRESTORM MATRIX WAS DESIGNED TO SYNCHRONIZE WITH A SINGLE GUIDING CONSCIOUSNESS.
THE FUSED FORM YOU AND JASON SHARE IS INHERENTLY UNSTABLE.
YEAH, BUT IT WORKS.
USUALLY.
"USUALLY" DOESN'T NEARLY GET US KILLED.
WHY DOES RONNIE GET TO BE IN CHARGE OF THE FIRESTORM MATRIX, PROFESSOR?
WHY DO I ALWAYS HAVE TO RIDE SHOTGUN?
I DON'T KNOW, JASON. THAT'S ONE REASON FOR THESE TESTS.
OF ALL THE INDIVIDUALS WHO MERGED WITH VARIATIONS OF THE FIRESTORM MATRIX, ONLY YOU AND RONALD SURVIVE.
THE FACT YOU SHARE THE MATRIX MUST BE KEY TO THAT SURVIVAL.

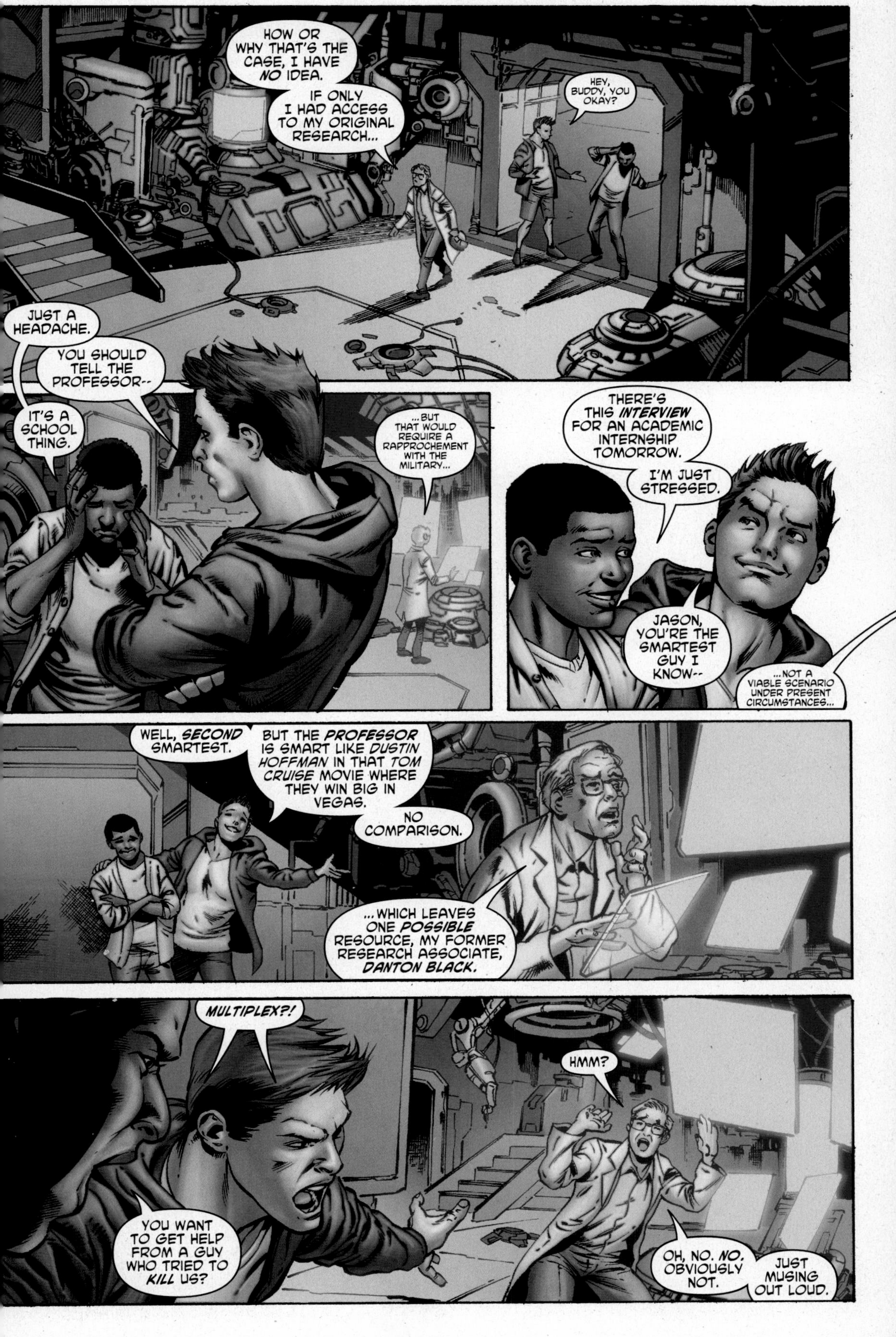
HOW OR WHY THAT'S THE CASE, I HAVE NO IDEA.
IF ONLY I HAD ACCESS TO MY ORIGINAL RESEARCH...
HEY, BUDDY, YOU OKAY?
JUST A HEADACHE.
YOU SHOULD TELL THE PROFESSOR--
IT'S A SCHOOL THING.
...BUT THAT WOULD REQUIRE A RAPPROCHEMENT WITH THE MILITARY...
THERE'S THIS INTERVIEW FOR AN ACADEMIC INTERNSHIP TOMORROW.
I'M JUST STRESSED.
JASON, YOU'RE THE SMARTEST GUY I KNOW--
...NOT A VIABLE SCENARIO UNDER PRESENT CIRCUMSTANCES...
WELL, SECOND SMARTEST.
BUT THE PROFESSOR IS SMART LIKE DUSTIN HOFFMAN IN THAT TOM CRUISE MOVIE WHERE THEY WIN BIG IN VEGAS.
NO COMPARISON.
...WHICH LEAVES ONE POSSIBLE RESOURCE, MY FORMER RESEARCH ASSOCIATE, DANTON BLACK.
MULTIPLEX?!
HMM?
YOU WANT TO GET HELP FROM A GUY WHO TRIED TO KILL US?
OH, NO. NO. OBVIOUSLY NOT.
JUST MUSING OUT LOUD.

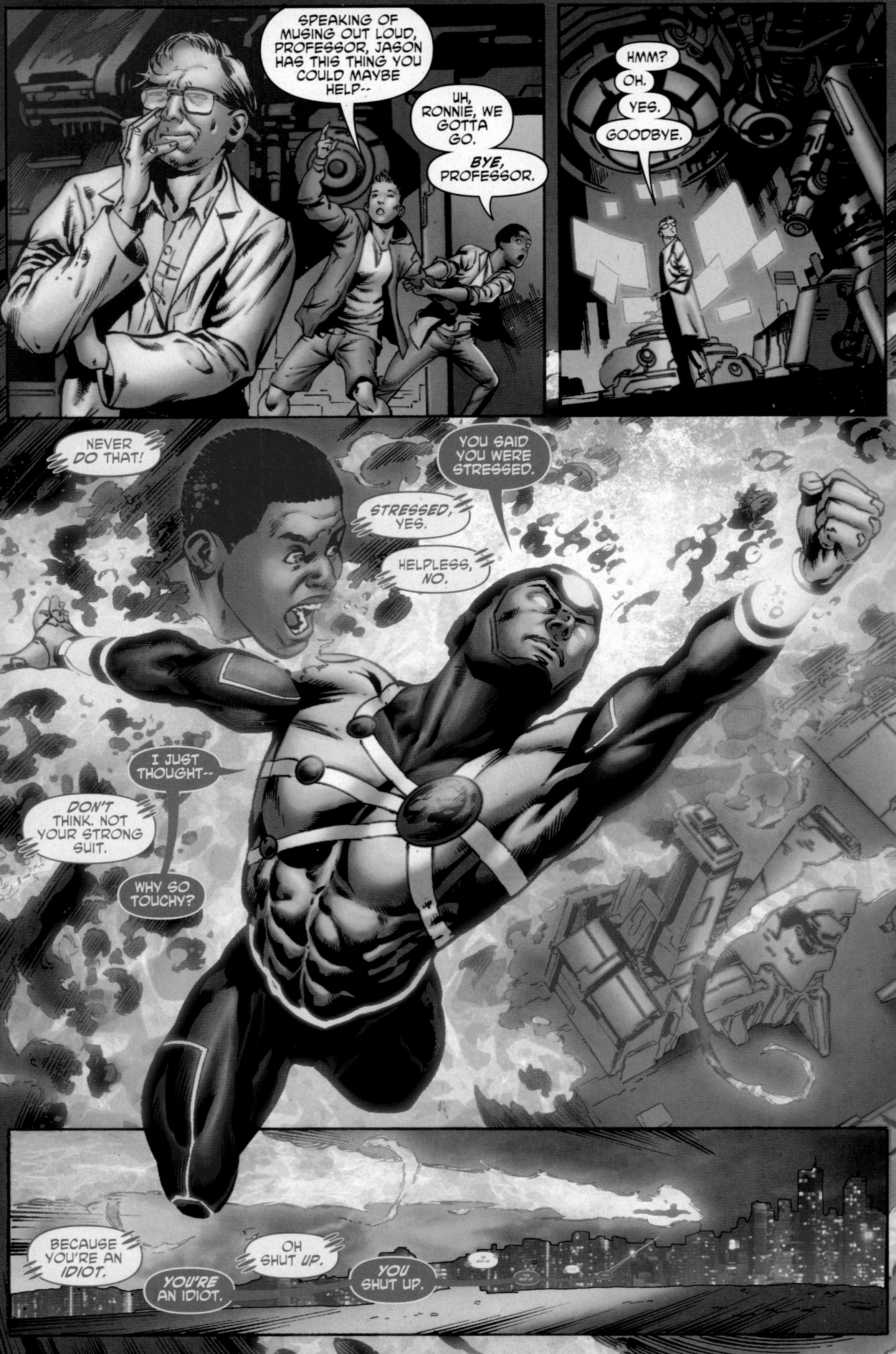
SPEAKING OF MUSING OUT LOUD, PROFESSOR, JASON HAS THIS THING YOU COULD MAYBE HELP--
UH, RONNIE, WE GOTTA GO.
BYE, PROFESSOR.
HMM?
OH.
YES.
GOODBYE.
NEVER DO THAT!
YOU SAID YOU WERE STRESSED.
STRESSED, YES.
HELPLESS, NO.
I JUST THOUGHT--
DON'T THINK. NOT YOUR STRONG SUIT.
WHY SO TOUCHY?
BECAUSE YOU'RE AN IDIOT.
YOU'RE AN IDIOT.
OH SHUT UP.
YOU SHUT UP.

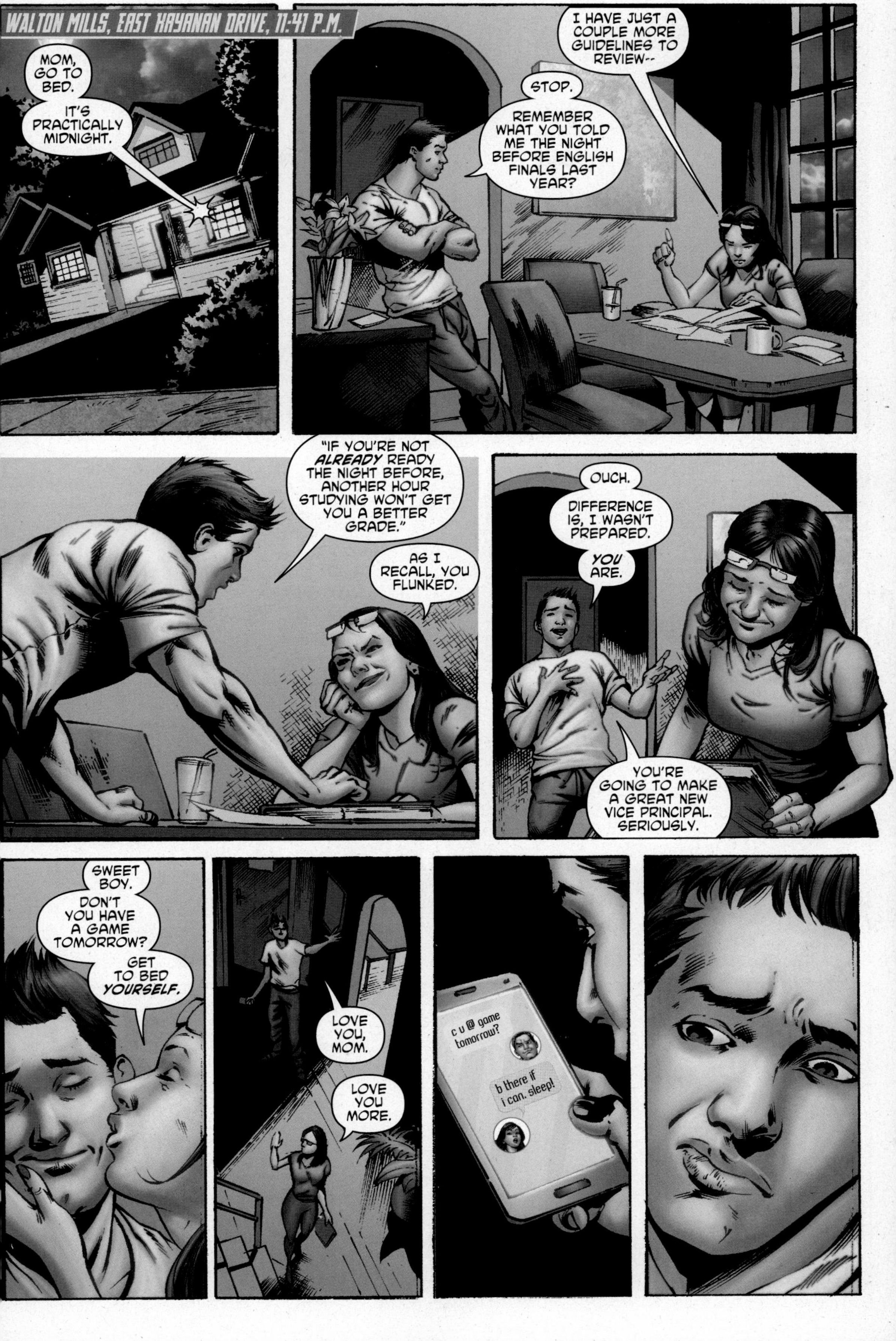
WALTON MILLS, EAST KAYANAN DRIVE, 11:41 P.M.
MOM, GO TO BED.
IT'S PRACTICALLY MIDNIGHT.
I HAVE JUST A COUPLE MORE GUIDELINES TO REVIEW--
STOP.
REMEMBER WHAT YOU TOLD ME THE NIGHT BEFORE ENGLISH FINALS LAST YEAR?
"IF YOU'RE NOT ALREADY READY THE NIGHT BEFORE, ANOTHER HOUR STUDYING WON'T GET YOU A BETTER GRADE."
AS I RECALL, YOU FLUNKED.
OUCH.
DIFFERENCE IS, I WASN'T PREPARED.
YOU ARE.
YOU'RE GOING TO MAKE A GREAT NEW VICE PRINCIPAL. SERIOUSLY.
SWEET BOY.
DON'T YOU HAVE A GAME TOMORROW?
GET TO BED YOURSELF.
LOVE YOU, MOM.
LOVE YOU MORE.
c u @ game tomorrow?
b there if i can. sleep!

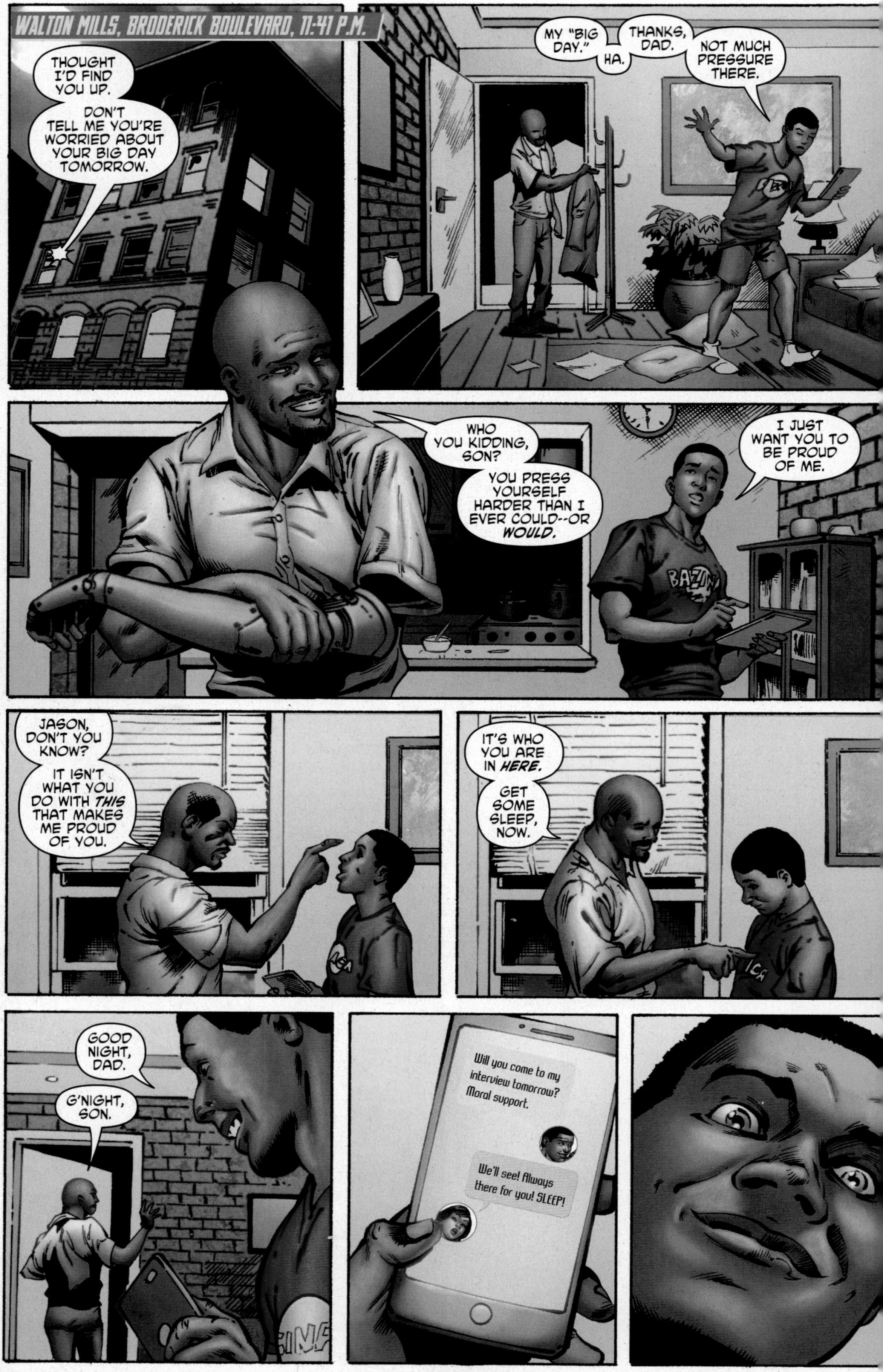

WALTON MILLS, BRODERICK BOULEVARD, 11:41 P.M.
THOUGHT I'D FIND YOU UP.
DON'T TELL ME YOU'RE WORRIED ABOUT YOUR BIG DAY TOMORROW.
MY "BIG DAY."
HA.
THANKS, DAD.
NOT MUCH PRESSURE THERE.
WHO YOU KIDDING, SON?
YOU PRESS YOURSELF HARDER THAN I EVER COULD--OR *WOULD.*
I JUST WANT YOU TO BE PROUD OF ME.
JASON, DON'T YOU KNOW?
IT ISN'T WHAT YOU DO WITH *THIS* THAT MAKES ME PROUD OF YOU.
IT'S WHO YOU ARE IN *HERE.*
GET SOME SLEEP, NOW.
GOOD NIGHT, DAD.
G'NIGHT, SON.
Will you come to my interview tomorrow? Moral support.
We'll see! Always there for you! SLEEP!

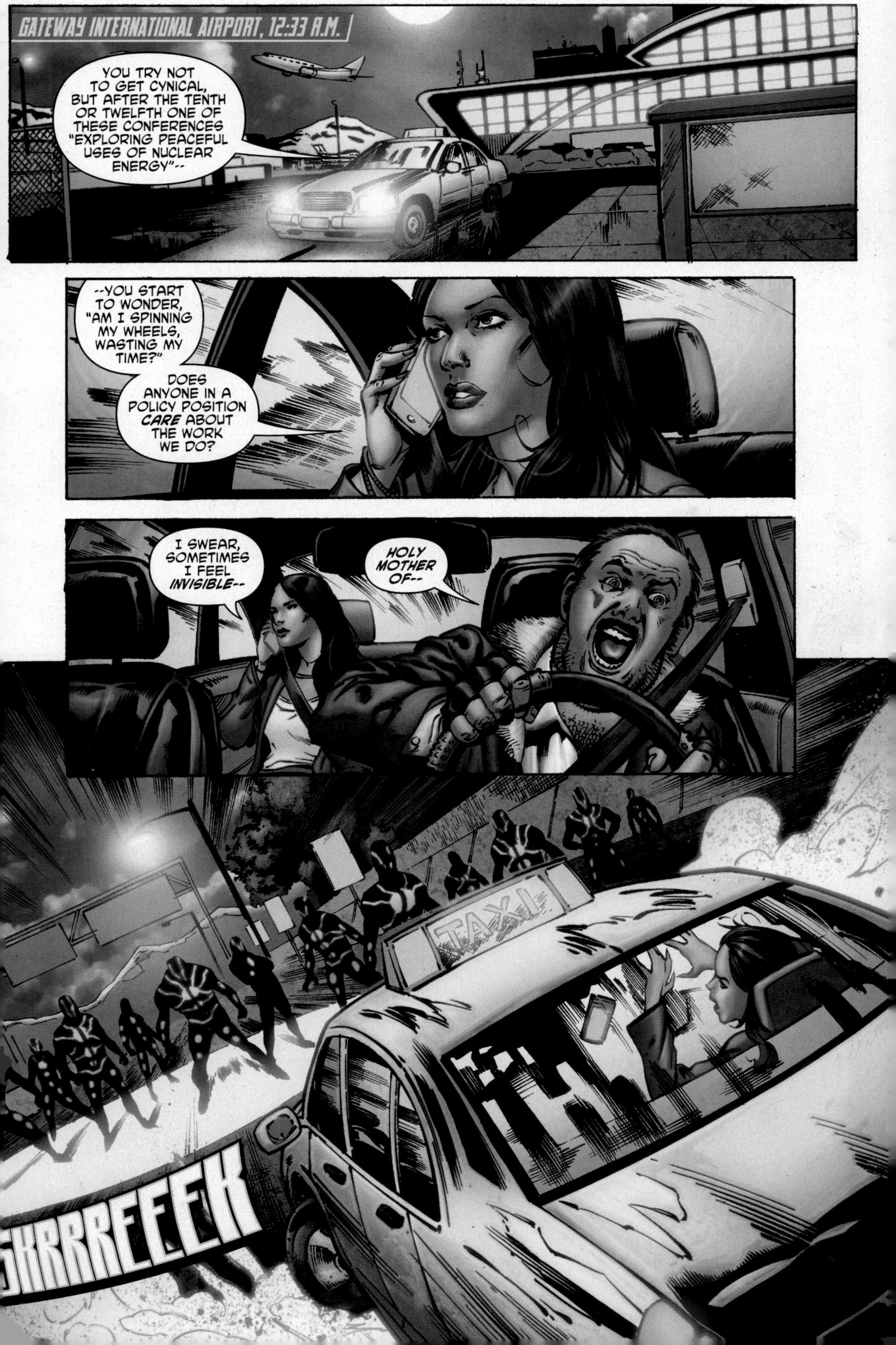
GATEWAY INTERNATIONAL AIRPORT, 12:33 A.M.
YOU TRY NOT TO GET CYNICAL, BUT AFTER THE TENTH OR TWELFTH ONE OF THESE CONFERENCES "EXPLORING PEACEFUL USES OF NUCLEAR ENERGY"--
--YOU START TO WONDER, "AM I SPINNING MY WHEELS, WASTING MY TIME?"
DOES ANYONE IN A POLICY POSITION CARE ABOUT THE WORK WE DO?
I SWEAR, SOMETIMES I FEEL INVISIBLE--
HOLY MOTHER OF--
TAXI
SKRRREEEK

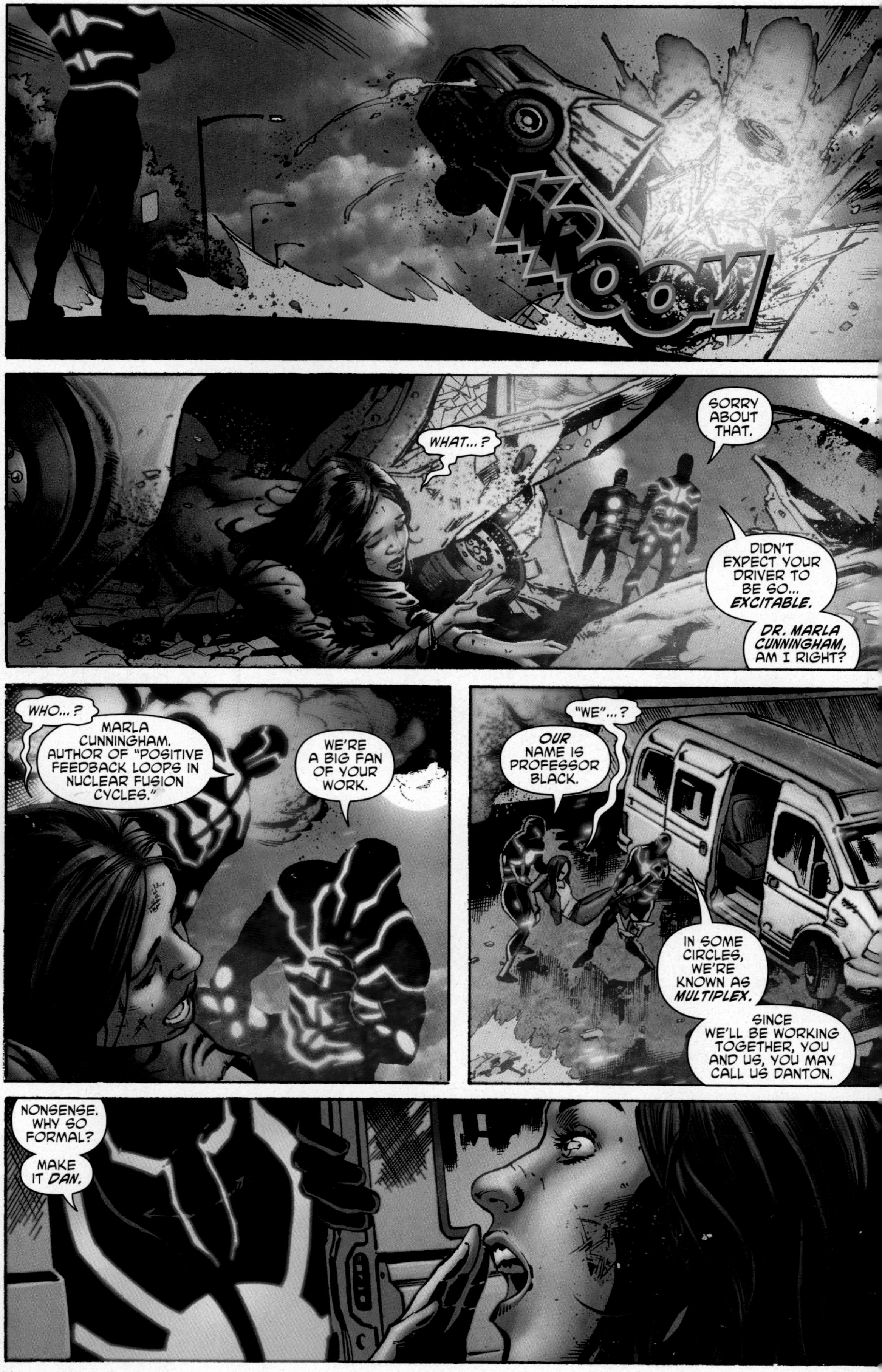
KROOOM
WHAT...?
SORRY ABOUT THAT.
DIDN'T EXPECT YOUR DRIVER TO BE SO... EXCITABLE.
DR. MARLA CUNNINGHAM, AM I RIGHT?
WHO...?
MARLA CUNNINGHAM. AUTHOR OF "POSITIVE FEEDBACK LOOPS IN NUCLEAR FUSION CYCLES."
WE'RE A BIG FAN OF YOUR WORK.
"WE"...?
OUR NAME IS PROFESSOR BLACK.
IN SOME CIRCLES, WE'RE KNOWN AS MULTIPLEX.
SINCE WE'LL BE WORKING TOGETHER, YOU AND US, YOU MAY CALL US DANTON.
NONSENSE. WHY SO FORMAL?
MAKE IT DAN.

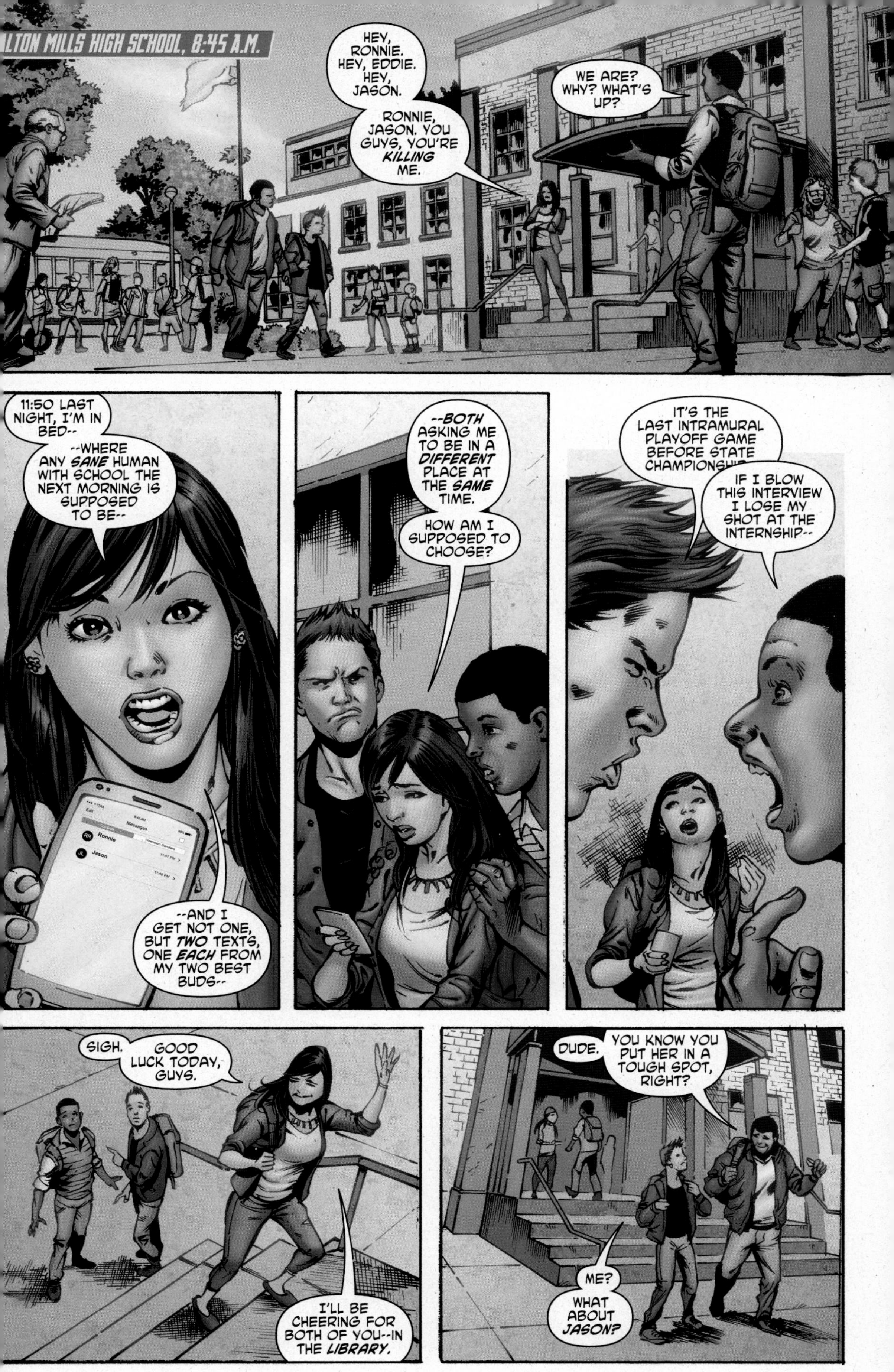

LTON MILLS HIGH SCHOOL, 8:45 A.M.
HEY, RONNIE. HEY, EDDIE. HEY, JASON.
RONNIE, JASON. YOU GUYS, YOU'RE KILLING ME.
WE ARE? WHY? WHAT'S UP?
11:50 LAST NIGHT, I'M IN BED--
--WHERE ANY SANE HUMAN WITH SCHOOL THE NEXT MORNING IS SUPPOSED TO BE--
--AND I GET NOT ONE, BUT TWO TEXTS, ONE EACH FROM MY TWO BEST BUDS--
--BOTH ASKING ME TO BE IN A DIFFERENT PLACE AT THE SAME TIME.
HOW AM I SUPPOSED TO CHOOSE?
IT'S THE LAST INTRAMURAL PLAYOFF GAME BEFORE STATE CHAMPIONSH--
IF I BLOW THIS INTERVIEW I LOSE MY SHOT AT THE INTERNSHIP--
SIGH.
GOOD LUCK TODAY, GUYS.
I'LL BE CHEERING FOR BOTH OF YOU--IN THE LIBRARY.
DUDE.
YOU KNOW YOU PUT HER IN A TOUGH SPOT, RIGHT?
ME? WHAT ABOUT JASON?

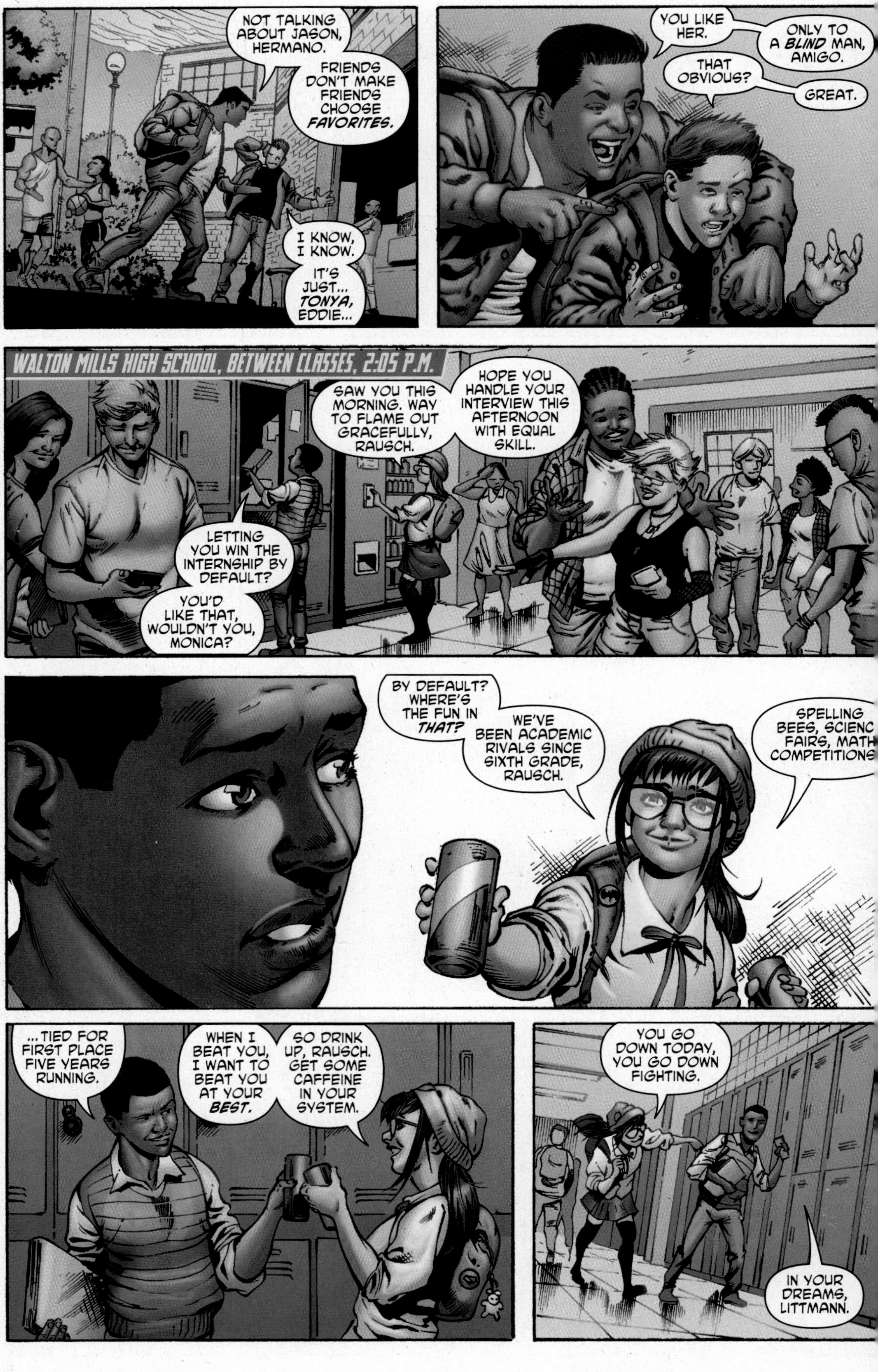

NOT TALKING ABOUT JASON, HERMANO.
FRIENDS DON'T MAKE FRIENDS CHOOSE *FAVORITES.*
I KNOW, I KNOW.
IT'S JUST... *TONYA,* EDDIE...
YOU LIKE HER.
THAT OBVIOUS?
ONLY TO A *BLIND* MAN, AMIGO.
GREAT.
WALTON MILLS HIGH SCHOOL, BETWEEN CLASSES, 2:05 P.M.
SAW YOU THIS MORNING. WAY TO FLAME OUT GRACEFULLY, RAUSCH.
HOPE YOU HANDLE YOUR INTERVIEW THIS AFTERNOON WITH EQUAL SKILL.
LETTING YOU WIN THE INTERNSHIP BY DEFAULT?
YOU'D LIKE THAT, WOULDN'T YOU, MONICA?
BY DEFAULT? WHERE'S THE FUN IN *THAT?*
WE'VE BEEN ACADEMIC RIVALS SINCE SIXTH GRADE, RAUSCH.
SPELLING BEES, SCIENC FAIRS, MATH COMPETITIONS
...TIED FOR FIRST PLACE FIVE YEARS RUNNING.
WHEN I BEAT YOU, I WANT TO BEAT YOU AT YOUR *BEST.*
SO DRINK UP, RAUSCH. GET SOME CAFFEINE IN YOUR SYSTEM.
YOU GO DOWN TODAY, YOU GO DOWN FIGHTING.
IN YOUR DREAMS, LITTMANN.

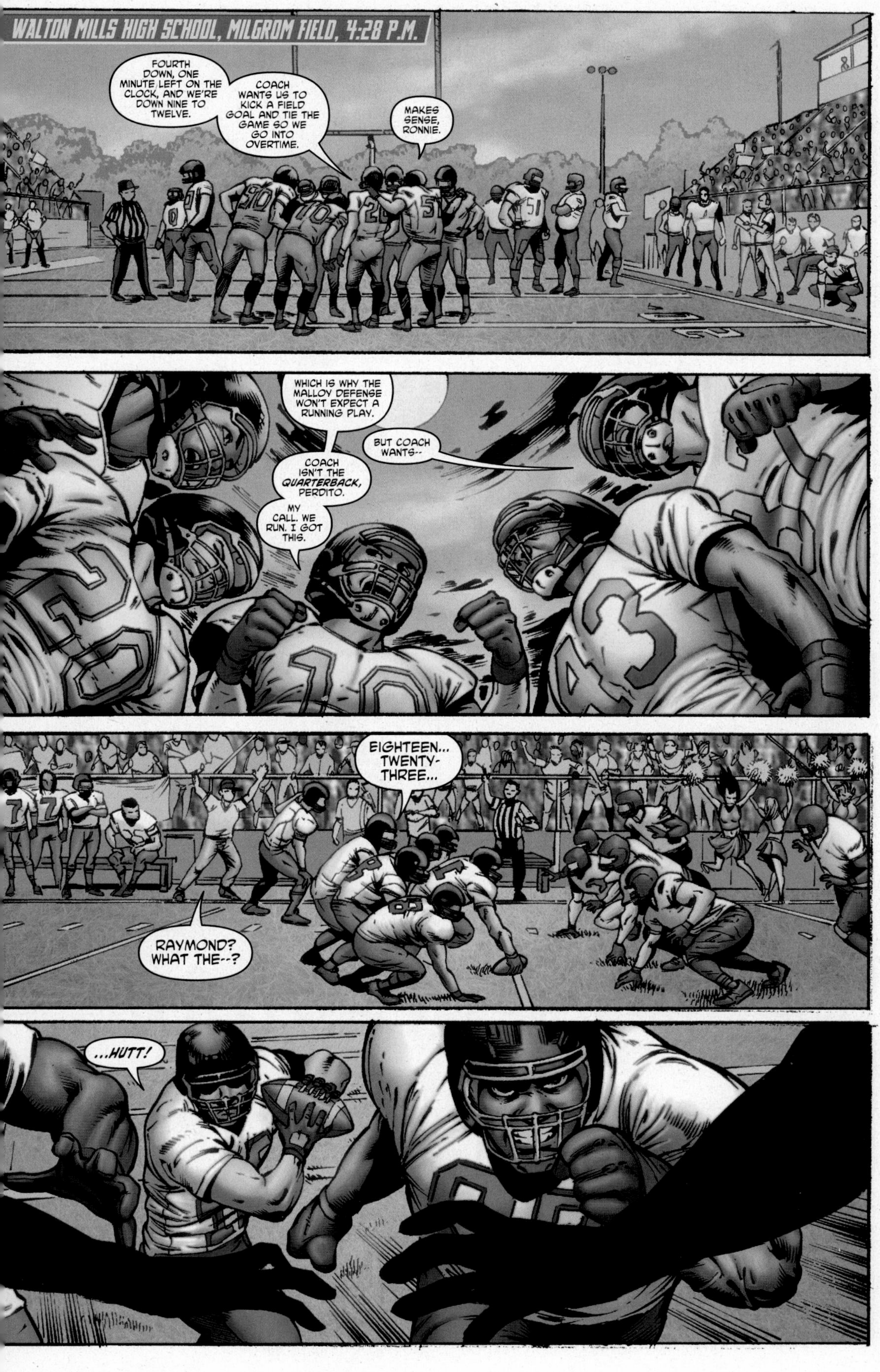
WALTON MILLS HIGH SCHOOL, MILGROM FIELD, 4:28 P.M.
FOURTH DOWN, ONE MINUTE LEFT ON THE CLOCK, AND WE'RE DOWN NINE TO TWELVE.
COACH WANTS US TO KICK A FIELD GOAL AND TIE THE GAME SO WE GO INTO OVERTIME.
MAKES SENSE, RONNIE.
WHICH IS WHY THE MALLOY DEFENSE WON'T EXPECT A RUNNING PLAY.
BUT COACH WANTS--
COACH ISN'T THE *QUARTERBACK,* PERDITO.
MY CALL. WE RUN. I GOT THIS.
EIGHTEEN... TWENTY-THREE...
RAYMOND? WHAT THE--?
...HUTT!

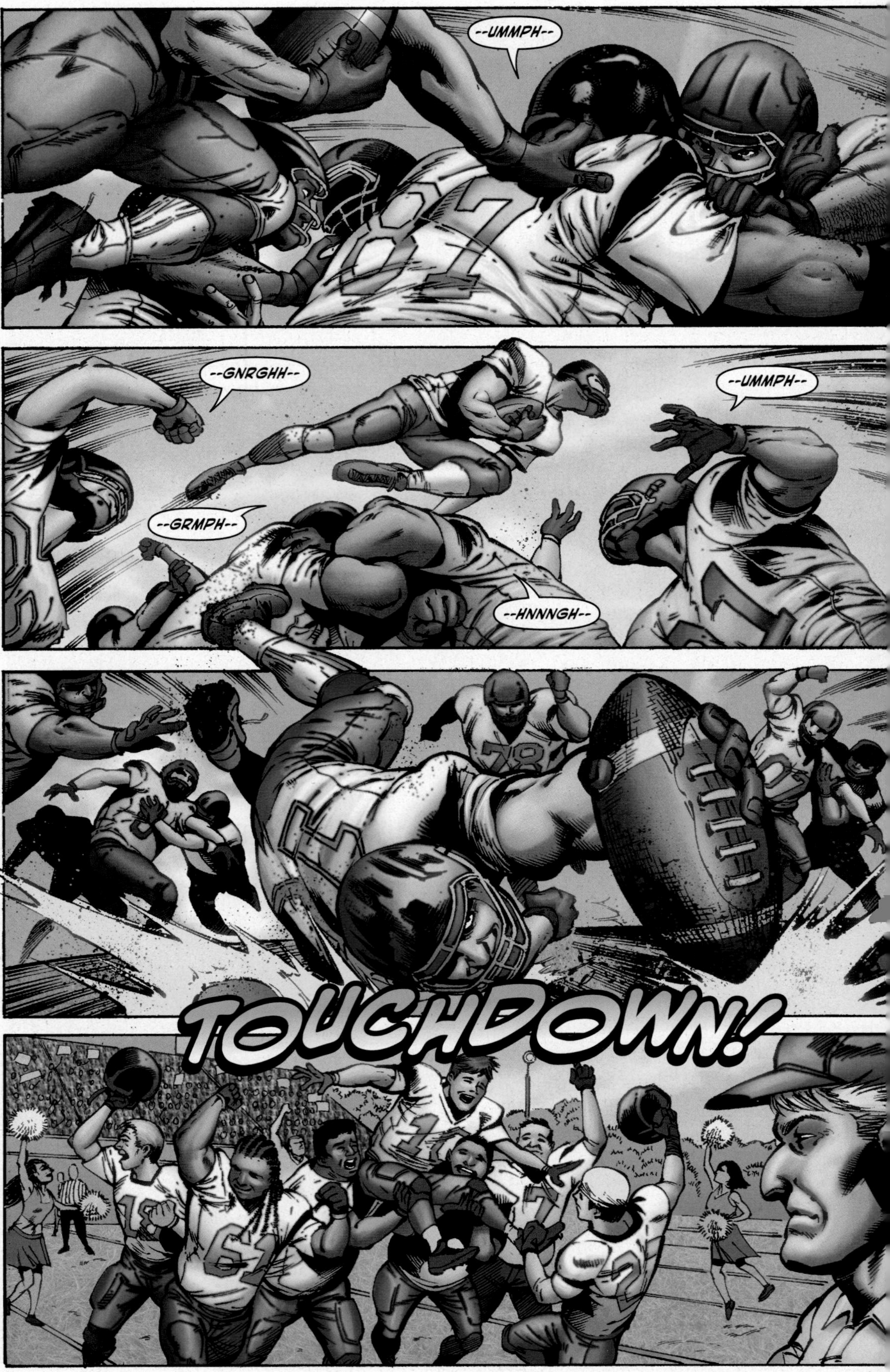
--UMMPH--
--GNRGHH--
--UMMPH--
--GRMPH--
--HNNNGH--
TOUCHDOWN!

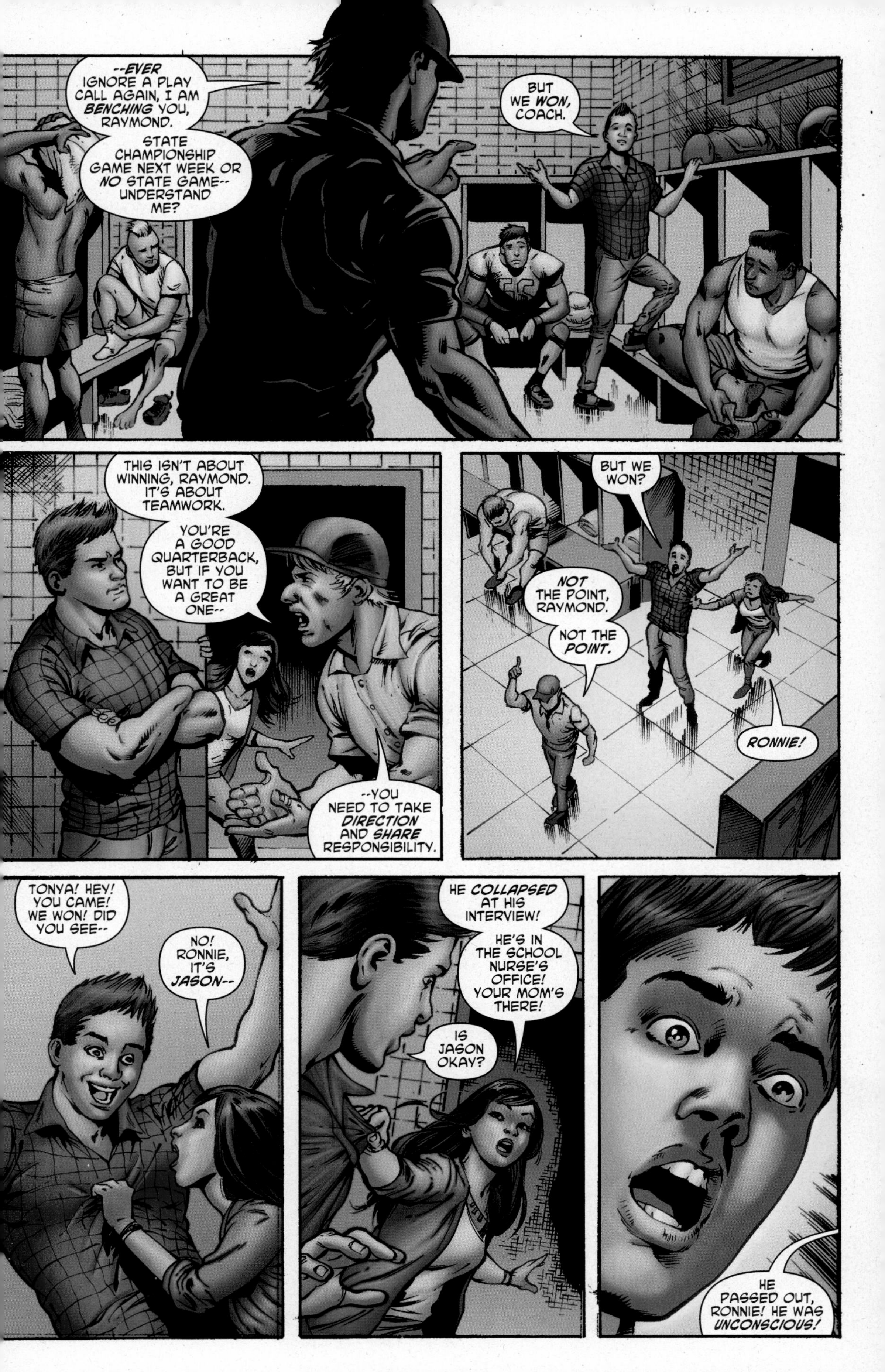
--EVER IGNORE A PLAY CALL AGAIN, I AM BENCHING YOU, RAYMOND.
STATE CHAMPIONSHIP GAME NEXT WEEK OR NO STATE GAME--UNDERSTAND ME?
BUT WE WON, COACH.
THIS ISN'T ABOUT WINNING, RAYMOND. IT'S ABOUT TEAMWORK.
YOU'RE A GOOD QUARTERBACK, BUT IF YOU WANT TO BE A GREAT ONE--
--YOU NEED TO TAKE DIRECTION AND SHARE RESPONSIBILITY.
BUT WE WON?
NOT THE POINT, RAYMOND.
NOT THE POINT.
RONNIE!
TONYA! HEY! YOU CAME! WE WON! DID YOU SEE--
NO! RONNIE, IT'S JASON--
HE COLLAPSED AT HIS INTERVIEW!
HE'S IN THE SCHOOL NURSE'S OFFICE! YOUR MOM'S THERE!
IS JASON OKAY?
HE PASSED OUT, RONNIE! HE WAS UNCONSCIOUS!

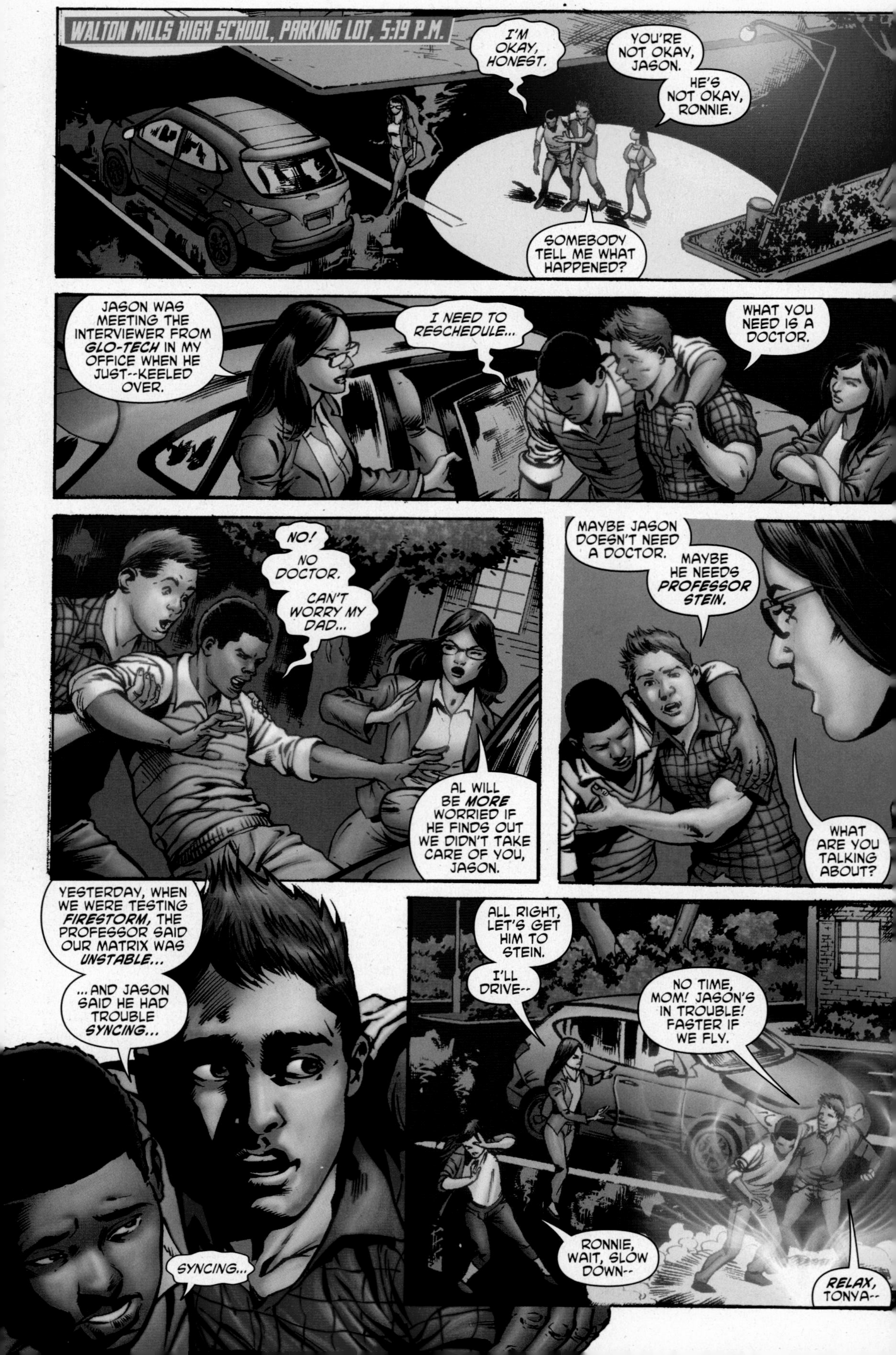
WALTON MILLS HIGH SCHOOL, PARKING LOT, 5:19 P.M.
I'M OKAY, HONEST.
YOU'RE NOT OKAY, JASON.
HE'S NOT OKAY, RONNIE.
SOMEBODY TELL ME WHAT HAPPENED?
JASON WAS MEETING THE INTERVIEWER FROM GLO-TECH IN MY OFFICE WHEN HE JUST--KEELED OVER.
I NEED TO RESCHEDULE...
WHAT YOU NEED IS A DOCTOR.
NO! NO DOCTOR.
CAN'T WORRY MY DAD...
AL WILL BE MORE WORRIED IF HE FINDS OUT WE DIDN'T TAKE CARE OF YOU, JASON.
MAYBE JASON DOESN'T NEED A DOCTOR.
MAYBE HE NEEDS PROFESSOR STEIN.
WHAT ARE YOU TALKING ABOUT?
YESTERDAY, WHEN WE WERE TESTING FIRESTORM, THE PROFESSOR SAID OUR MATRIX WAS UNSTABLE...
...AND JASON SAID HE HAD TROUBLE SYNCING...
SYNCING...
ALL RIGHT, LET'S GET HIM TO STEIN.
I'LL DRIVE--
NO TIME, MOM! JASON'S IN TROUBLE! FASTER IF WE FLY.
RONNIE, WAIT, SLOW DOWN--
RELAX, TONYA--

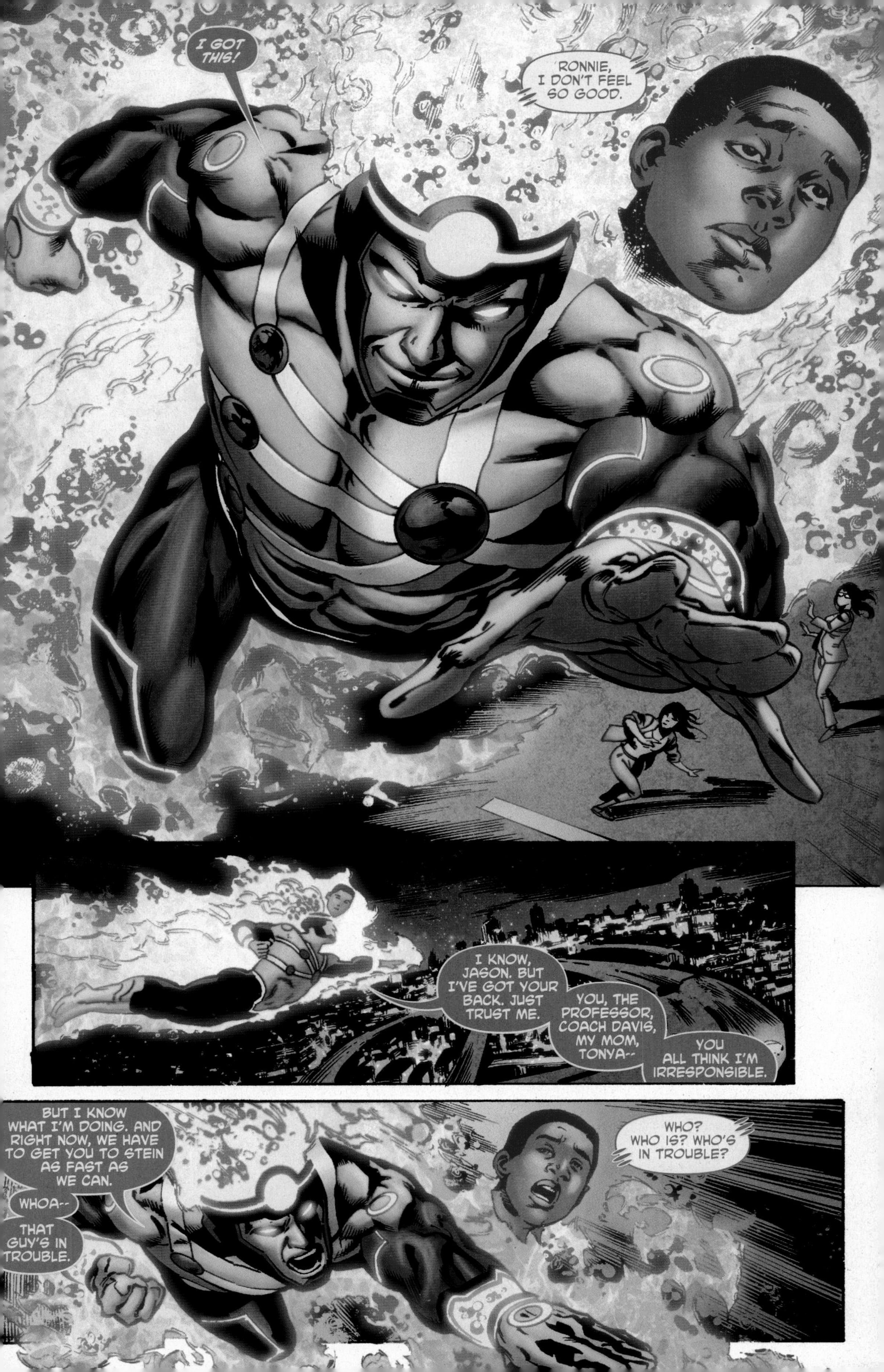

I GOT THIS!
RONNIE, I DON'T FEEL SO GOOD.
I KNOW, JASON. BUT I'VE GOT YOUR BACK. JUST TRUST ME.
YOU, THE PROFESSOR, COACH DAVIS, MY MOM, TONYA--
YOU ALL THINK I'M IRRESPONSIBLE.
BUT I KNOW WHAT I'M DOING. AND RIGHT NOW, WE HAVE TO GET YOU TO STEIN AS FAST AS WE CAN.
WHOA--
THAT GUY'S IN TROUBLE.
WHO? WHO IS? WHO'S IN TROUBLE?

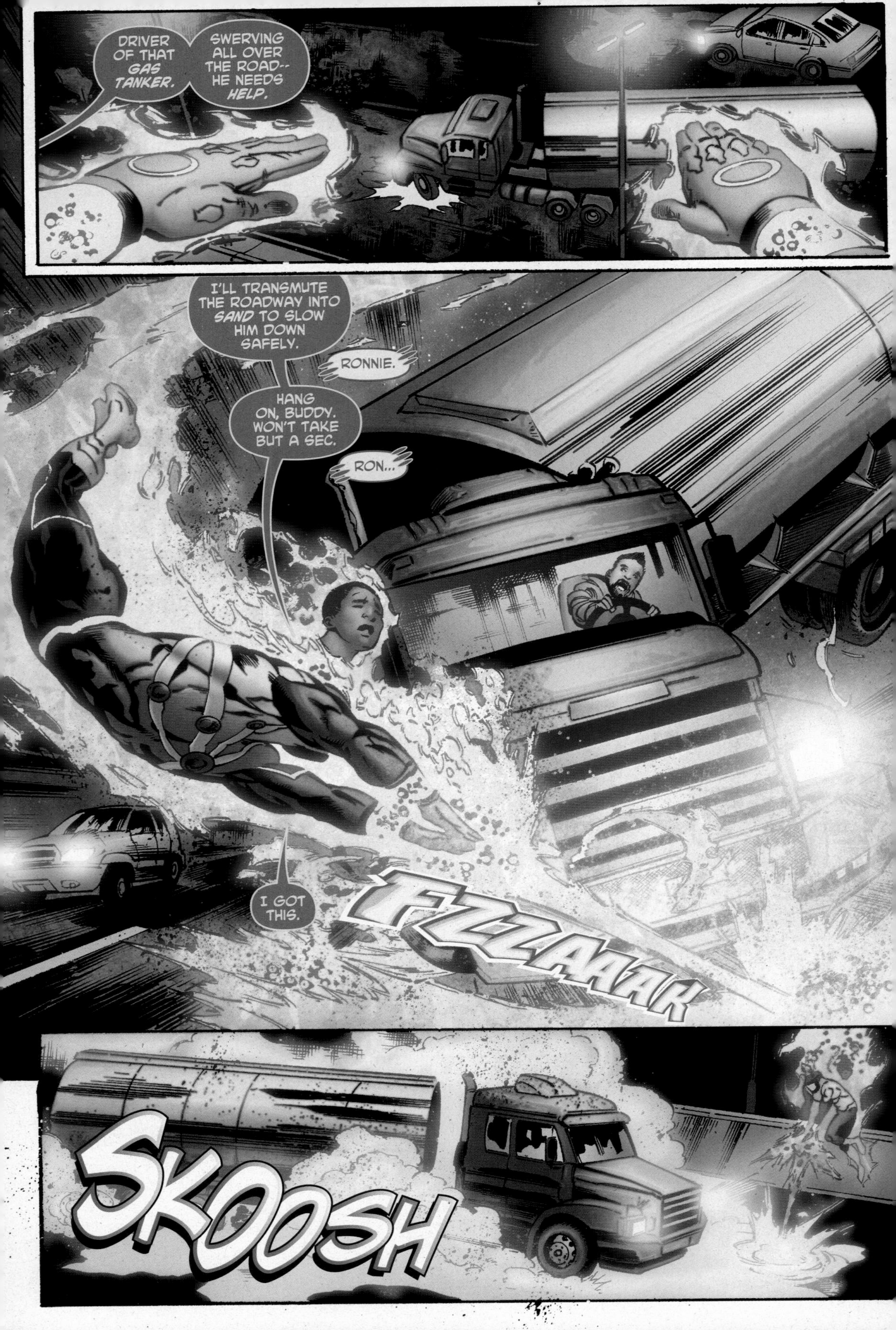

DRIVER OF THAT GAS TANKER.
SWERVING ALL OVER THE ROAD-- HE NEEDS HELP.
I'LL TRANSMUTE THE ROADWAY INTO SAND TO SLOW HIM DOWN SAFELY.
RONNIE.
HANG ON, BUDDY. WON'T TAKE BUT A SEC.
RON...
I GOT THIS.
FZZAAAK
SKOOSH

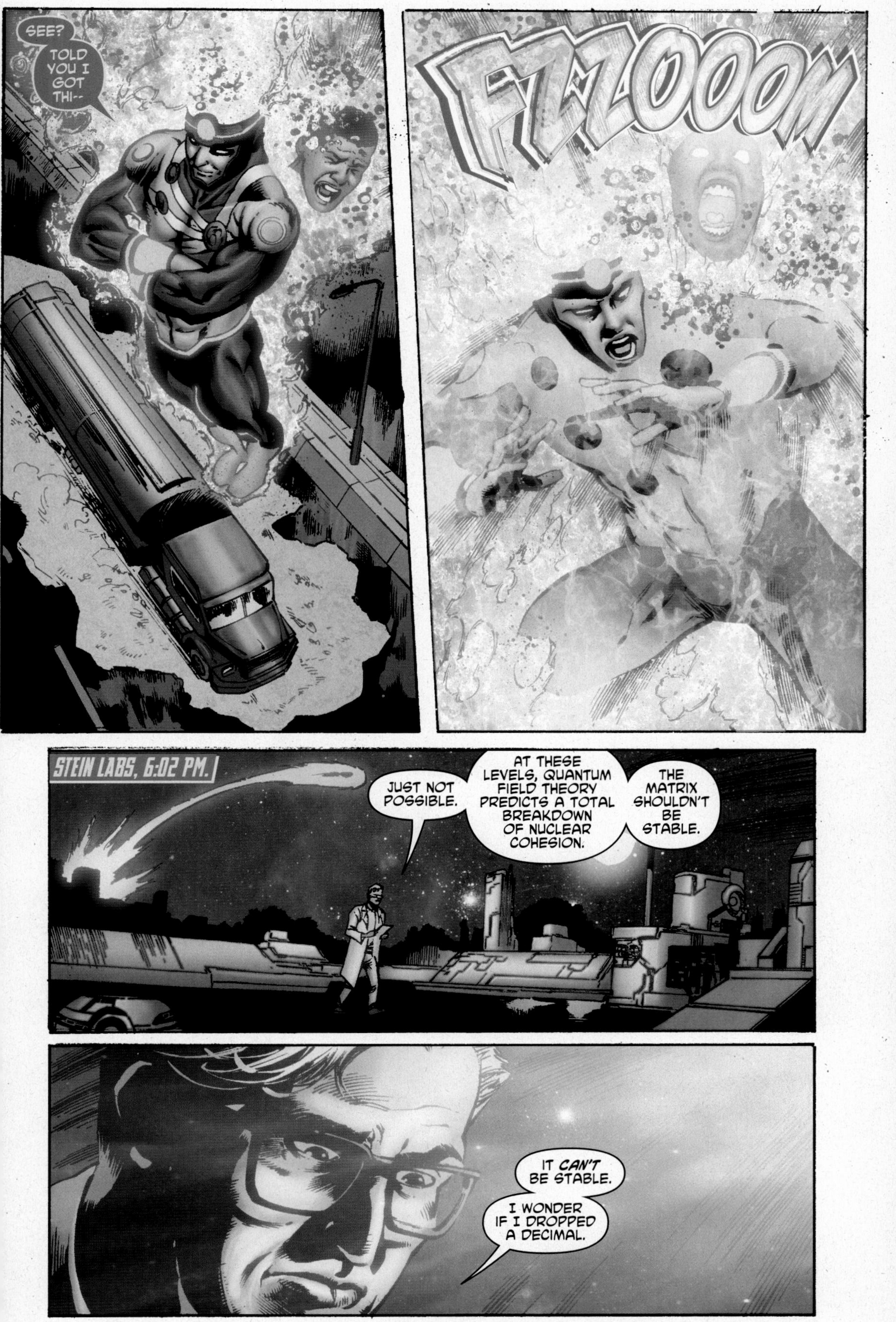
SEE?
TOLD YOU I GOT THI--
FZZOOOM
STEIN LABS, 6:02 PM.
JUST NOT POSSIBLE.
AT THESE LEVELS, QUANTUM FIELD THEORY PREDICTS A TOTAL BREAKDOWN OF NUCLEAR COHESION.
THE MATRIX SHOULDN'T BE STABLE.
IT CAN'T BE STABLE.
I WONDER IF I DROPPED A DECIMAL.

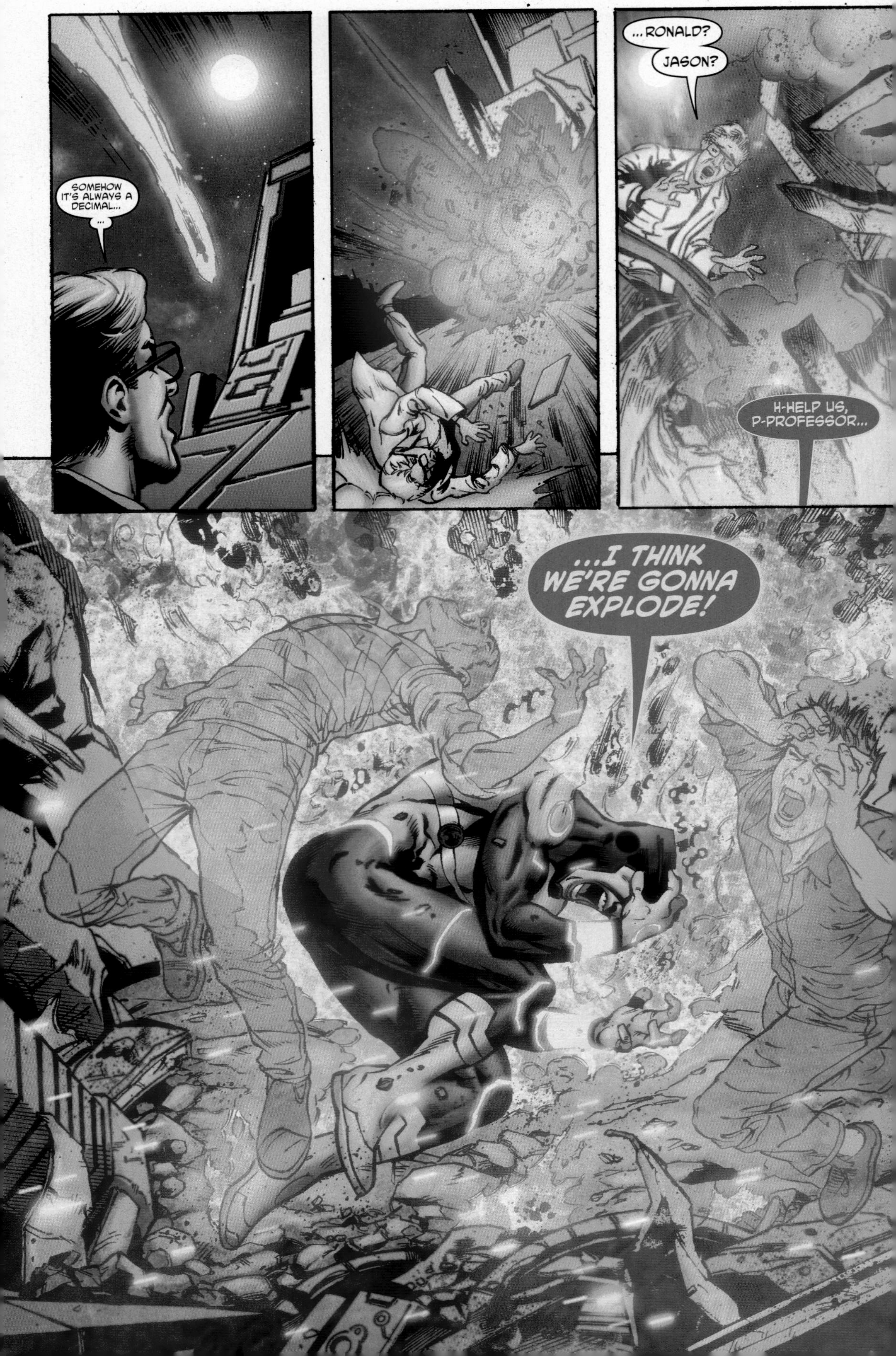
SOMEHOW IT'S ALWAYS A DECIMAL...
...
...RONALD?
JASON?
H-HELP US, P-PROFESSOR...
...I THINK WE'RE GONNA EXPLODE!

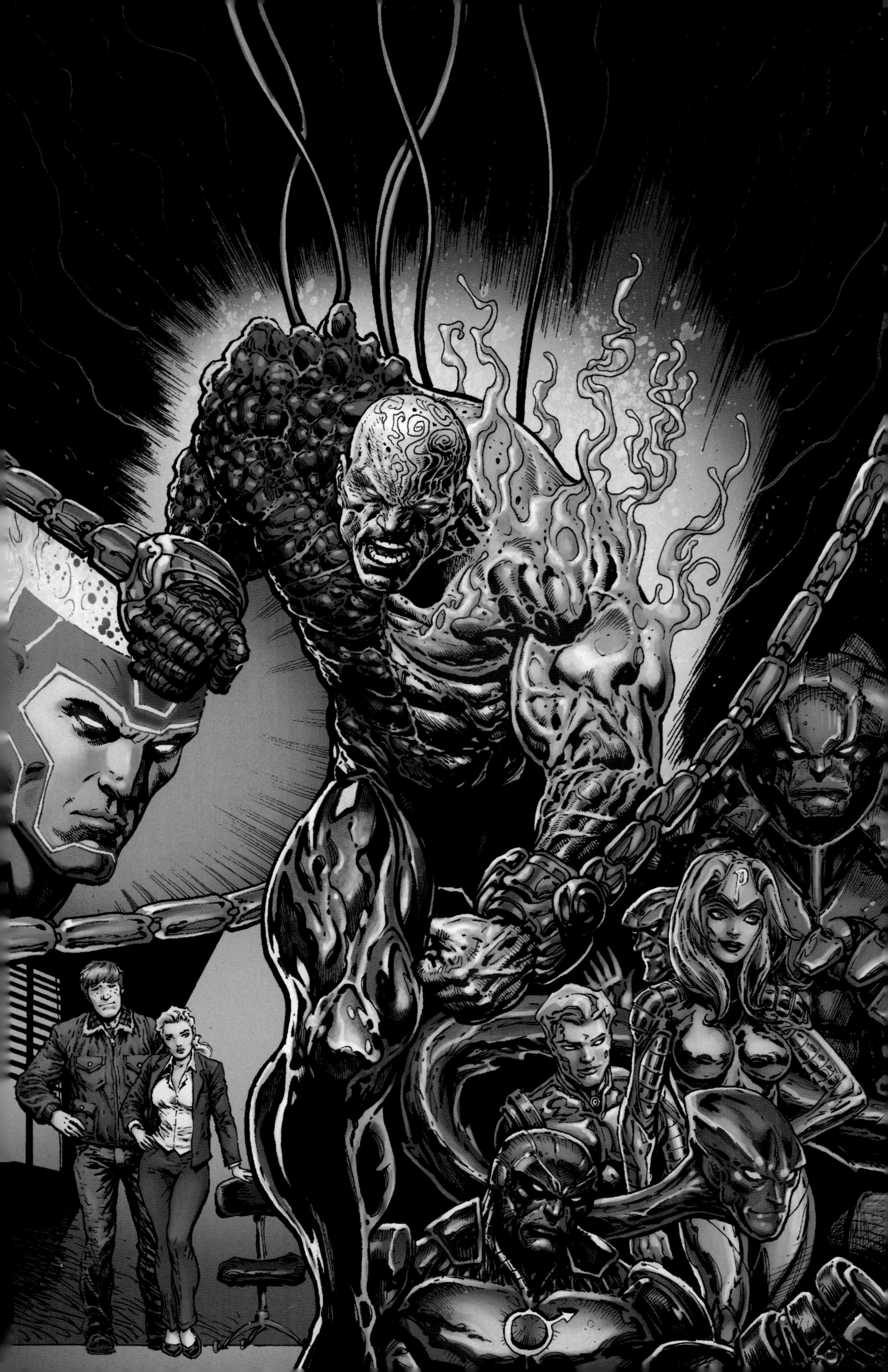

GERRY CONWAY writer EDUARDO PANSICA penciller ROB HUNTER inker ANDREW DALHOUSE colorist COREY BREEN letterer
LIAM SHARP with CHRIS SOTOMAYOR cover

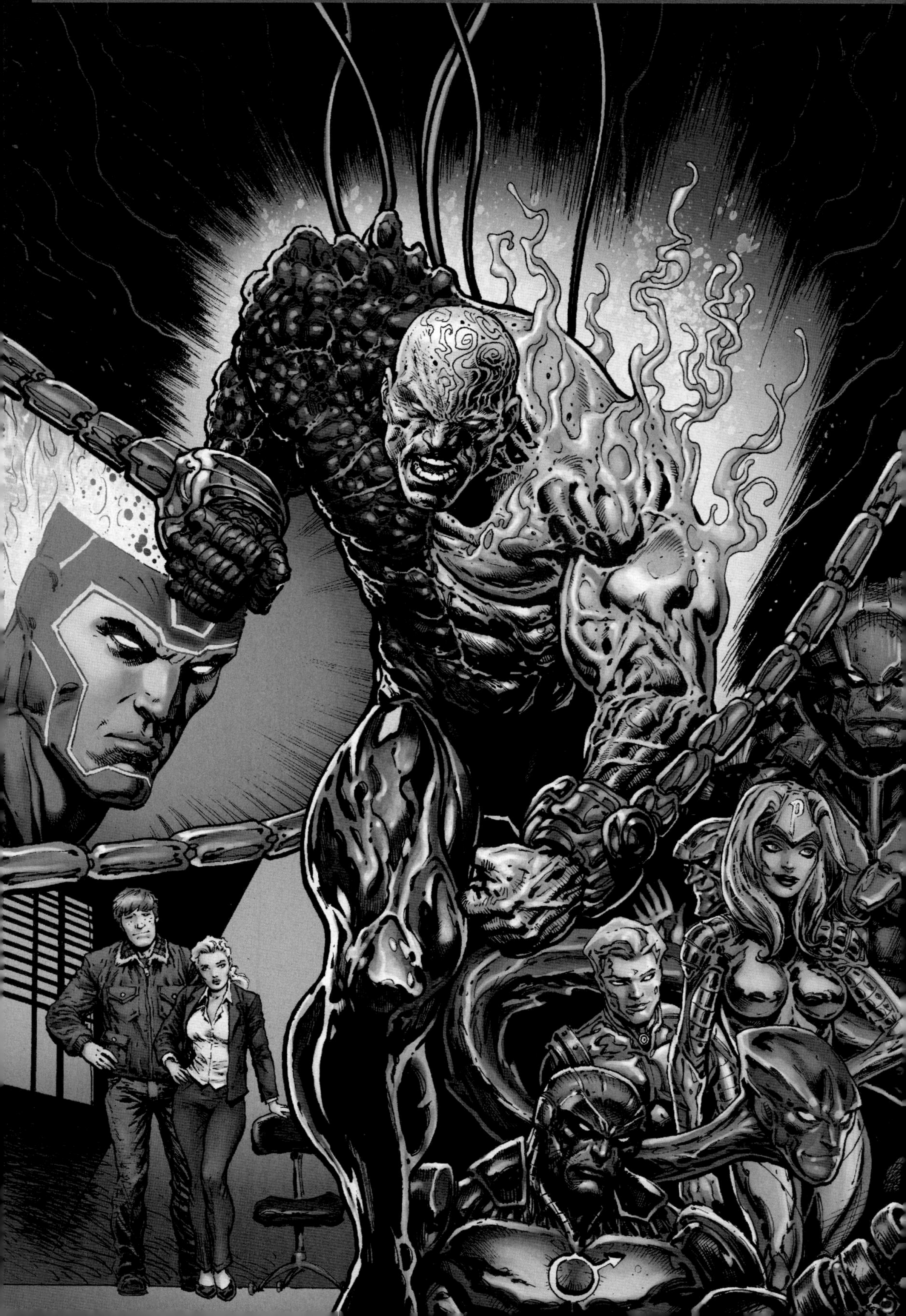

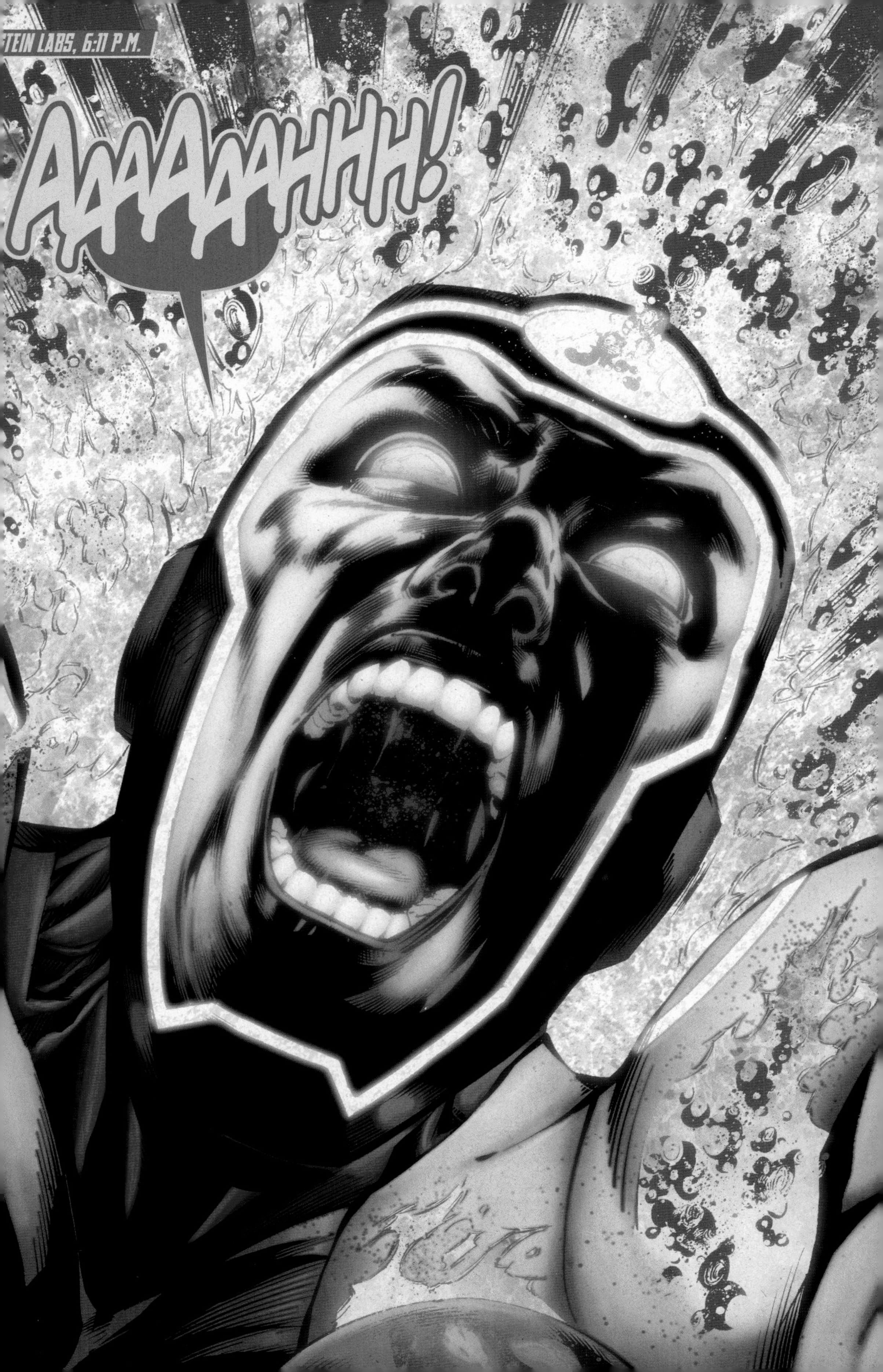
TEIN LABS, 6:11 P.M.
AAAAAAHHH!

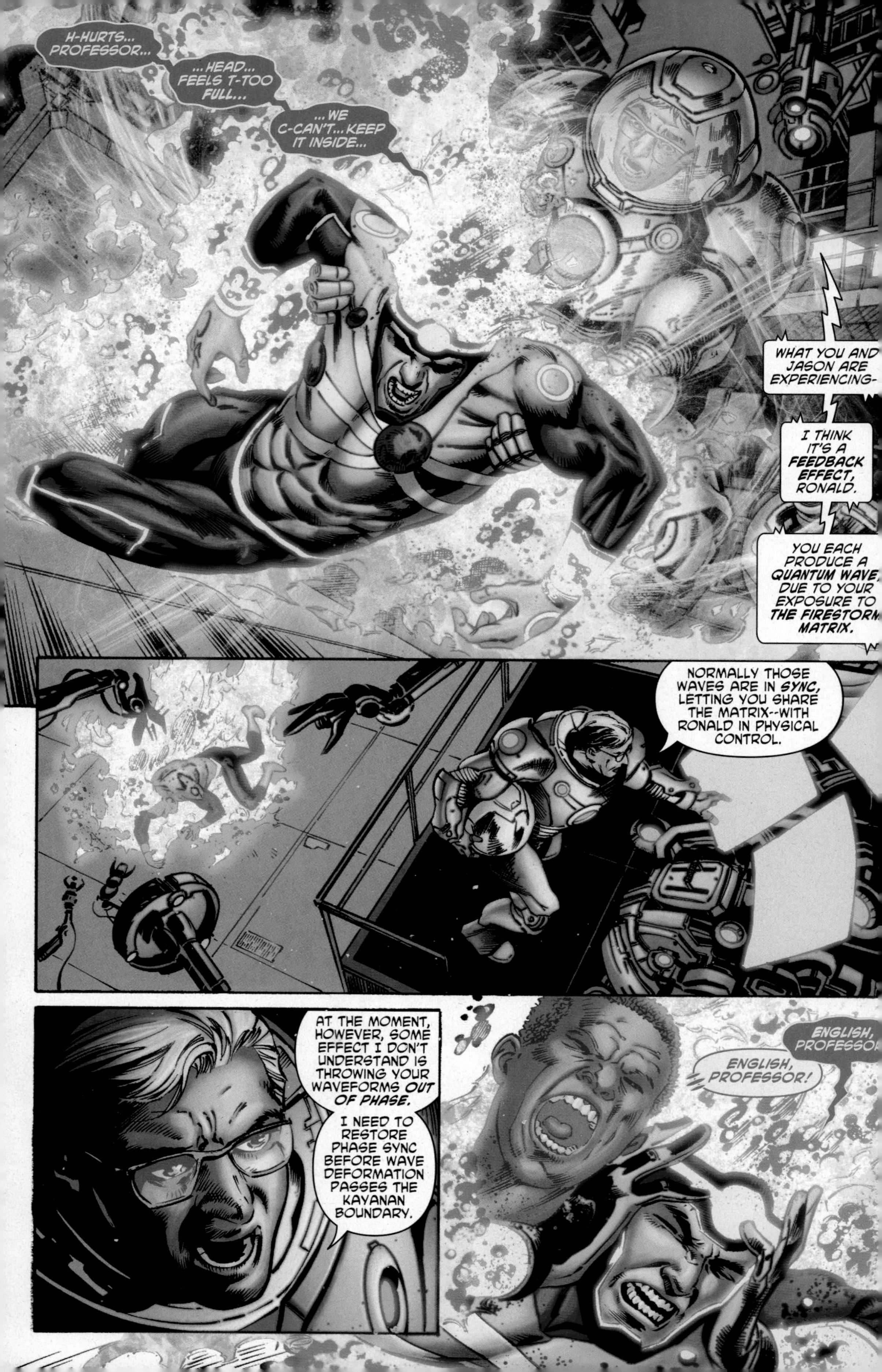
H-HURTS... PROFESSOR...
...HEAD... FEELS T-TOO FULL...
...WE C-CAN'T...KEEP IT INSIDE...
WHAT YOU AND JASON ARE EXPERIENCING-
I THINK IT'S A FEEDBACK EFFECT, RONALD.
YOU EACH PRODUCE A QUANTUM WAVE, DUE TO YOUR EXPOSURE TO THE FIRESTORM MATRIX.
NORMALLY THOSE WAVES ARE IN SYNC, LETTING YOU SHARE THE MATRIX--WITH RONALD IN PHYSICAL CONTROL.
AT THE MOMENT, HOWEVER, SOME EFFECT I DON'T UNDERSTAND IS THROWING YOUR WAVEFORMS OUT OF PHASE.
I NEED TO RESTORE PHASE SYNC BEFORE WAVE DEFORMATION PASSES THE KAYANAN BOUNDARY.
ENGLISH, PROFESSOR!
ENGLISH, PROFESSOR!

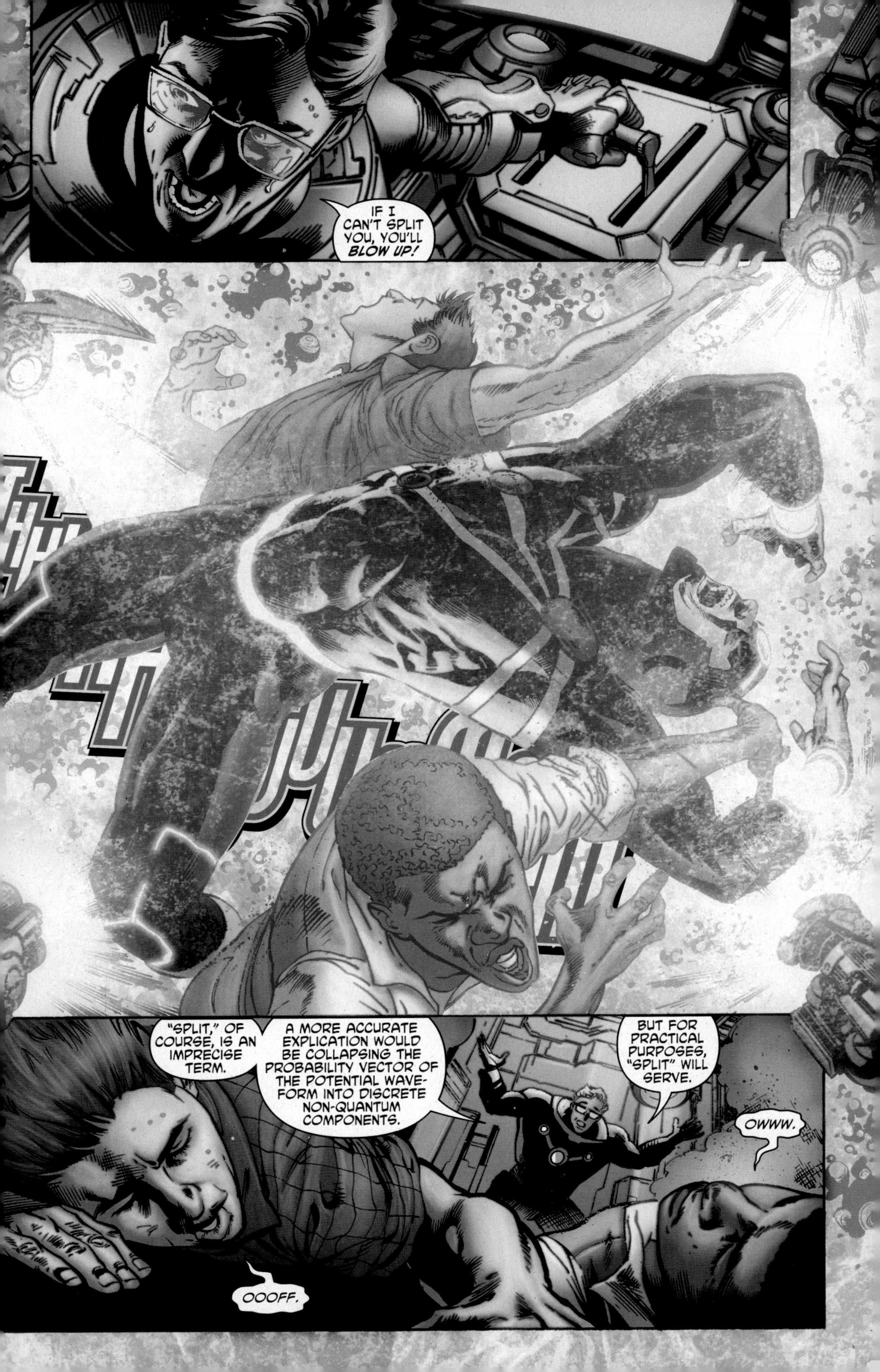
IF I CAN'T SPLIT YOU, YOU'LL *BLOW UP!*
"SPLIT," OF COURSE, IS AN IMPRECISE TERM.
A MORE ACCURATE EXPLICATION WOULD BE COLLAPSING THE PROBABILITY VECTOR OF THE POTENTIAL WAVE-FORM INTO DISCRETE NON-QUANTUM COMPONENTS.
BUT FOR PRACTICAL PURPOSES, "SPLIT" WILL SERVE.
OWWW.
OOOFF.

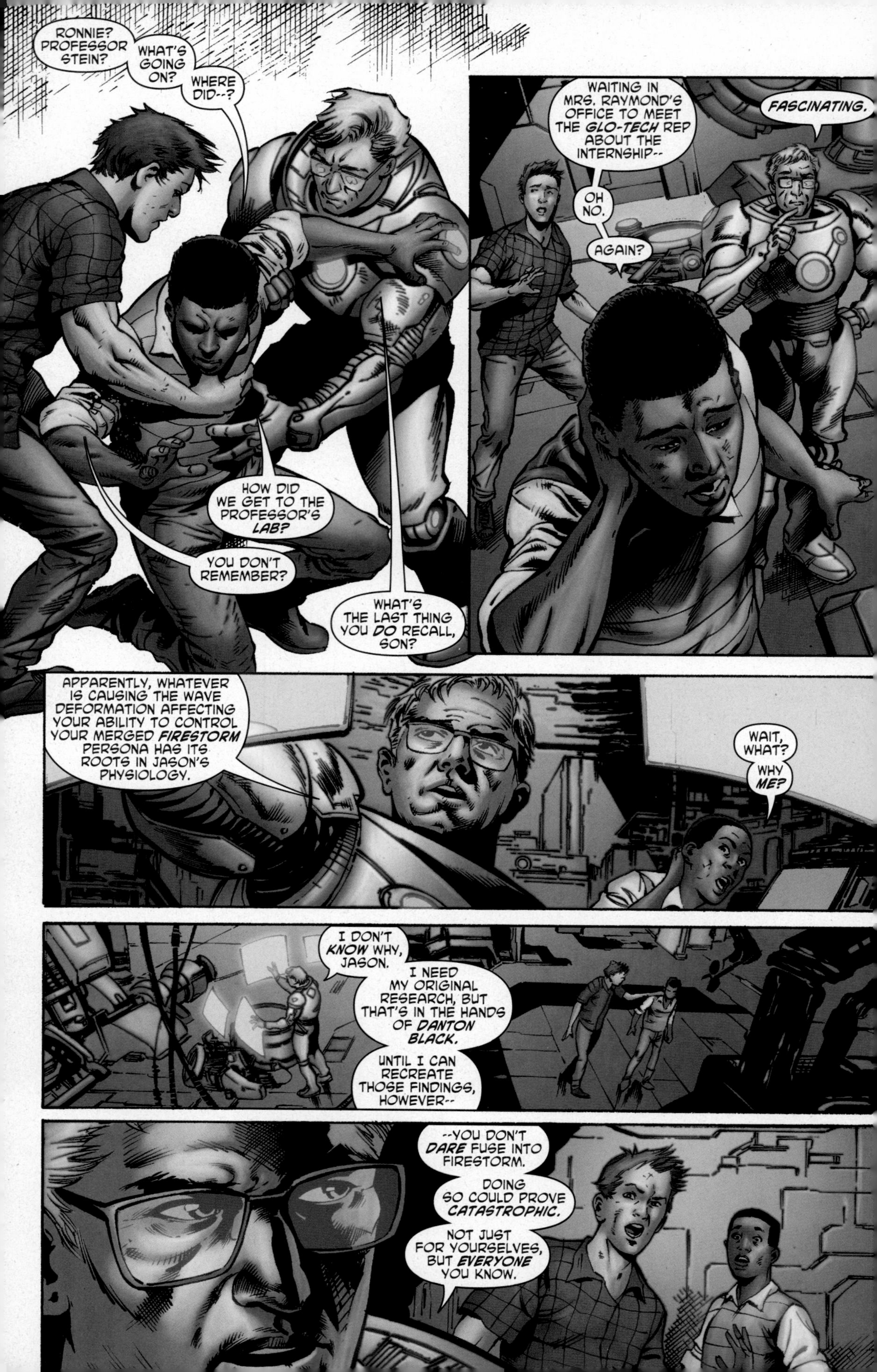
RONNIE? PROFESSOR STEIN?
WHAT'S GOING ON?
WHERE DID--?
HOW DID WE GET TO THE PROFESSOR'S LAB?
YOU DON'T REMEMBER?
WHAT'S THE LAST THING YOU DO RECALL, SON?
WAITING IN MRS. RAYMOND'S OFFICE TO MEET THE GLO-TECH REP ABOUT THE INTERNSHIP--
OH NO.
AGAIN?
FASCINATING.
APPARENTLY, WHATEVER IS CAUSING THE WAVE DEFORMATION AFFECTING YOUR ABILITY TO CONTROL YOUR MERGED FIRESTORM PERSONA HAS ITS ROOTS IN JASON'S PHYSIOLOGY.
WAIT, WHAT?
WHY ME?
I DON'T KNOW WHY, JASON.
I NEED MY ORIGINAL RESEARCH, BUT THAT'S IN THE HANDS OF DANTON BLACK.
UNTIL I CAN RECREATE THOSE FINDINGS, HOWEVER--
--YOU DON'T DARE FUSE INTO FIRESTORM.
DOING SO COULD PROVE CATASTROPHIC.
NOT JUST FOR YOURSELVES, BUT EVERYONE YOU KNOW.

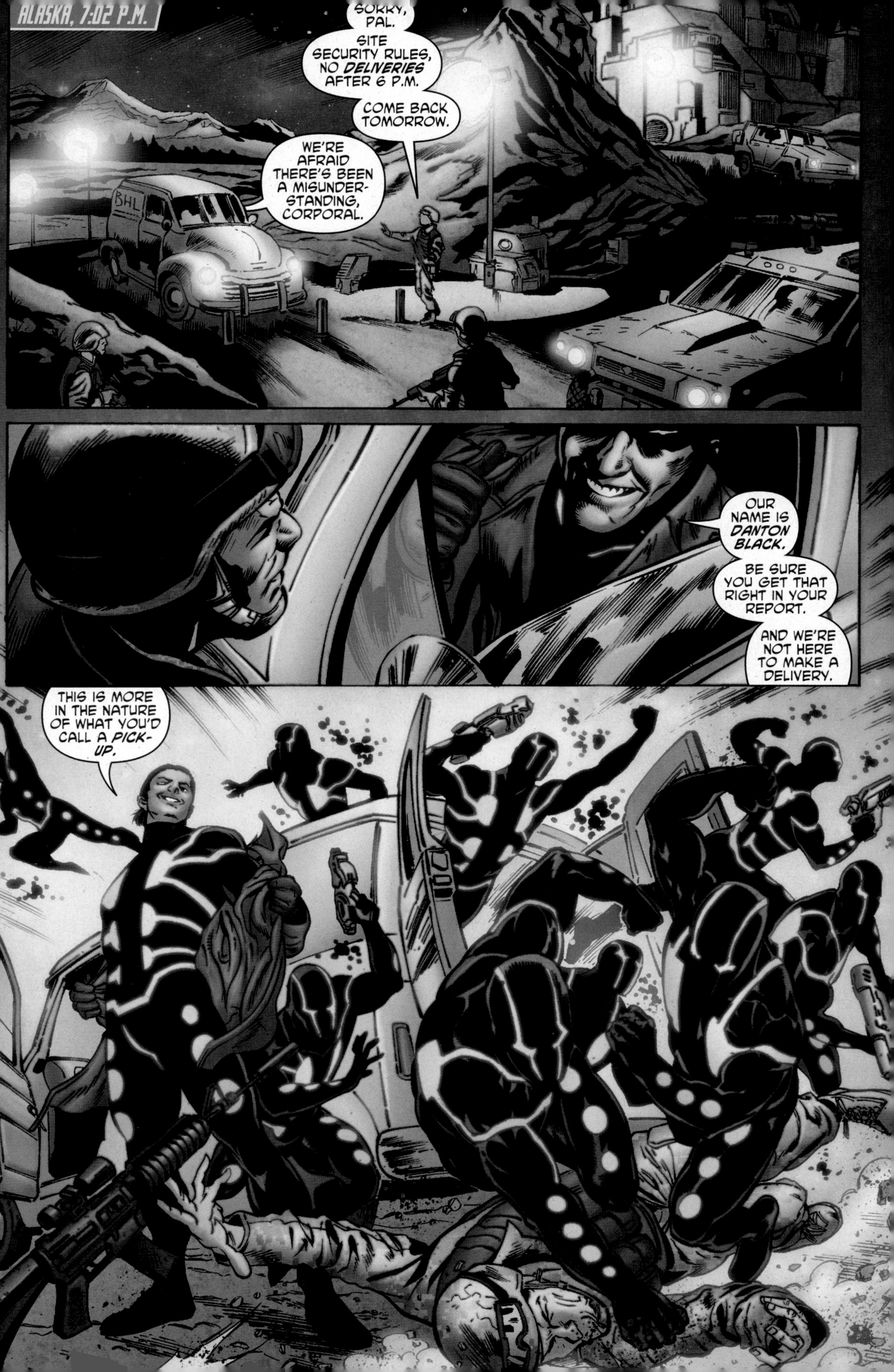
ALASKA, 7:02 P.M.
SORRY, PAL.
SITE SECURITY RULES, NO DELIVERIES AFTER 6 P.M.
COME BACK TOMORROW.
WE'RE AFRAID THERE'S BEEN A MISUNDER-STANDING, CORPORAL.
BHL
OUR NAME IS DANTON BLACK.
BE SURE YOU GET THAT RIGHT IN YOUR REPORT.
AND WE'RE NOT HERE TO MAKE A DELIVERY.
THIS IS MORE IN THE NATURE OF WHAT YOU'D CALL A PICK-UP.

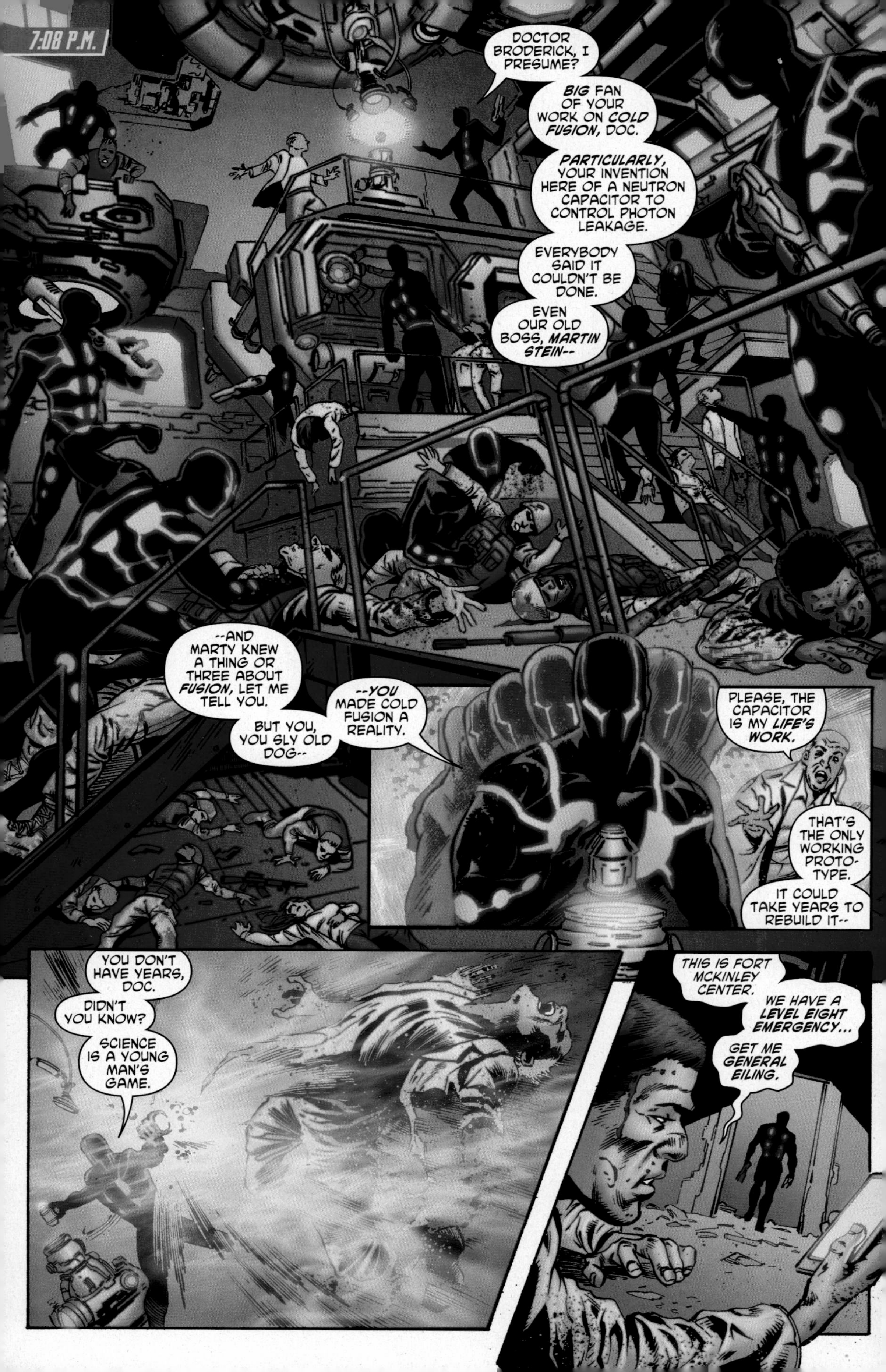

7:08 P.M.
DOCTOR BRODERICK, I PRESUME?
BIG FAN OF YOUR WORK ON COLD FUSION, DOC.
PARTICULARLY, YOUR INVENTION HERE OF A NEUTRON CAPACITOR TO CONTROL PHOTON LEAKAGE.
EVERYBODY SAID IT COULDN'T BE DONE.
EVEN OUR OLD BOSS, MARTIN STEIN--
--AND MARTY KNEW A THING OR THREE ABOUT FUSION, LET ME TELL YOU.
BUT YOU, YOU SLY OLD DOG--
--YOU MADE COLD FUSION A REALITY.
PLEASE, THE CAPACITOR IS MY LIFE'S WORK.
THAT'S THE ONLY WORKING PROTO-TYPE.
IT COULD TAKE YEARS TO REBUILD IT--
YOU DON'T HAVE YEARS, DOC.
DIDN'T YOU KNOW?
SCIENCE IS A YOUNG MAN'S GAME.
THIS IS FORT MCKINLEY CENTER.
WE HAVE A LEVEL EIGHT EMERGENCY...
GET ME GENERAL EILING.

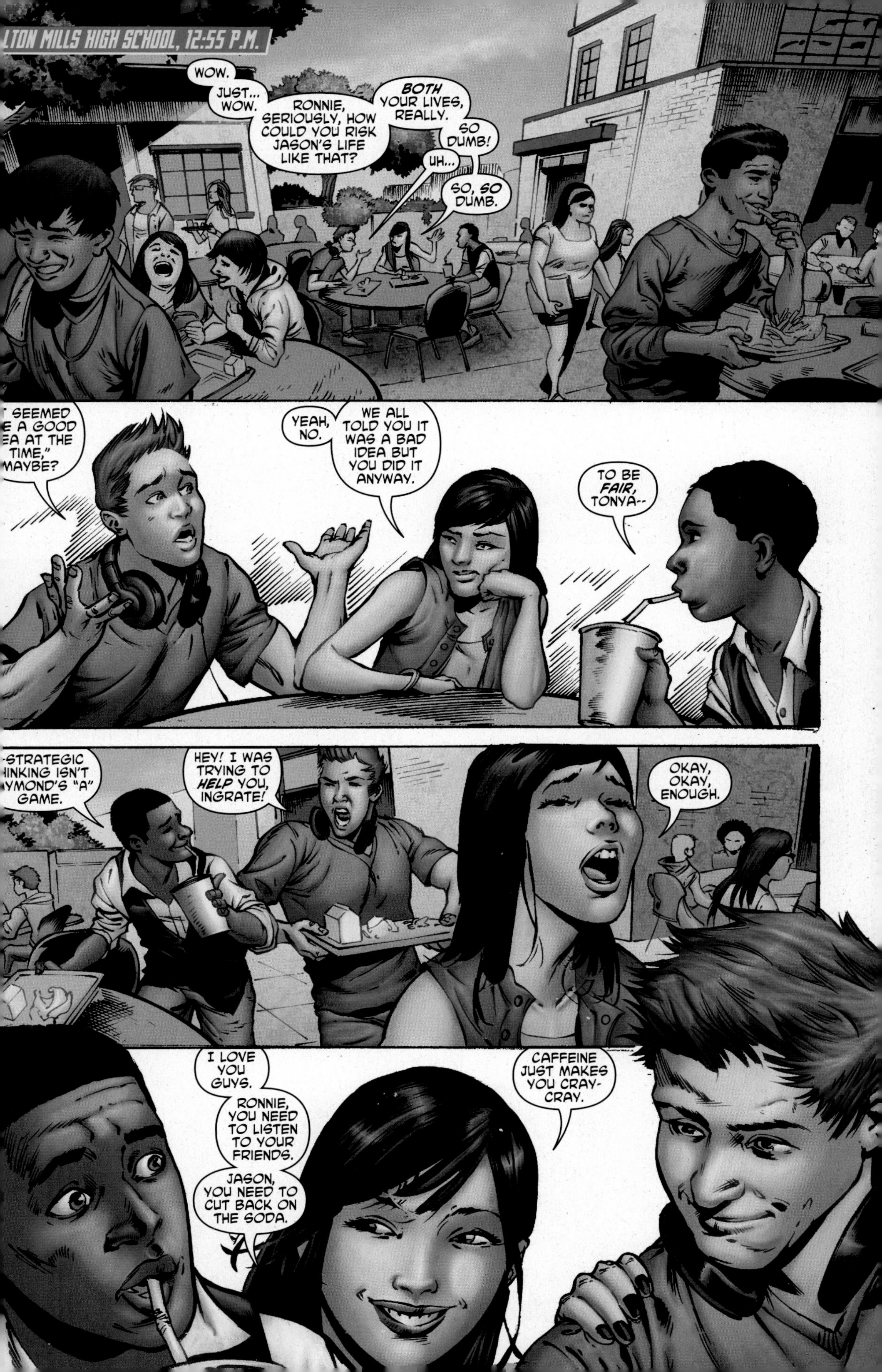
LTON MILLS HIGH SCHOOL, 12:55 P.M.
WOW.
JUST... WOW.
RONNIE, SERIOUSLY, HOW COULD YOU RISK JASON'S LIFE LIKE THAT?
BOTH YOUR LIVES, REALLY.
SO DUMB!
UH...
SO, SO DUMB.
T SEEMED E A GOOD EA AT THE TIME," MAYBE?
YEAH, NO.
WE ALL TOLD YOU IT WAS A BAD IDEA BUT YOU DID IT ANYWAY.
TO BE FAIR, TONYA--
-STRATEGIC HINKING ISN'T YMOND'S "A" GAME.
HEY! I WAS TRYING TO HELP YOU, INGRATE!
OKAY, OKAY, ENOUGH.
I LOVE YOU GUYS.
RONNIE, YOU NEED TO LISTEN TO YOUR FRIENDS.
JASON, YOU NEED TO CUT BACK ON THE SODA.
CAFFEINE JUST MAKES YOU CRAY-CRAY.

TONYA, YOU'RE RIGHT.

I DO NEED MORE TIME WITH MY FRIENDS.

SO, I WAS THINKING, MAYBE YOU AND ME, WE COULD HANG OUT SOMETIME, Y'KNOW, WATCH SOME *NETFLIX*, MAYBE CHILL--

WHOA, WAIT--

TONYA WAS MY FRIEND FIRST.

WE WERE ON THE *DEBATE TEAM* IN JUNIOR HIGH.

IF ANYBODY'S GOING TO MAYBE CHIL AND NETFL WE ARE.

MAYBE YOU KNEW HER FIRST BUT *I* ASKED HER FIRST.

YOU'RE CALLING *DIBS* ON A DATE?

YOU SNOOZE, YOU *LOSE.*

WHAT ARE YOU, *TWELVE?*

UH, GUYS? YOU DO KNOW I'M *GAY,* RIGHT?

BOYS.

SOMETIMES YOU HAVE TO HIT THEM WITH A BRICK.

WHAT?!

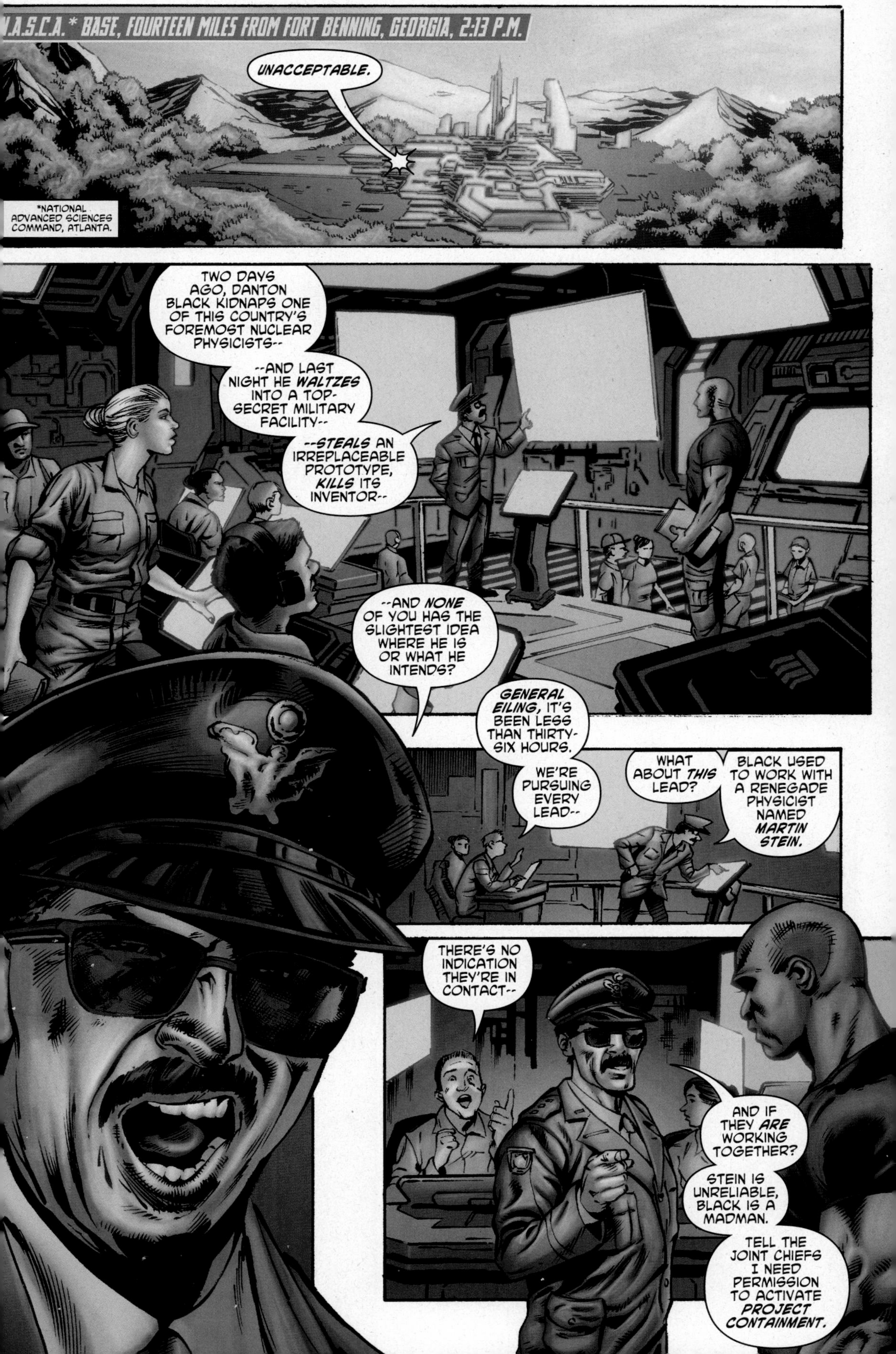
N.A.S.C.A.* BASE, FOURTEEN MILES FROM FORT BENNING, GEORGIA, 2:13 P.M.
UNACCEPTABLE.
*NATIONAL ADVANCED SCIENCES COMMAND, ATLANTA.
TWO DAYS AGO, DANTON BLACK KIDNAPS ONE OF THIS COUNTRY'S FOREMOST NUCLEAR PHYSICISTS--
--AND LAST NIGHT HE WALTZES INTO A TOP-SECRET MILITARY FACILITY--
--STEALS AN IRREPLACEABLE PROTOTYPE, KILLS ITS INVENTOR--
--AND NONE OF YOU HAS THE SLIGHTEST IDEA WHERE HE IS OR WHAT HE INTENDS?
GENERAL EILING, IT'S BEEN LESS THAN THIRTY-SIX HOURS.
WE'RE PURSUING EVERY LEAD--
WHAT ABOUT THIS LEAD?
BLACK USED TO WORK WITH A RENEGADE PHYSICIST NAMED MARTIN STEIN.
THERE'S NO INDICATION THEY'RE IN CONTACT--
AND IF THEY ARE WORKING TOGETHER?
STEIN IS UNRELIABLE, BLACK IS A MADMAN.
TELL THE JOINT CHIEFS I NEED PERMISSION TO ACTIVATE PROJECT CONTAINMENT.

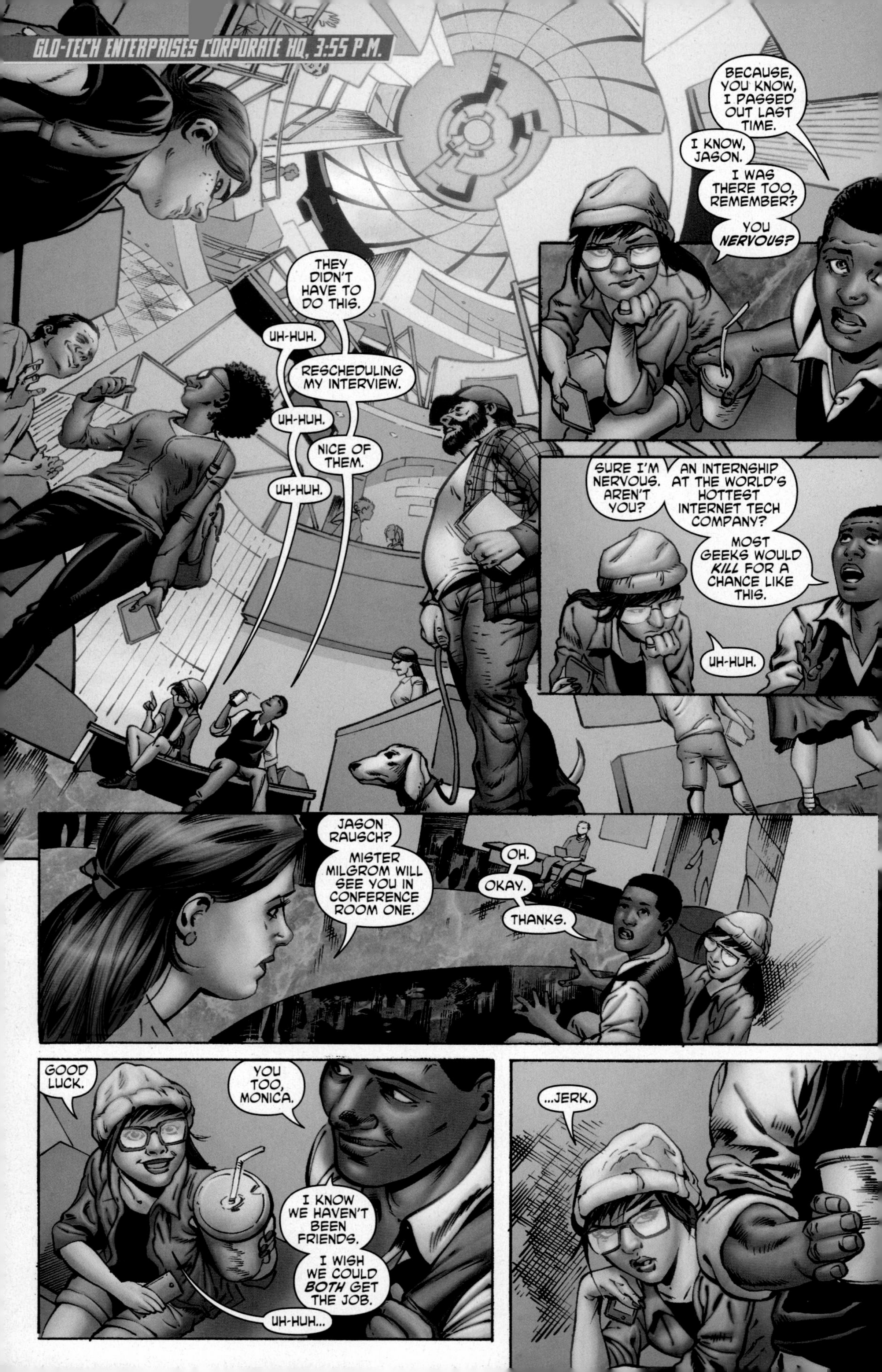
GLO-TECH ENTERPRISES CORPORATE HQ, 3:55 P.M.
THEY DIDN'T HAVE TO DO THIS.
UH-HUH.
RESCHEDULING MY INTERVIEW.
UH-HUH.
NICE OF THEM.
UH-HUH.
BECAUSE, YOU KNOW, I PASSED OUT LAST TIME.
I KNOW, JASON.
I WAS THERE TOO, REMEMBER?
YOU NERVOUS?
SURE I'M NERVOUS. AREN'T YOU?
AN INTERNSHIP AT THE WORLD'S HOTTEST INTERNET TECH COMPANY?
MOST GEEKS WOULD KILL FOR A CHANCE LIKE THIS.
UH-HUH.
JASON RAUSCH?
MISTER MILGROM WILL SEE YOU IN CONFERENCE ROOM ONE.
OH.
OKAY.
THANKS.
GOOD LUCK.
YOU TOO, MONICA.
I KNOW WE HAVEN'T BEEN FRIENDS.
I WISH WE COULD BOTH GET THE JOB.
UH-HUH...
...JERK.

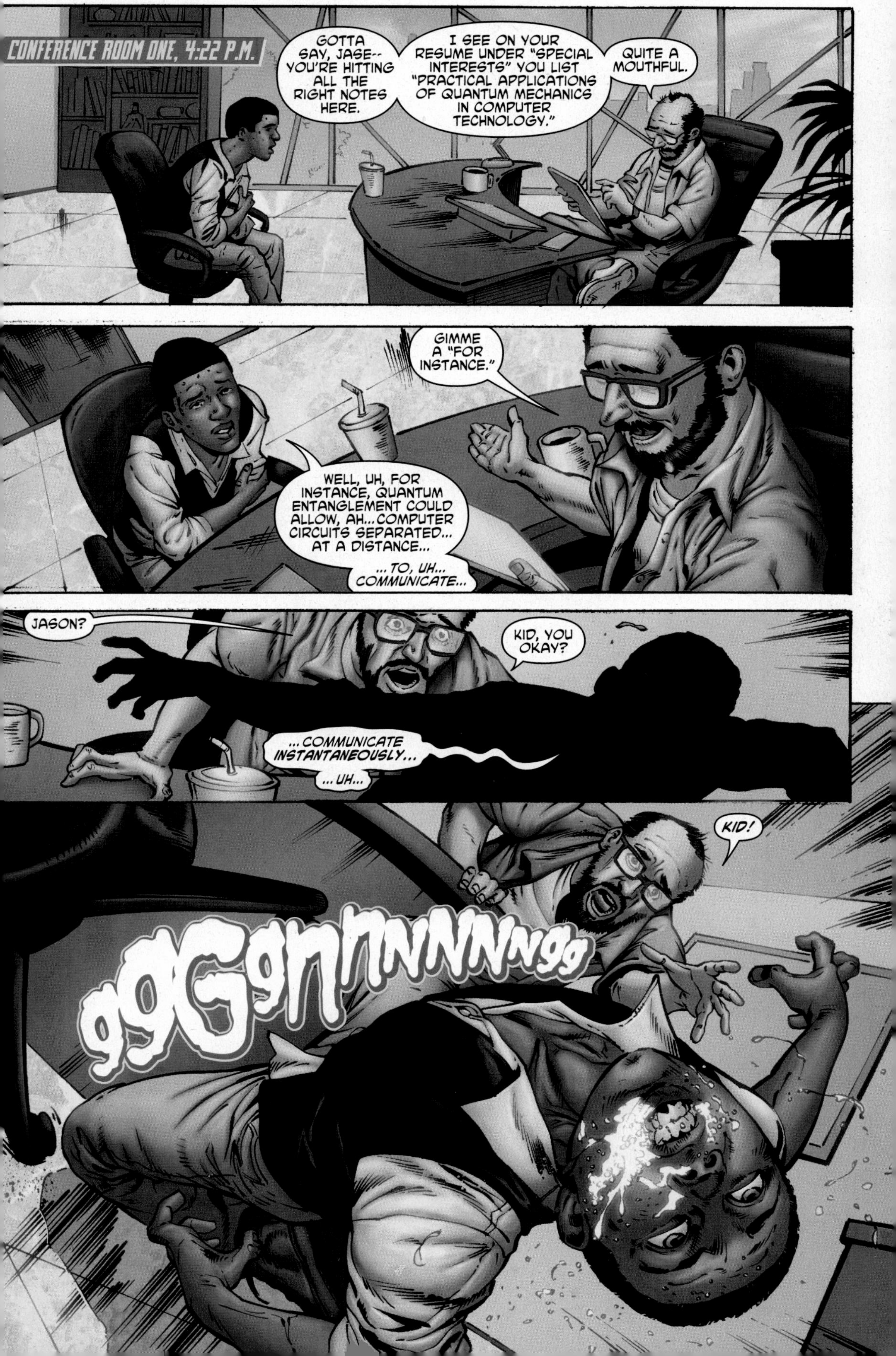
CONFERENCE ROOM ONE, 4:22 P.M.
GOTTA SAY, JASE-- YOU'RE HITTING ALL THE RIGHT NOTES HERE.
I SEE ON YOUR RESUME UNDER "SPECIAL INTERESTS" YOU LIST "PRACTICAL APPLICATIONS OF QUANTUM MECHANICS IN COMPUTER TECHNOLOGY."
QUITE A MOUTHFUL.
GIMME A "FOR INSTANCE."
WELL, UH, FOR INSTANCE, QUANTUM ENTANGLEMENT COULD ALLOW, AH...COMPUTER CIRCUITS SEPARATED... AT A DISTANCE...
...TO, UH... COMMUNICATE...
JASON?
KID, YOU OKAY?
...COMMUNICATE INSTANTANEOUSLY...
...UH...
KID!
ggGgnnnnnngg

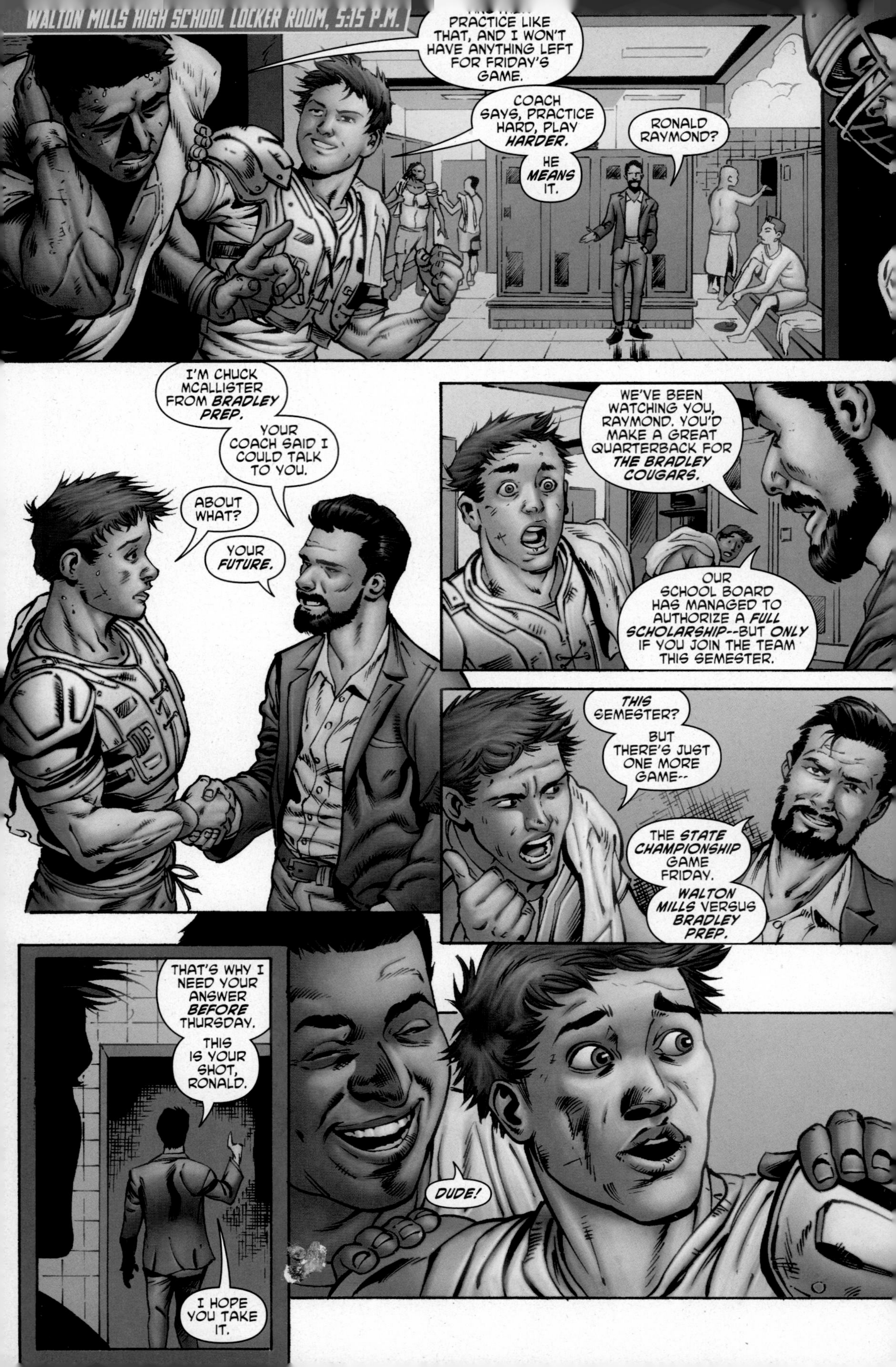

WALTON MILLS HIGH SCHOOL LOCKER ROOM, 5:15 P.M.
PRACTICE LIKE THAT, AND I WON'T HAVE ANYTHING LEFT FOR FRIDAY'S GAME.
COACH SAYS, PRACTICE HARD, PLAY HARDER.
HE MEANS IT.
RONALD RAYMOND?
I'M CHUCK MCALLISTER FROM BRADLEY PREP.
YOUR COACH SAID I COULD TALK TO YOU.
ABOUT WHAT?
YOUR FUTURE.
WE'VE BEEN WATCHING YOU, RAYMOND. YOU'D MAKE A GREAT QUARTERBACK FOR THE BRADLEY COUGARS.
OUR SCHOOL BOARD HAS MANAGED TO AUTHORIZE A FULL SCHOLARSHIP--BUT ONLY IF YOU JOIN THE TEAM THIS SEMESTER.
THIS SEMESTER?
BUT THERE'S JUST ONE MORE GAME--
THE STATE CHAMPIONSHIP GAME FRIDAY.
WALTON MILLS VERSUS BRADLEY PREP.
THAT'S WHY I NEED YOUR ANSWER BEFORE THURSDAY.
THIS IS YOUR SHOT, RONALD.
I HOPE YOU TAKE IT.
DUDE!

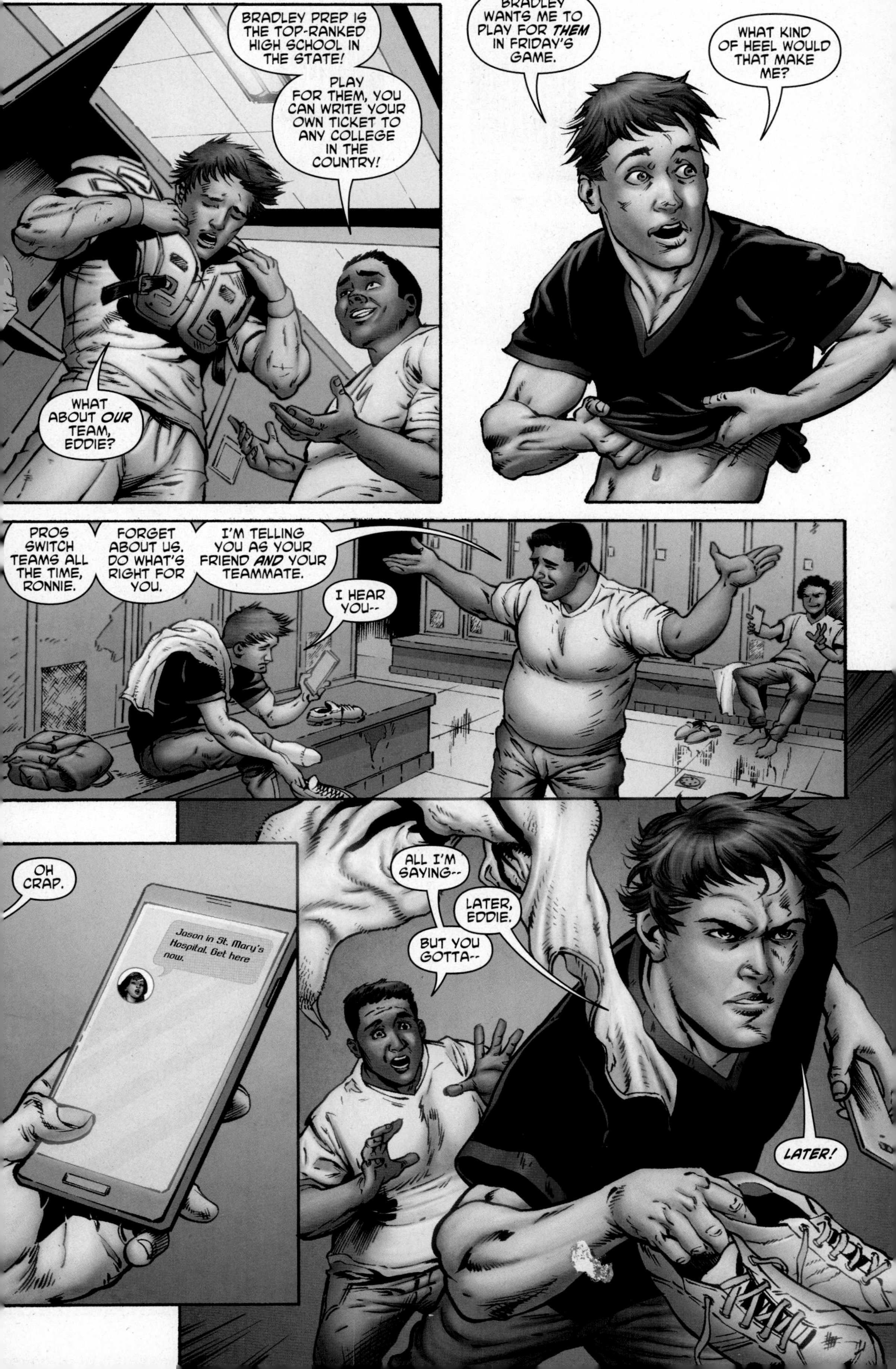
BRADLEY PREP IS THE TOP-RANKED HIGH SCHOOL IN THE STATE!
PLAY FOR THEM, YOU CAN WRITE YOUR OWN TICKET TO ANY COLLEGE IN THE COUNTRY!
WHAT ABOUT *OUR* TEAM, EDDIE?
BRADLEY WANTS ME TO PLAY FOR *THEM* IN FRIDAY'S GAME.
WHAT KIND OF HEEL WOULD THAT MAKE ME?
PROS SWITCH TEAMS ALL THE TIME, RONNIE.
FORGET ABOUT US. DO WHAT'S RIGHT FOR YOU.
I'M TELLING YOU AS YOUR FRIEND *AND* YOUR TEAMMATE.
I HEAR YOU--
OH CRAP.
Jason in St. Mary's Hospital. Get here now.
ALL I'M SAYING--
LATER, EDDIE.
BUT YOU GOTTA--
LATER!

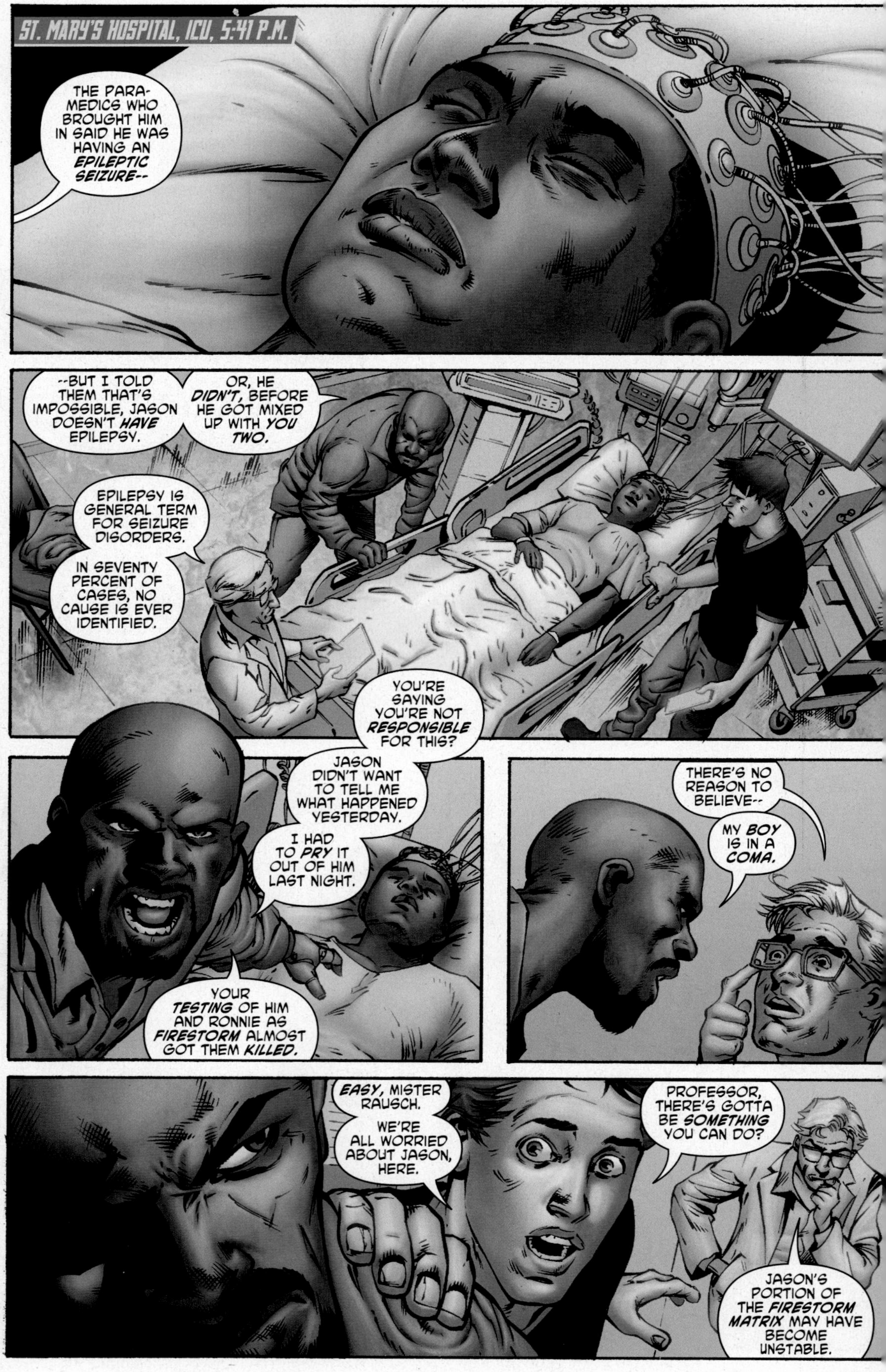

ST. MARY'S HOSPITAL, ICU, 5:41 P.M.
THE PARAMEDICS WHO BROUGHT HIM IN SAID HE WAS HAVING AN EPILEPTIC SEIZURE--
--BUT I TOLD THEM THAT'S IMPOSSIBLE, JASON DOESN'T HAVE EPILEPSY.
OR, HE DIDN'T, BEFORE HE GOT MIXED UP WITH YOU TWO.
EPILEPSY IS GENERAL TERM FOR SEIZURE DISORDERS.
IN SEVENTY PERCENT OF CASES, NO CAUSE IS EVER IDENTIFIED.
YOU'RE SAYING YOU'RE NOT RESPONSIBLE FOR THIS?
JASON DIDN'T WANT TO TELL ME WHAT HAPPENED YESTERDAY.
I HAD TO PRY IT OUT OF HIM LAST NIGHT.
YOUR TESTING OF HIM AND RONNIE AS FIRESTORM ALMOST GOT THEM KILLED.
THERE'S NO REASON TO BELIEVE--
MY BOY IS IN A COMA.
EASY, MISTER RAUSCH.
WE'RE ALL WORRIED ABOUT JASON, HERE.
PROFESSOR, THERE'S GOTTA BE SOMETHING YOU CAN DO?
JASON'S PORTION OF THE FIRESTORM MATRIX MAY HAVE BECOME UNSTABLE.

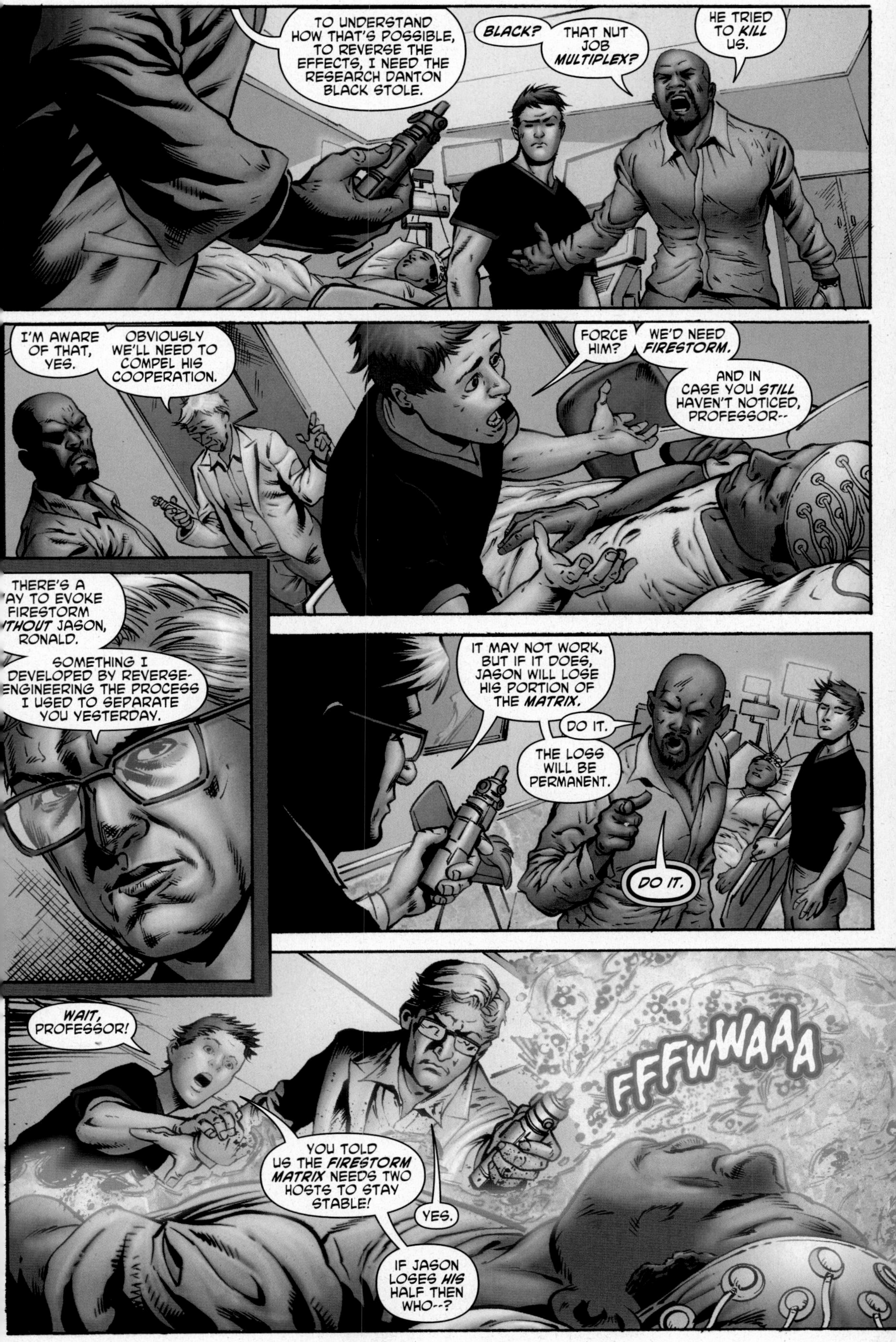
TO UNDERSTAND HOW THAT'S POSSIBLE, TO REVERSE THE EFFECTS, I NEED THE RESEARCH DANTON BLACK STOLE.
BLACK?
THAT NUT JOB MULTIPLEX?
HE TRIED TO KILL US.
I'M AWARE OF THAT, YES.
OBVIOUSLY WE'LL NEED TO COMPEL HIS COOPERATION.
FORCE HIM?
WE'D NEED FIRESTORM.
AND IN CASE YOU STILL HAVEN'T NOTICED, PROFESSOR--
THERE'S A WAY TO EVOKE FIRESTORM WITHOUT JASON, RONALD.
SOMETHING I DEVELOPED BY REVERSE-ENGINEERING THE PROCESS I USED TO SEPARATE YOU YESTERDAY.
IT MAY NOT WORK, BUT IF IT DOES, JASON WILL LOSE HIS PORTION OF THE MATRIX.
DO IT.
THE LOSS WILL BE PERMANENT.
DO IT.
WAIT, PROFESSOR!
FFFWWAAAA
YOU TOLD US THE FIRESTORM MATRIX NEEDS TWO HOSTS TO STAY STABLE!
YES.
IF JASON LOSES HIS HALF THEN WHO--?

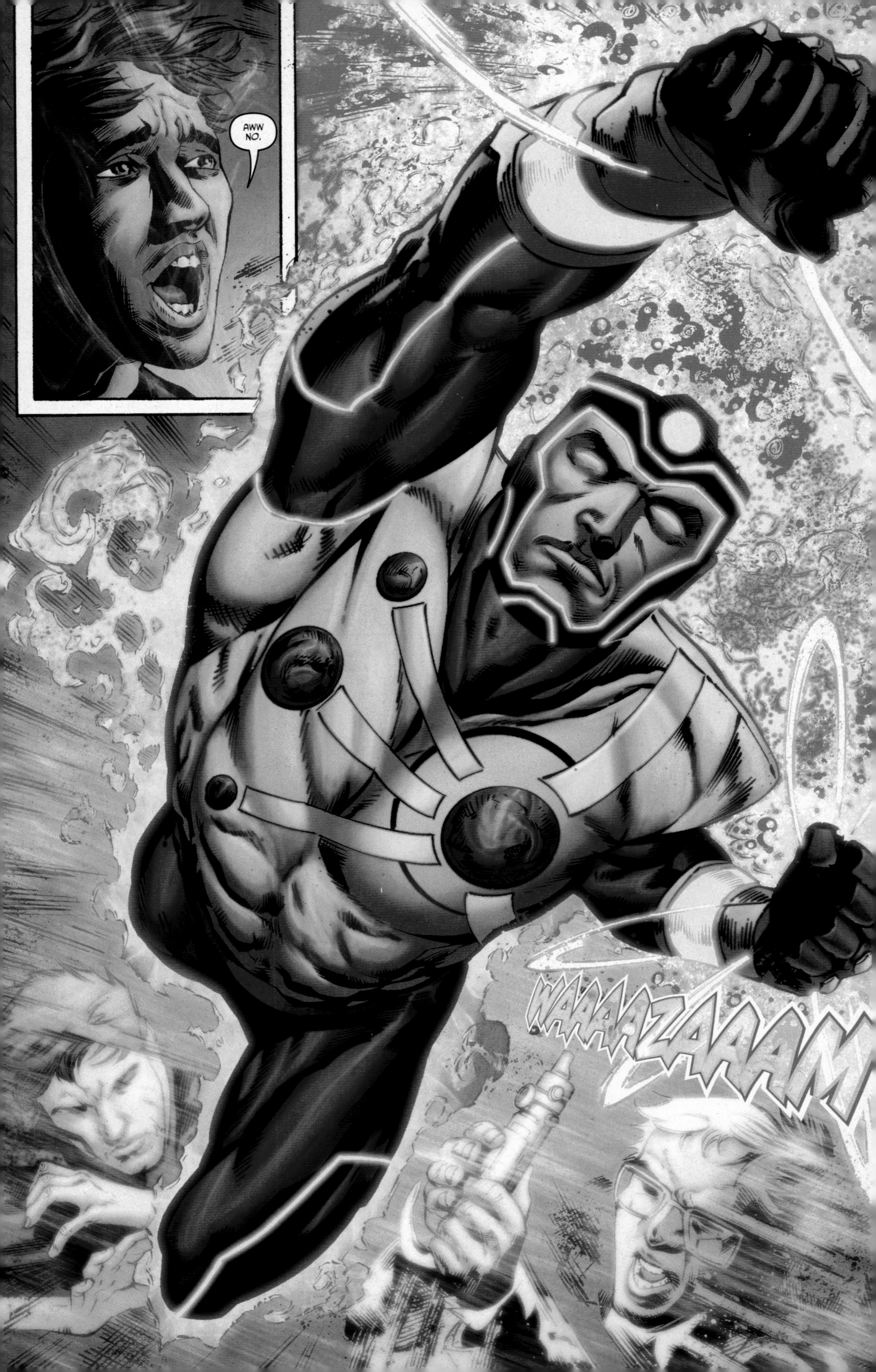
AWW NO.
WAAAAZAAAAM

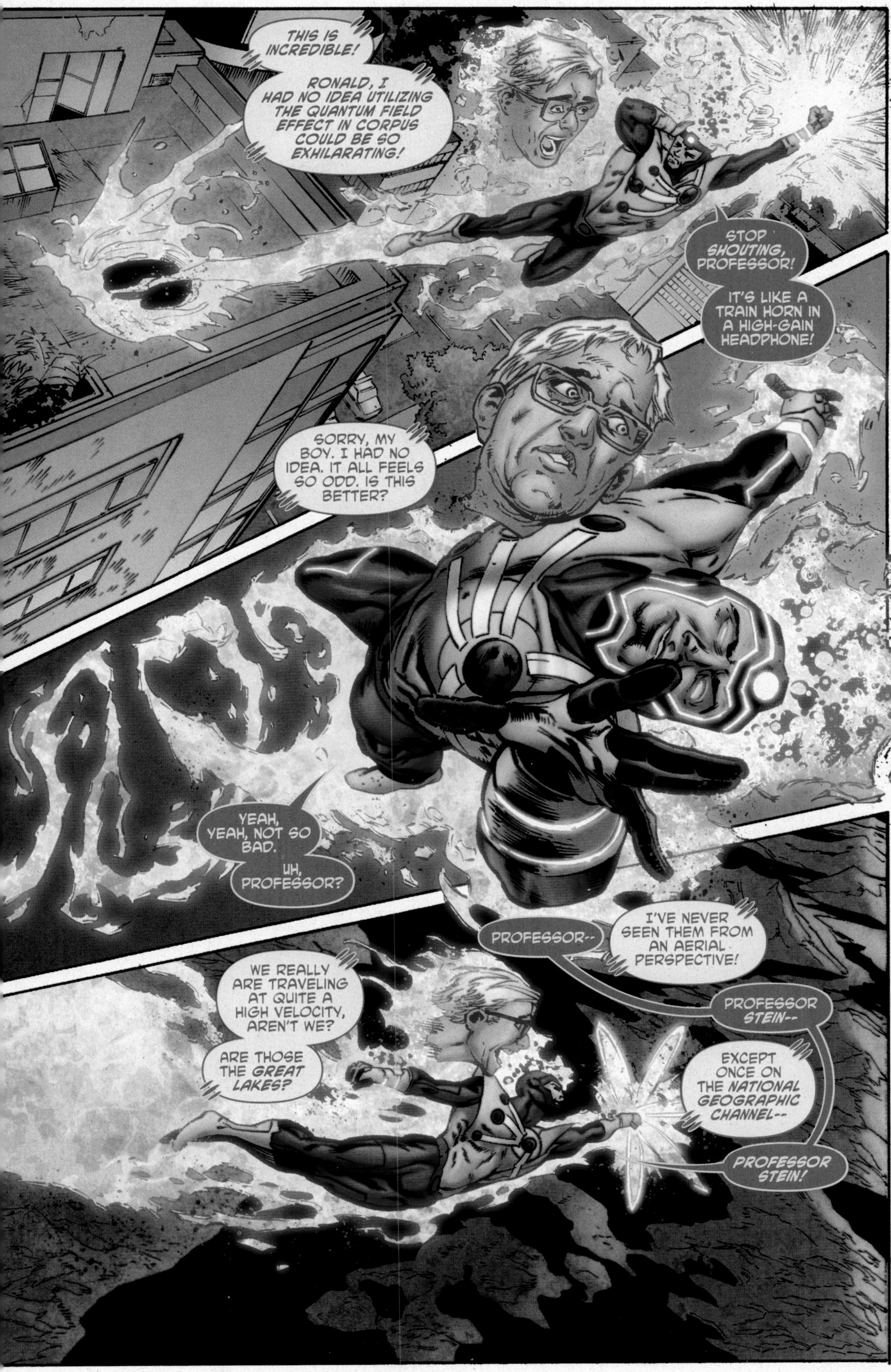
THIS IS INCREDIBLE!
RONALD, I HAD NO IDEA UTILIZING THE QUANTUM FIELD EFFECT IN CORPUS COULD BE SO EXHILARATING!
STOP SHOUTING, PROFESSOR!
IT'S LIKE A TRAIN HORN IN A HIGH-GAIN HEADPHONE!
SORRY, MY BOY. I HAD NO IDEA. IT ALL FEELS SO ODD. IS THIS BETTER?
YEAH, YEAH, NOT SO BAD.
UH, PROFESSOR?
WE REALLY ARE TRAVELING AT QUITE A HIGH VELOCITY, AREN'T WE?
ARE THOSE THE *GREAT LAKES*?
PROFESSOR--
I'VE NEVER SEEN THEM FROM AN AERIAL PERSPECTIVE!
PROFESSOR *STEIN*--
EXCEPT ONCE ON THE *NATIONAL GEOGRAPHIC CHANNEL*--
PROFESSOR STEIN!

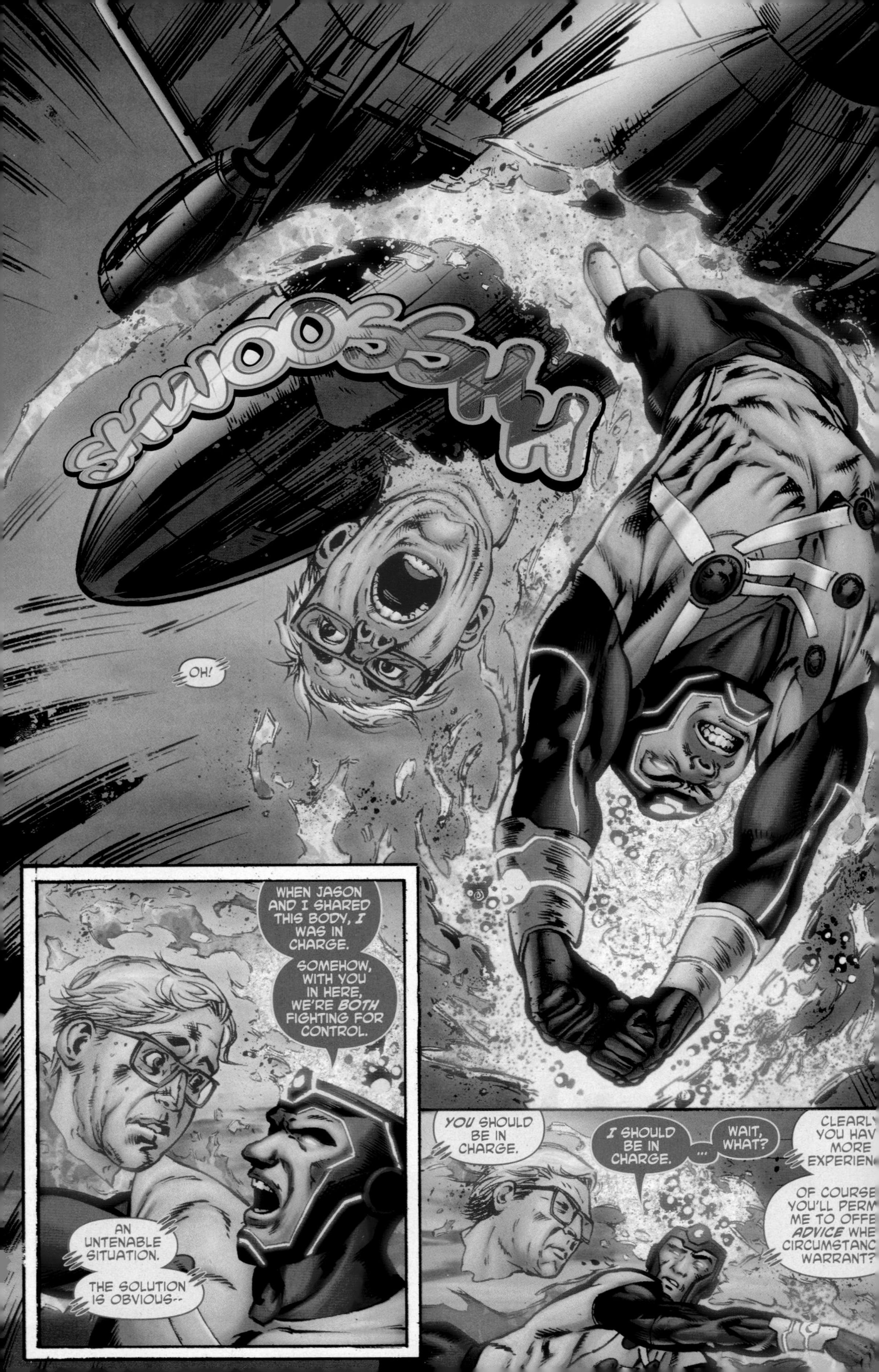
OH!
WHEN JASON AND I SHARED THIS BODY, *I* WAS IN CHARGE.
SOMEHOW, WITH YOU IN HERE, WE'RE *BOTH* FIGHTING FOR CONTROL.
AN UNTENABLE SITUATION.
THE SOLUTION IS OBVIOUS--
YOU SHOULD BE IN CHARGE.
I SHOULD BE IN CHARGE.
...
WAIT, WHAT?
CLEARL YOU HAV MORE EXPERIEN
OF COURSE YOU'LL PERM ME TO OFFE *ADVICE* WHE CIRCUMSTANC WARRANT?

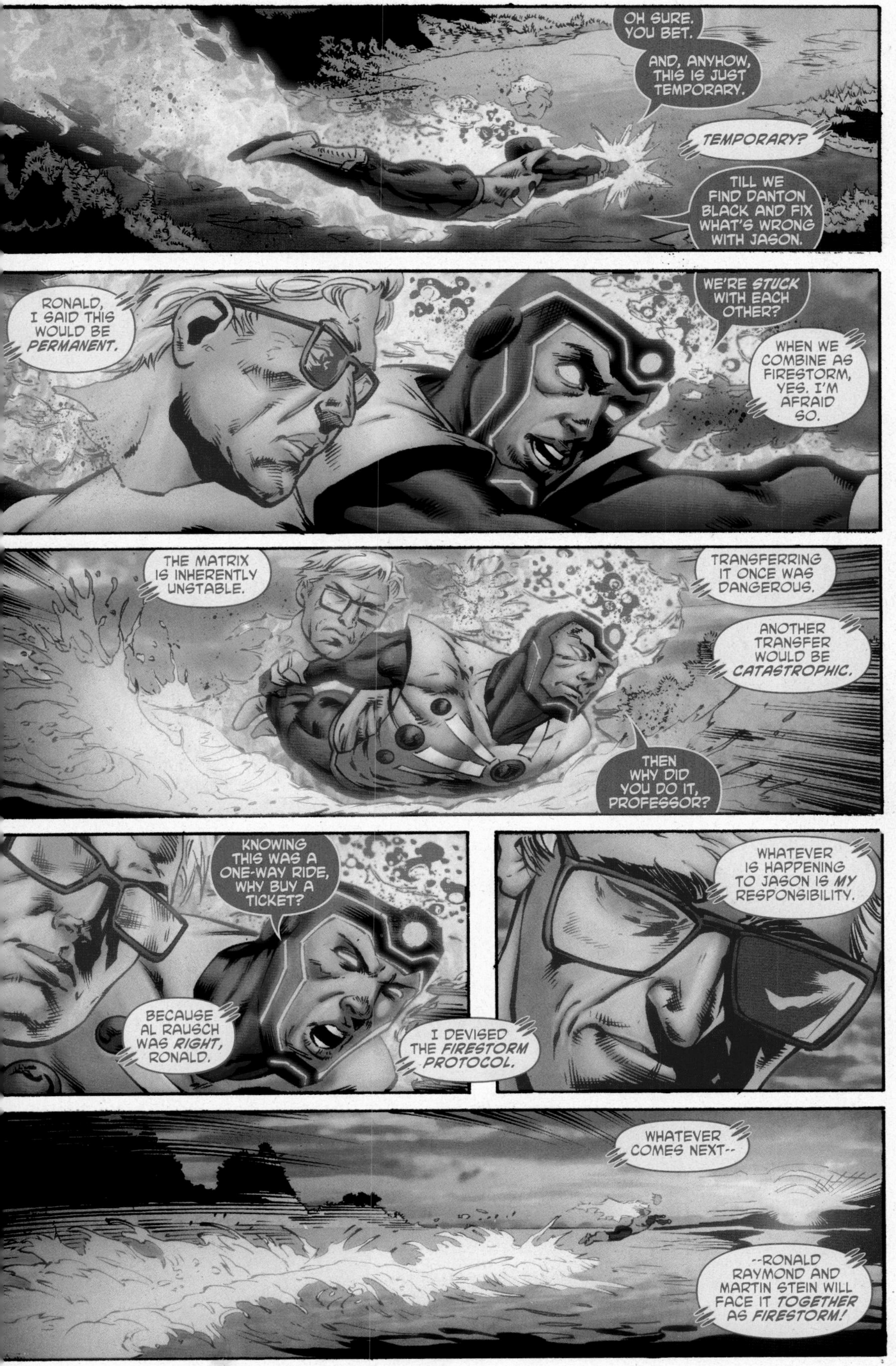

OH SURE. YOU BET.
AND, ANYHOW, THIS IS JUST TEMPORARY.
TEMPORARY?
TILL WE FIND DANTON BLACK AND FIX WHAT'S WRONG WITH JASON.
RONALD, I SAID THIS WOULD BE PERMANENT.
WE'RE STUCK WITH EACH OTHER?
WHEN WE COMBINE AS FIRESTORM, YES. I'M AFRAID SO.
THE MATRIX IS INHERENTLY UNSTABLE.
TRANSFERRING IT ONCE WAS DANGEROUS.
ANOTHER TRANSFER WOULD BE CATASTROPHIC.
THEN WHY DID YOU DO IT, PROFESSOR?
KNOWING THIS WAS A ONE-WAY RIDE, WHY BUY A TICKET?
BECAUSE AL RAUSCH WAS RIGHT, RONALD.
I DEVISED THE FIRESTORM PROTOCOL.
WHATEVER IS HAPPENING TO JASON IS MY RESPONSIBILITY.
WHATEVER COMES NEXT--
--RONALD RAYMOND AND MARTIN STEIN WILL FACE IT TOGETHER AS FIRESTORM!

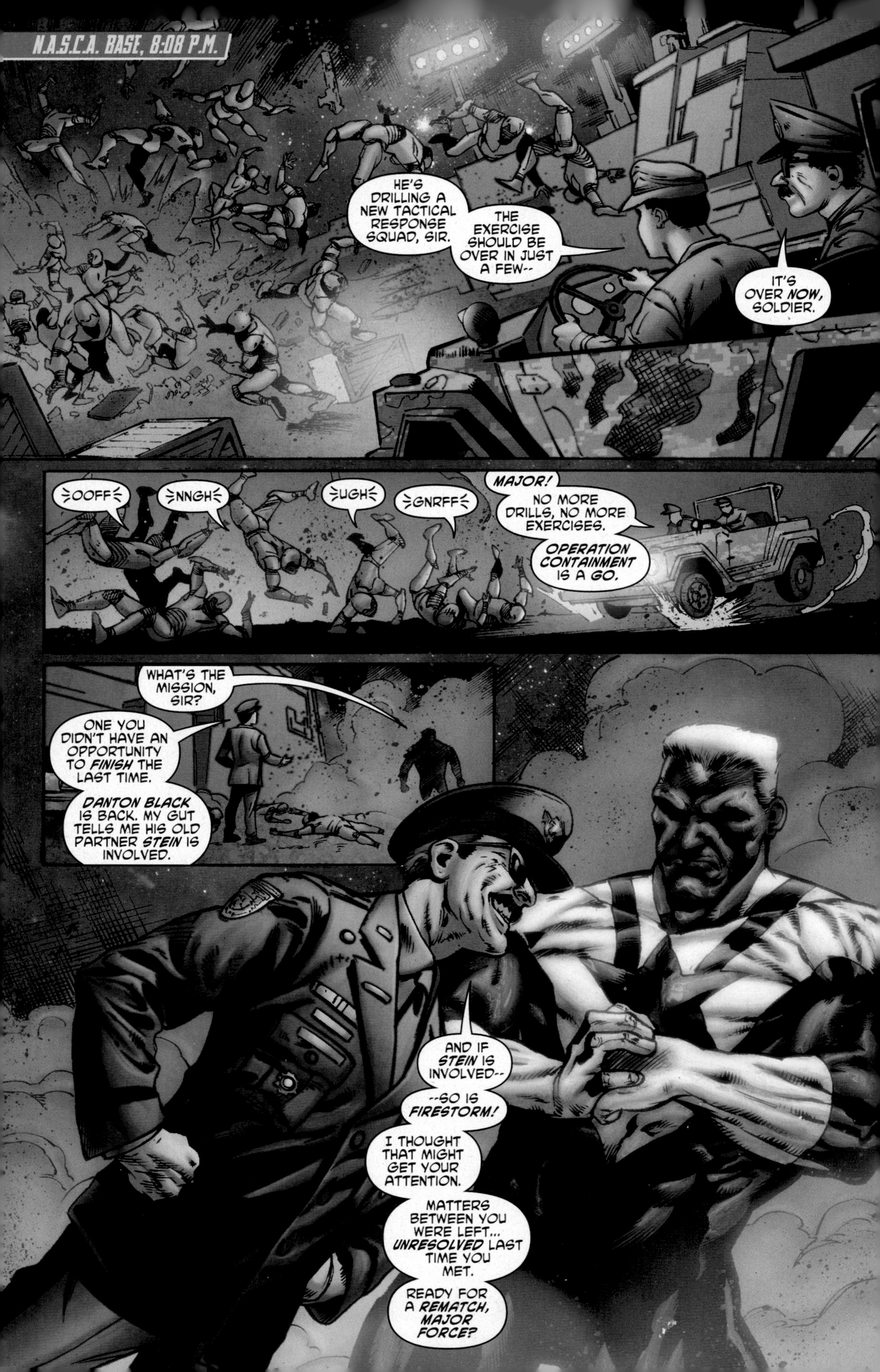
N.A.S.C.A. BASE, 8:08 P.M.
HE'S DRILLING A NEW TACTICAL RESPONSE SQUAD, SIR.
THE EXERCISE SHOULD BE OVER IN JUST A FEW--
IT'S OVER NOW, SOLDIER.
OOFF
NNGH
UGH
GNRFF
MAJOR!
NO MORE DRILLS, NO MORE EXERCISES.
OPERATION CONTAINMENT IS A GO.
WHAT'S THE MISSION, SIR?
ONE YOU DIDN'T HAVE AN OPPORTUNITY TO FINISH THE LAST TIME.
DANTON BLACK IS BACK. MY GUT TELLS ME HIS OLD PARTNER STEIN IS INVOLVED.
AND IF STEIN IS INVOLVED--
--SO IS FIRESTORM!
I THOUGHT THAT MIGHT GET YOUR ATTENTION.
MATTERS BETWEEN YOU WERE LEFT... UNRESOLVED LAST TIME YOU MET.
READY FOR A REMATCH, MAJOR FORCE?

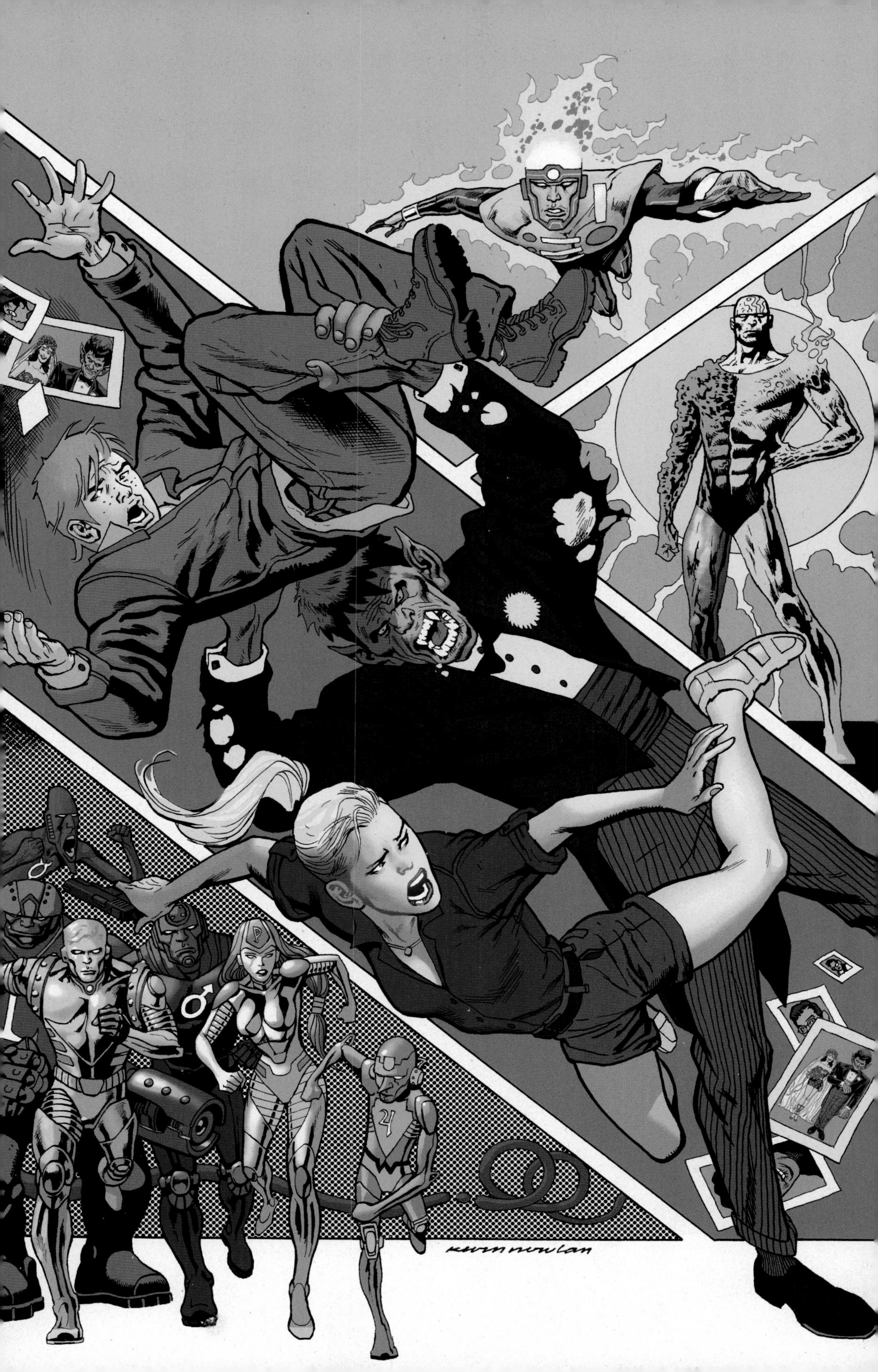
kevin nowlan

GERRY CONWAY writer EDUARDO PANSICA penciller ROB HUNTER inker ANDREW DALHOUSE colorist COREY BREEN letterer
KEVIN NOWLAN cover

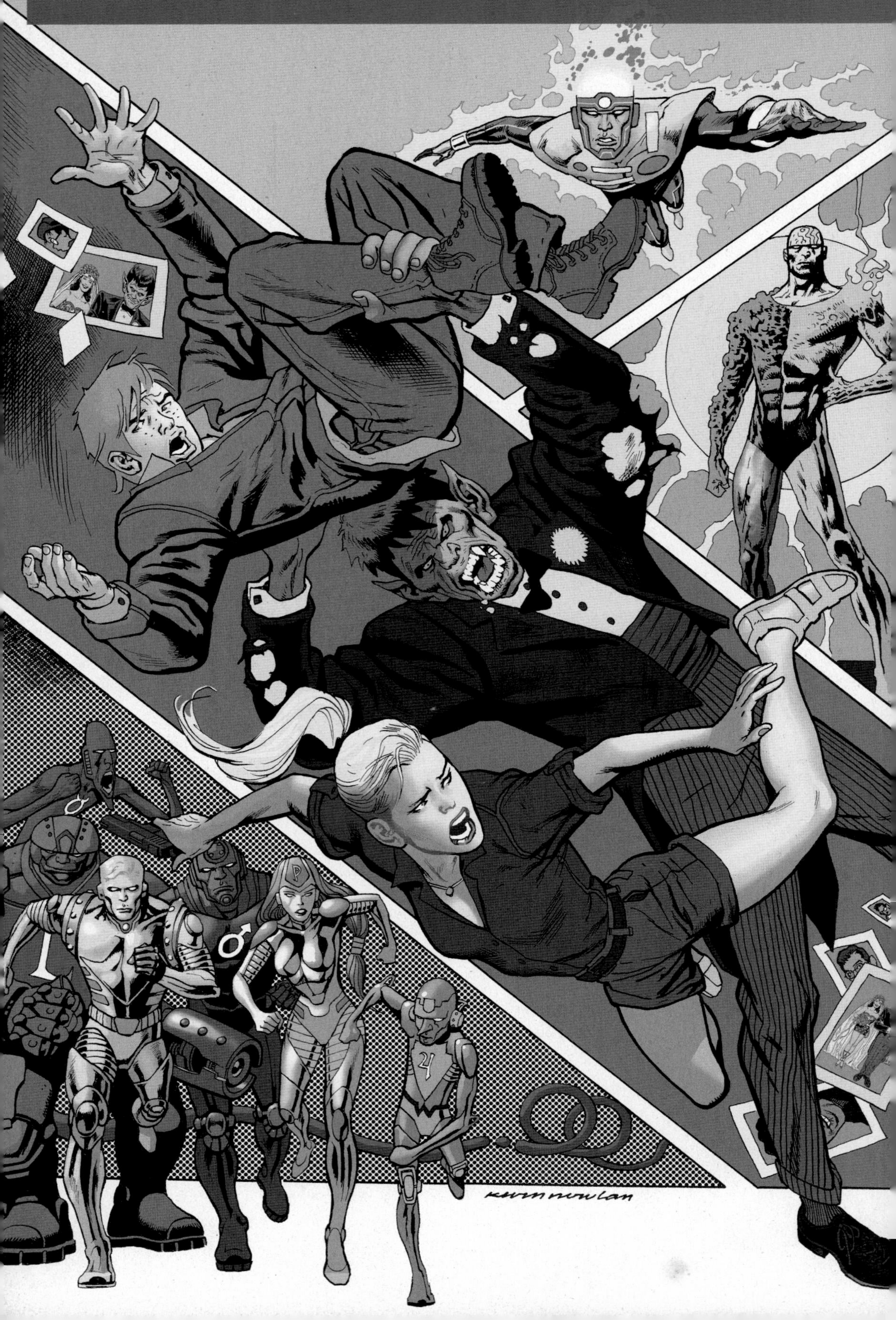
kevin nowlan

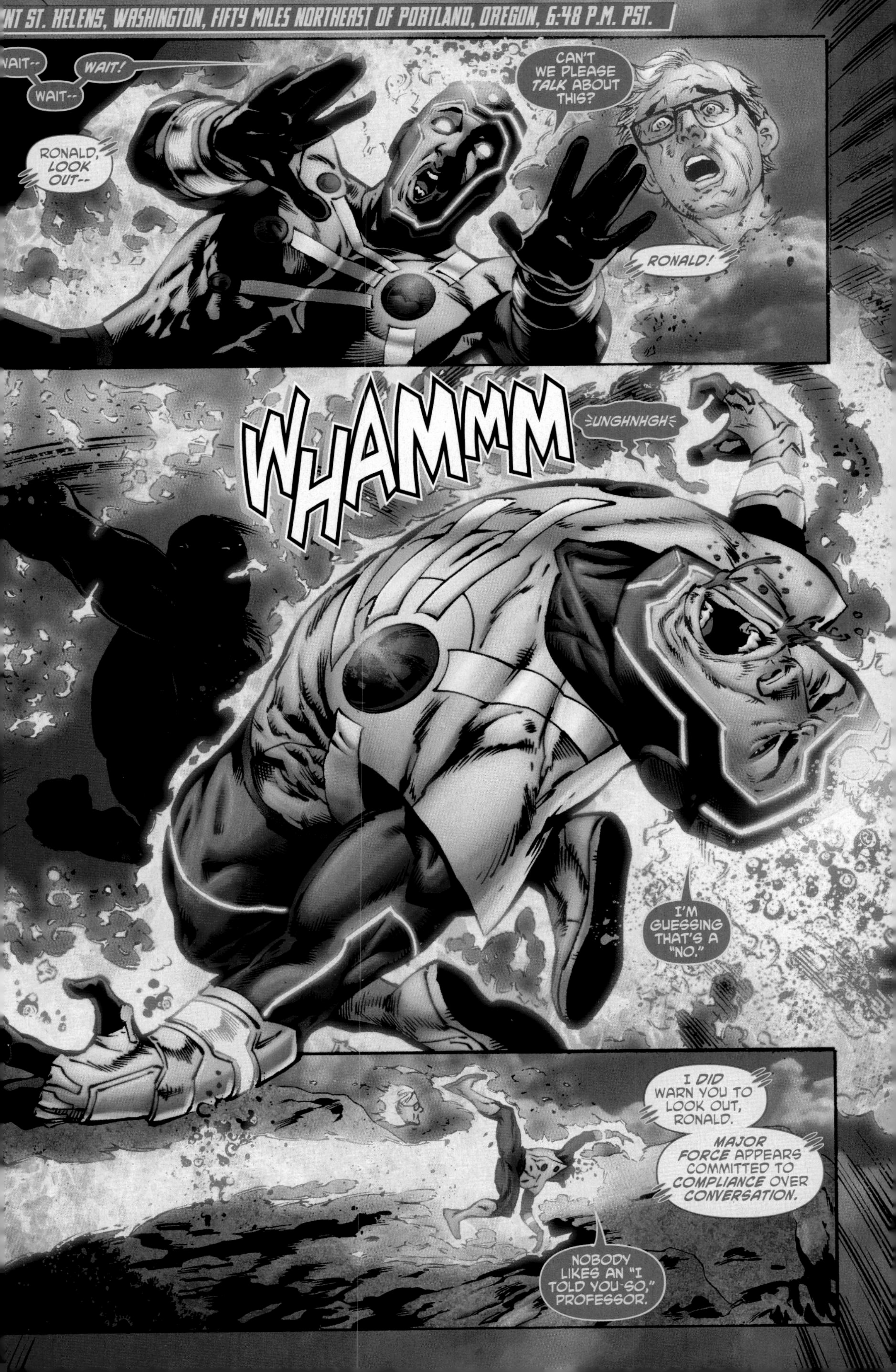

NT ST. HELENS, WASHINGTON, FIFTY MILES NORTHEAST OF PORTLAND, OREGON, 6:48 P.M. PST.
WAIT--
WAIT--
WAIT!
CAN'T WE PLEASE TALK ABOUT THIS?
RONALD, LOOK OUT--
RONALD!
WHAMMM
UNGHNHGH
I'M GUESSING THAT'S A "NO."
I DID WARN YOU TO LOOK OUT, RONALD.
MAJOR FORCE APPEARS COMMITTED TO COMPLIANCE OVER CONVERSATION.
NOBODY LIKES AN "I TOLD YOU-SO," PROFESSOR.

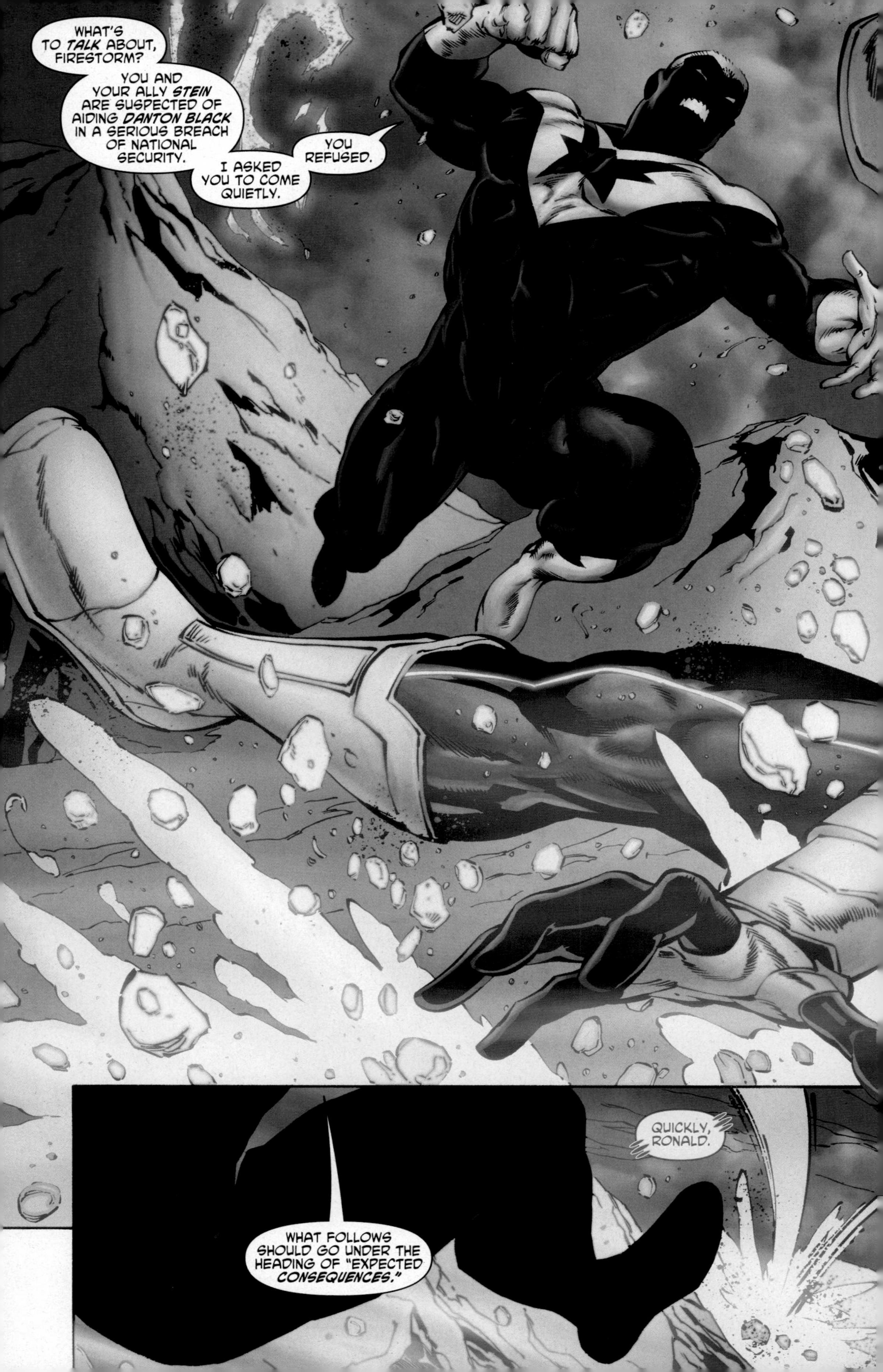
WHAT'S TO TALK ABOUT, FIRESTORM?
YOU AND YOUR ALLY STEIN ARE SUSPECTED OF AIDING DANTON BLACK IN A SERIOUS BREACH OF NATIONAL SECURITY.
I ASKED YOU TO COME QUIETLY.
YOU REFUSED.
QUICKLY, RONALD.
WHAT FOLLOWS SHOULD GO UNDER THE HEADING OF "EXPECTED CONSEQUENCES."

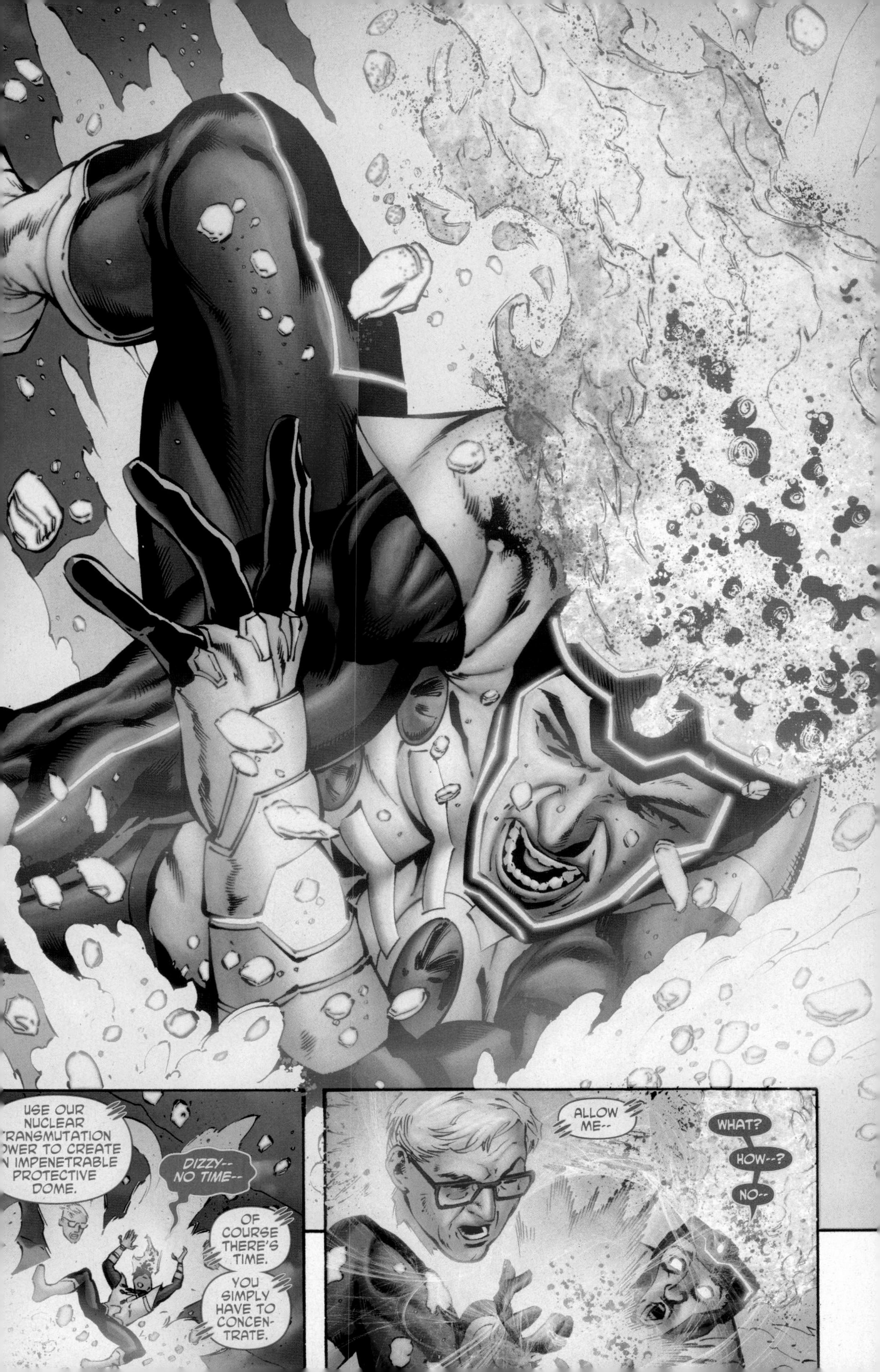
USE OUR NUCLEAR TRANSMUTATION POWER TO CREATE AN IMPENETRABLE PROTECTIVE DOME.
DIZZY-- NO TIME--
OF COURSE THERE'S TIME.
YOU SIMPLY HAVE TO CONCENTRATE.
ALLOW ME--
WHAT?
HOW--?
NO--

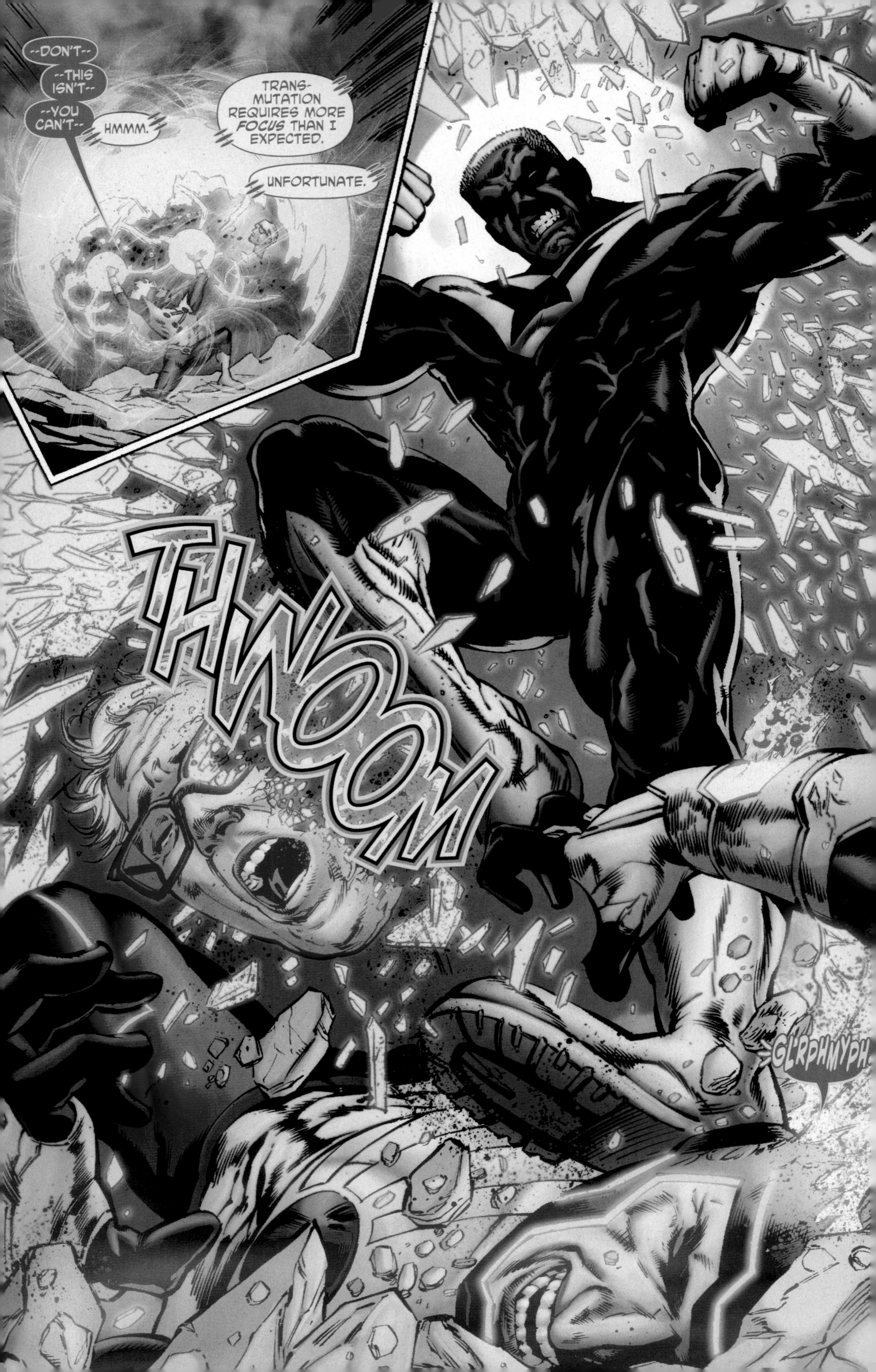
--DON'T--
--THIS ISN'T--
--YOU CAN'T--
HMMM.
TRANS-MUTATION REQUIRES MORE *FOCUS* THAN I EXPECTED.
UNFORTUNATE.
THWOOM
GLRPHMYPH

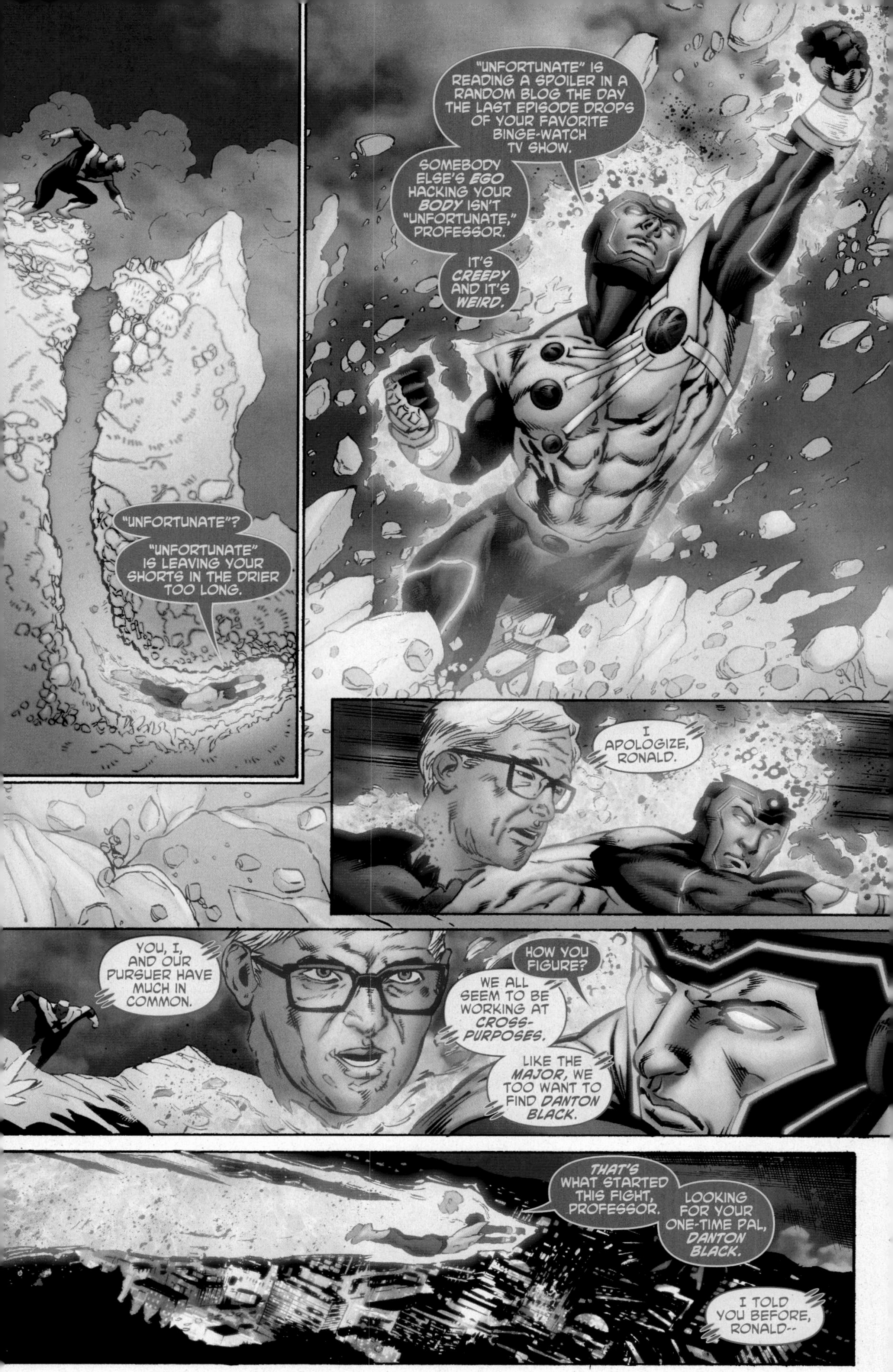
"UNFORTUNATE" IS READING A SPOILER IN A RANDOM BLOG THE DAY THE LAST EPISODE DROPS OF YOUR FAVORITE BINGE-WATCH TV SHOW.
SOMEBODY ELSE'S *EGO* HACKING YOUR *BODY* ISN'T "UNFORTUNATE," PROFESSOR.
IT'S *CREEPY* AND IT'S *WEIRD*.
"UNFORTUNATE"?
"UNFORTUNATE" IS LEAVING YOUR SHORTS IN THE DRIER TOO LONG.
I APOLOGIZE, RONALD.
YOU, I, AND OUR PURSUER HAVE MUCH IN COMMON.
HOW YOU FIGURE?
WE ALL SEEM TO BE WORKING AT *CROSS-PURPOSES*.
LIKE THE *MAJOR*, WE TOO WANT TO FIND *DANTON BLACK*.
THAT'S WHAT STARTED THIS FIGHT, PROFESSOR.
LOOKING FOR YOUR ONE-TIME PAL, *DANTON BLACK*.
I TOLD YOU BEFORE, RONALD--

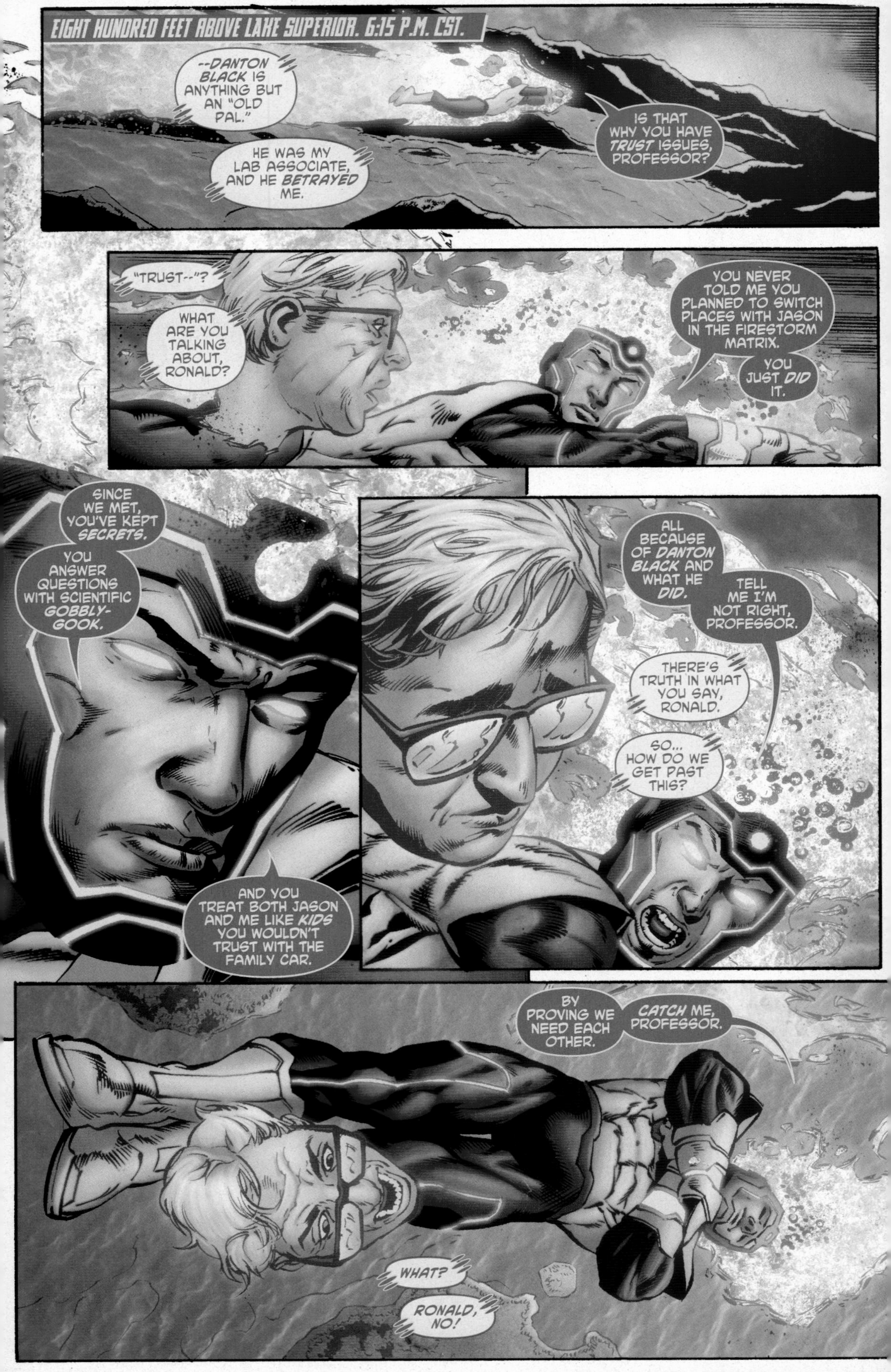
EIGHT HUNDRED FEET ABOVE LAKE SUPERIOR. 6:15 P.M. CST.
--DANTON BLACK IS ANYTHING BUT AN "OLD PAL."
HE WAS MY LAB ASSOCIATE, AND HE BETRAYED ME.
IS THAT WHY YOU HAVE TRUST ISSUES, PROFESSOR?
"TRUST--"?
WHAT ARE YOU TALKING ABOUT, RONALD?
YOU NEVER TOLD ME YOU PLANNED TO SWITCH PLACES WITH JASON IN THE FIRESTORM MATRIX.
YOU JUST DID IT.
SINCE WE MET, YOU'VE KEPT SECRETS.
YOU ANSWER QUESTIONS WITH SCIENTIFIC GOBBLY-GOOK.
AND YOU TREAT BOTH JASON AND ME LIKE KIDS YOU WOULDN'T TRUST WITH THE FAMILY CAR.
ALL BECAUSE OF DANTON BLACK AND WHAT HE DID.
TELL ME I'M NOT RIGHT, PROFESSOR.
THERE'S TRUTH IN WHAT YOU SAY, RONALD.
SO... HOW DO WE GET PAST THIS?
BY PROVING WE NEED EACH OTHER.
CATCH ME, PROFESSOR.
WHAT?
RONALD, NO!

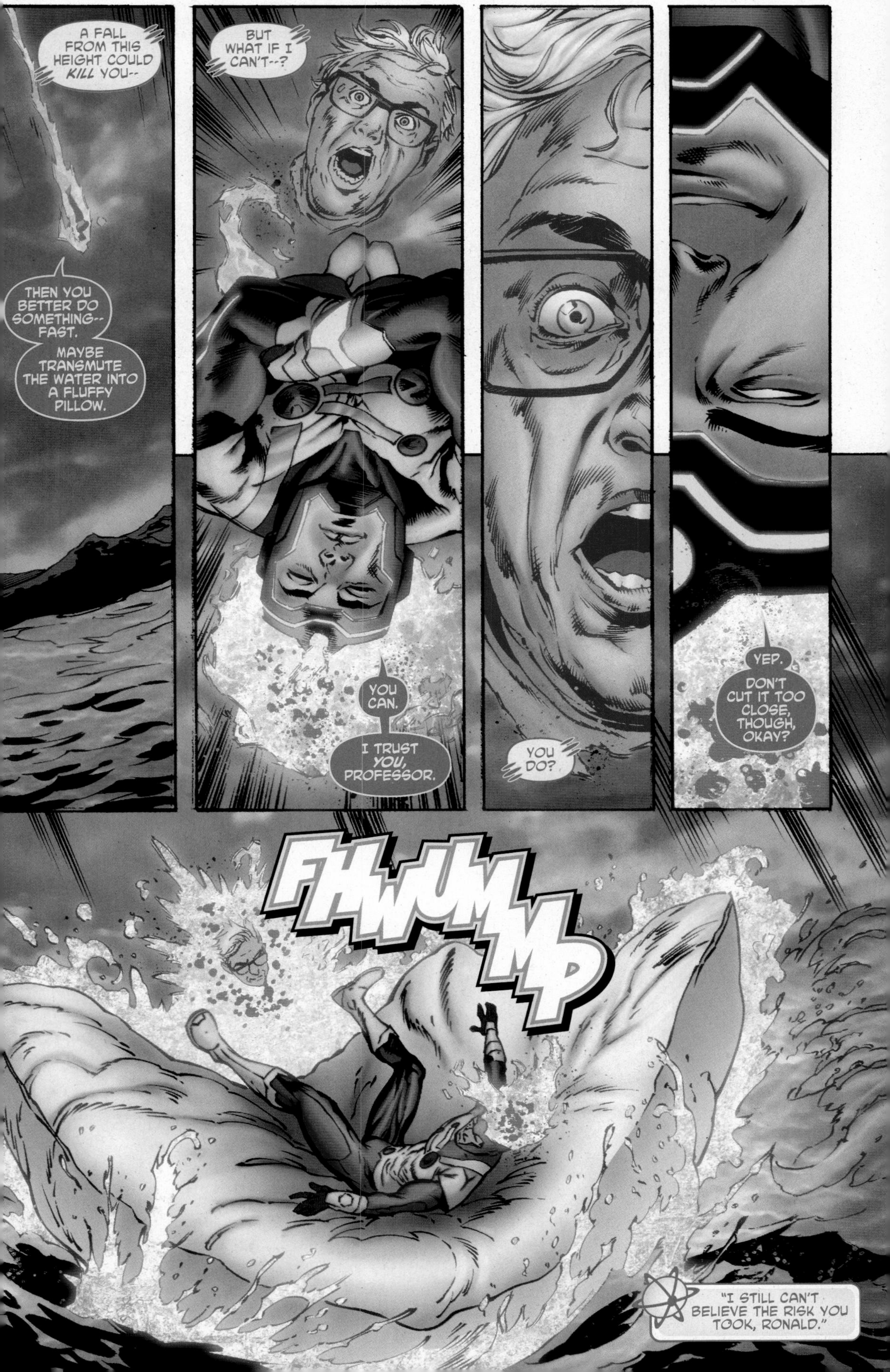
A FALL FROM THIS HEIGHT COULD KILL YOU--
THEN YOU BETTER DO SOMETHING-- FAST.
MAYBE TRANSMUTE THE WATER INTO A FLUFFY PILLOW.
BUT WHAT IF I CAN'T--?
YOU CAN.
I TRUST YOU, PROFESSOR.
YOU DO?
YEP.
DON'T CUT IT TOO CLOSE, THOUGH, OKAY?
FHWUMMP
"I STILL CAN'T BELIEVE THE RISK YOU TOOK, RONALD."

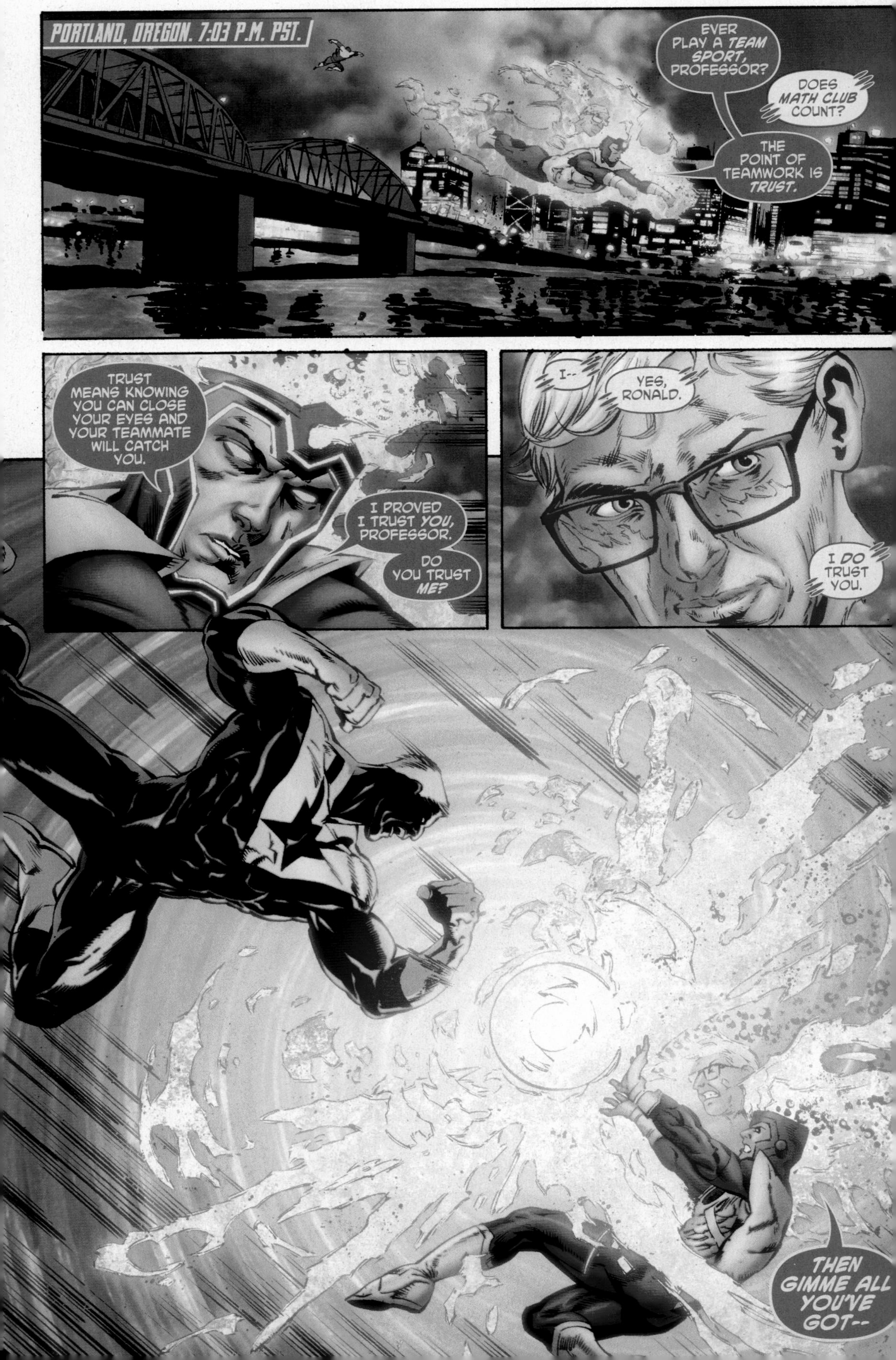
PORTLAND, OREGON. 7:03 P.M. PST.
EVER PLAY A TEAM SPORT, PROFESSOR?
DOES MATH CLUB COUNT?
THE POINT OF TEAMWORK IS TRUST.
TRUST MEANS KNOWING YOU CAN CLOSE YOUR EYES AND YOUR TEAMMATE WILL CATCH YOU.
I PROVED I TRUST YOU, PROFESSOR.
DO YOU TRUST ME?
I--
YES, RONALD.
I DO TRUST YOU.
THEN GIMME ALL YOU'VE GOT--

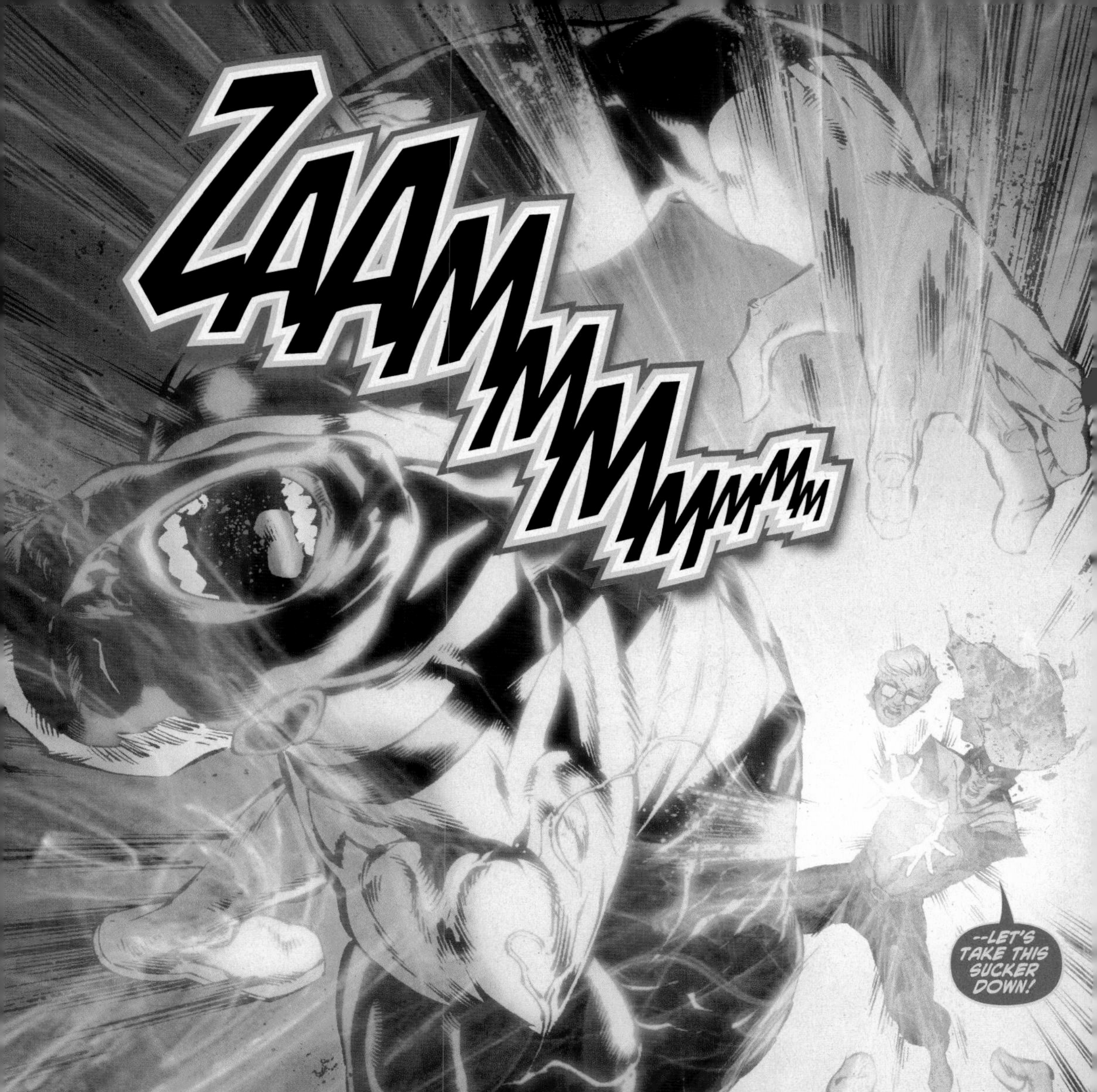
ZAAMMMMMMM
--LET'S TAKE THIS SUCKER DOWN!

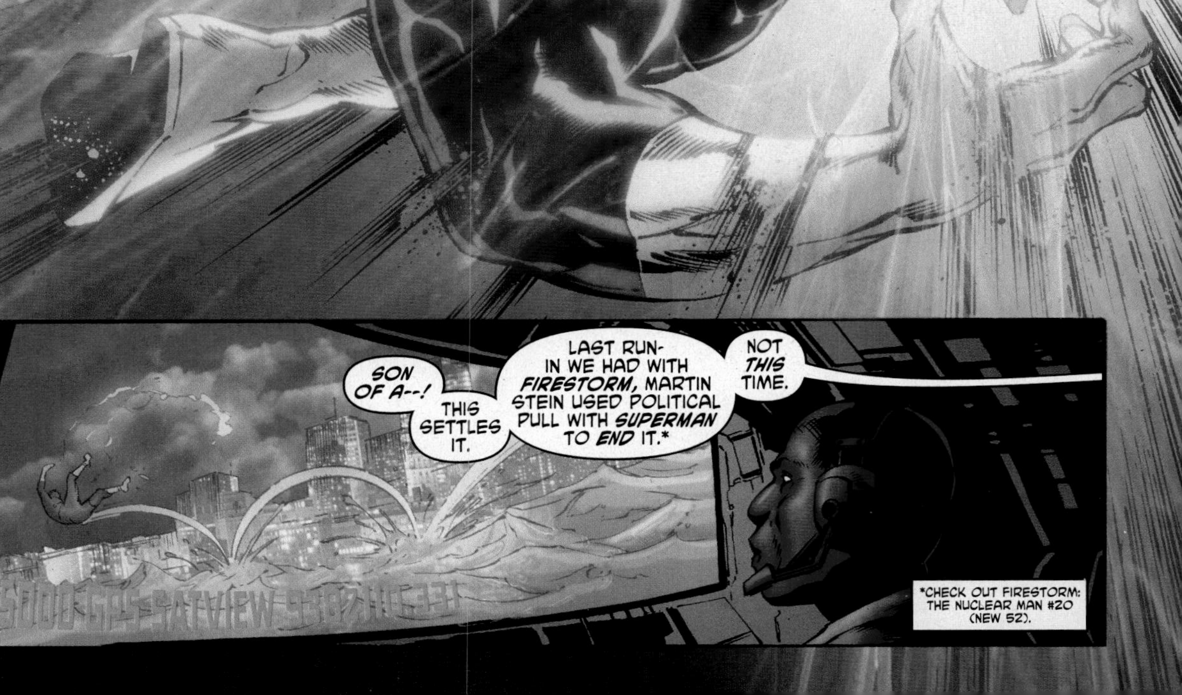
SON OF A--!
THIS SETTLES IT.
LAST RUN-IN WE HAD WITH *FIRESTORM*, MARTIN STEIN USED POLITICAL PULL WITH *SUPERMAN* TO *END* IT.*
NOT *THIS* TIME.

*CHECK OUT FIRESTORM: THE NUCLEAR MAN #20 (NEW 52).

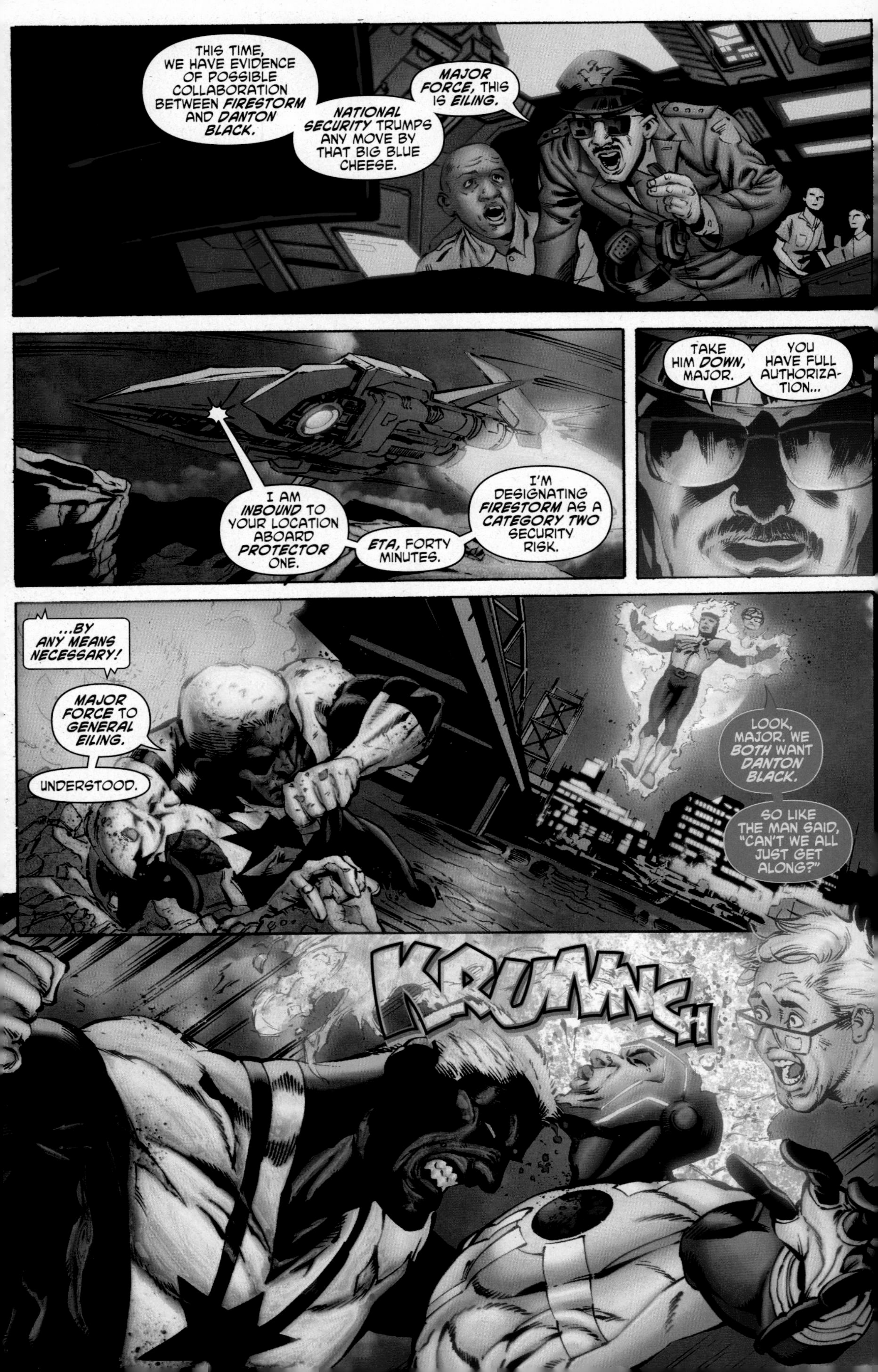

THIS TIME, WE HAVE EVIDENCE OF POSSIBLE COLLABORATION BETWEEN FIRESTORM AND DANTON BLACK.
MAJOR FORCE, THIS IS EILING.
NATIONAL SECURITY TRUMPS ANY MOVE BY THAT BIG BLUE CHEESE.
I AM INBOUND TO YOUR LOCATION ABOARD PROTECTOR ONE.
ETA, FORTY MINUTES.
I'M DESIGNATING FIRESTORM AS A CATEGORY TWO SECURITY RISK.
TAKE HIM DOWN, MAJOR.
YOU HAVE FULL AUTHORIZATION...
...BY ANY MEANS NECESSARY!
MAJOR FORCE TO GENERAL EILING.
UNDERSTOOD.
LOOK, MAJOR. WE BOTH WANT DANTON BLACK.
SO LIKE THE MAN SAID, "CAN'T WE ALL JUST GET ALONG?"
KRUNNCH

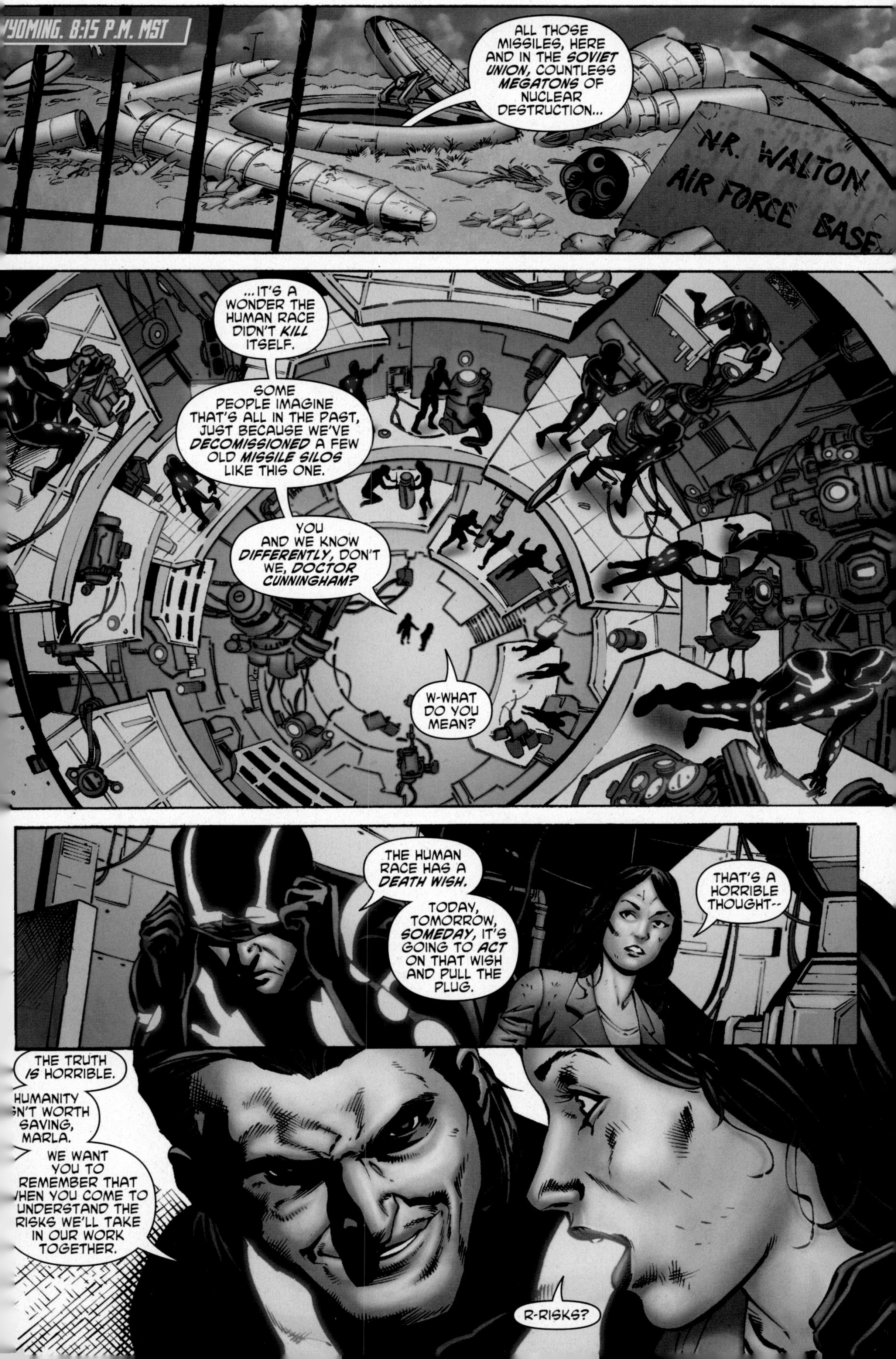

YOMING. 8:15 P.M. MST
ALL THOSE MISSILES, HERE AND IN THE SOVIET UNION, COUNTLESS MEGATONS OF NUCLEAR DESTRUCTION...
N.R. WALTON AIR FORCE BASE
...IT'S A WONDER THE HUMAN RACE DIDN'T KILL ITSELF.
SOME PEOPLE IMAGINE THAT'S ALL IN THE PAST, JUST BECAUSE WE'VE DECOMISSIONED A FEW OLD MISSILE SILOS LIKE THIS ONE.
YOU AND WE KNOW DIFFERENTLY, DON'T WE, DOCTOR CUNNINGHAM?
W-WHAT DO YOU MEAN?
THE HUMAN RACE HAS A DEATH WISH.
TODAY, TOMORROW, SOMEDAY, IT'S GOING TO ACT ON THAT WISH AND PULL THE PLUG.
THAT'S A HORRIBLE THOUGHT--
THE TRUTH IS HORRIBLE.
HUMANITY SN'T WORTH SAVING, MARLA.
WE WANT YOU TO REMEMBER THAT WHEN YOU COME TO UNDERSTAND THE RISKS WE'LL TAKE IN OUR WORK TOGETHER.
R-RISKS?

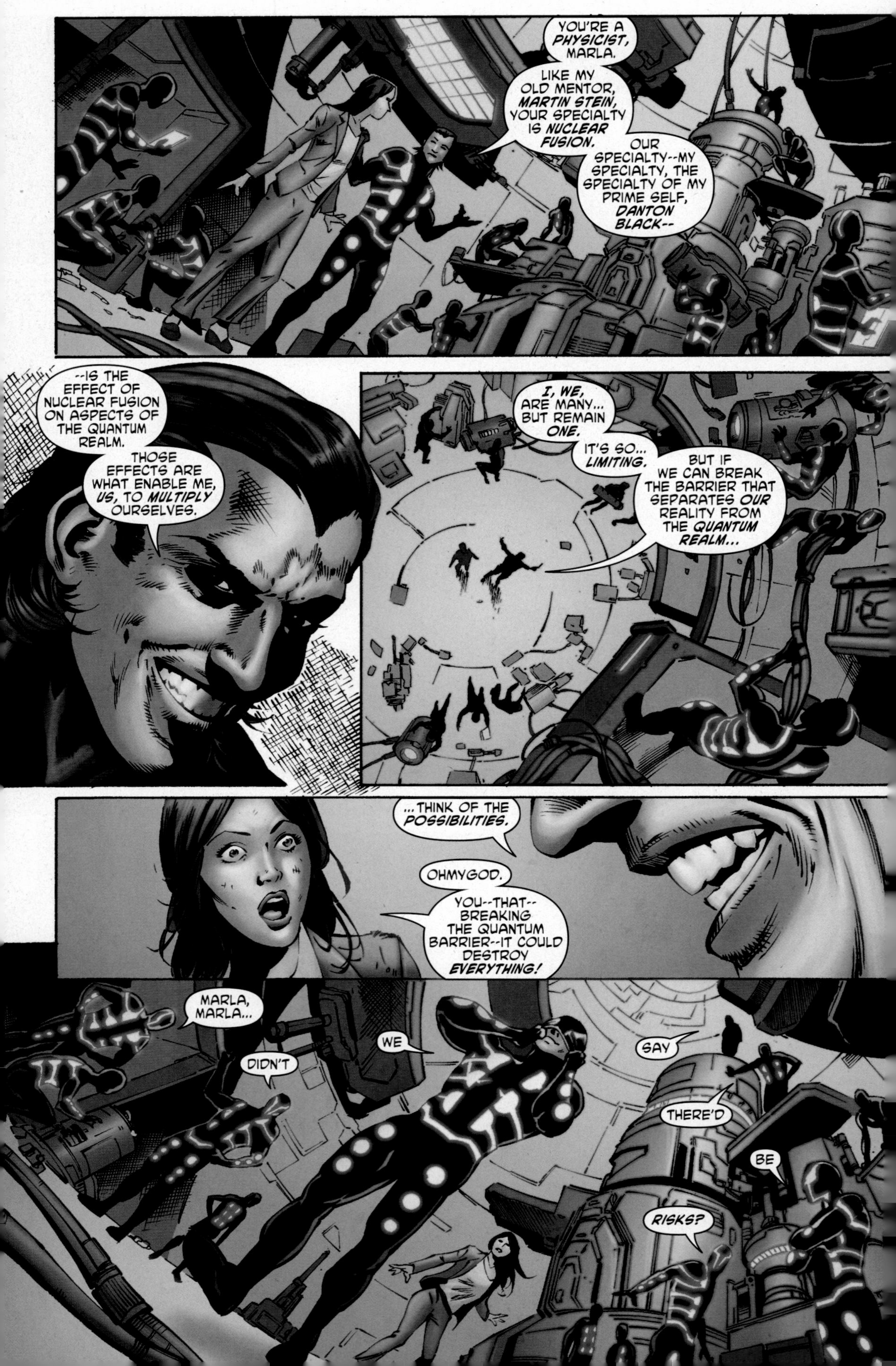
YOU'RE A PHYSICIST, MARLA.
LIKE MY OLD MENTOR, MARTIN STEIN, YOUR SPECIALTY IS NUCLEAR FUSION.
OUR SPECIALTY--MY SPECIALTY, THE SPECIALTY OF MY PRIME SELF, DANTON BLACK--
--IS THE EFFECT OF NUCLEAR FUSION ON ASPECTS OF THE QUANTUM REALM.
THOSE EFFECTS ARE WHAT ENABLE ME, US, TO MULTIPLY OURSELVES.
I, WE, ARE MANY... BUT REMAIN ONE.
IT'S SO... LIMITING.
BUT IF WE CAN BREAK THE BARRIER THAT SEPARATES OUR REALITY FROM THE QUANTUM REALM...
...THINK OF THE POSSIBILITIES.
OHMYGOD.
YOU--THAT--BREAKING THE QUANTUM BARRIER--IT COULD DESTROY EVERYTHING!
MARLA, MARLA...
DIDN'T
WE
SAY
THERE'D
BE
RISKS?

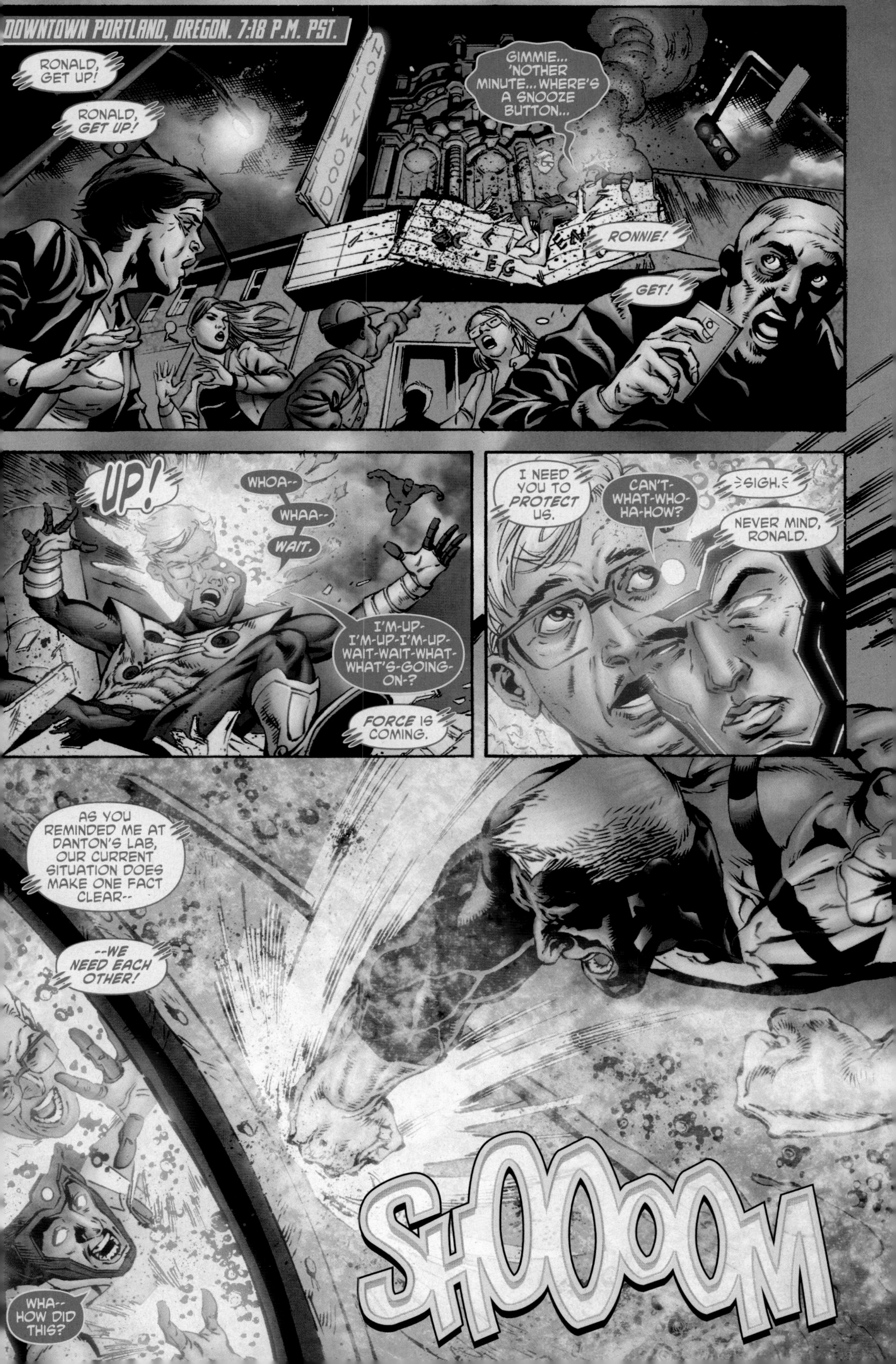
DOWNTOWN PORTLAND, OREGON. 7:18 P.M. PST.
RONALD, GET UP!
RONALD, GET UP!
GIMMIE... 'NOTHER MINUTE... WHERE'S A SNOOZE BUTTON...
HOLLYWOOD
RONNIE!
GET!
UP!
WHOA--
WHAA--
WAIT.
I'M-UP-I'M-UP-I'M-UP-WAIT-WAIT-WHAT-WHAT'S-GOING-ON-?
FORCE IS COMING.
I NEED YOU TO PROTECT US.
CAN'T-WHAT-WHO-HA-HOW?
SIGH.
NEVER MIND, RONALD.
AS YOU REMINDED ME AT DANTON'S LAB, OUR CURRENT SITUATION DOES MAKE ONE FACT CLEAR--
--WE NEED EACH OTHER!
WHA-- HOW DID THIS?
SHOOOOM

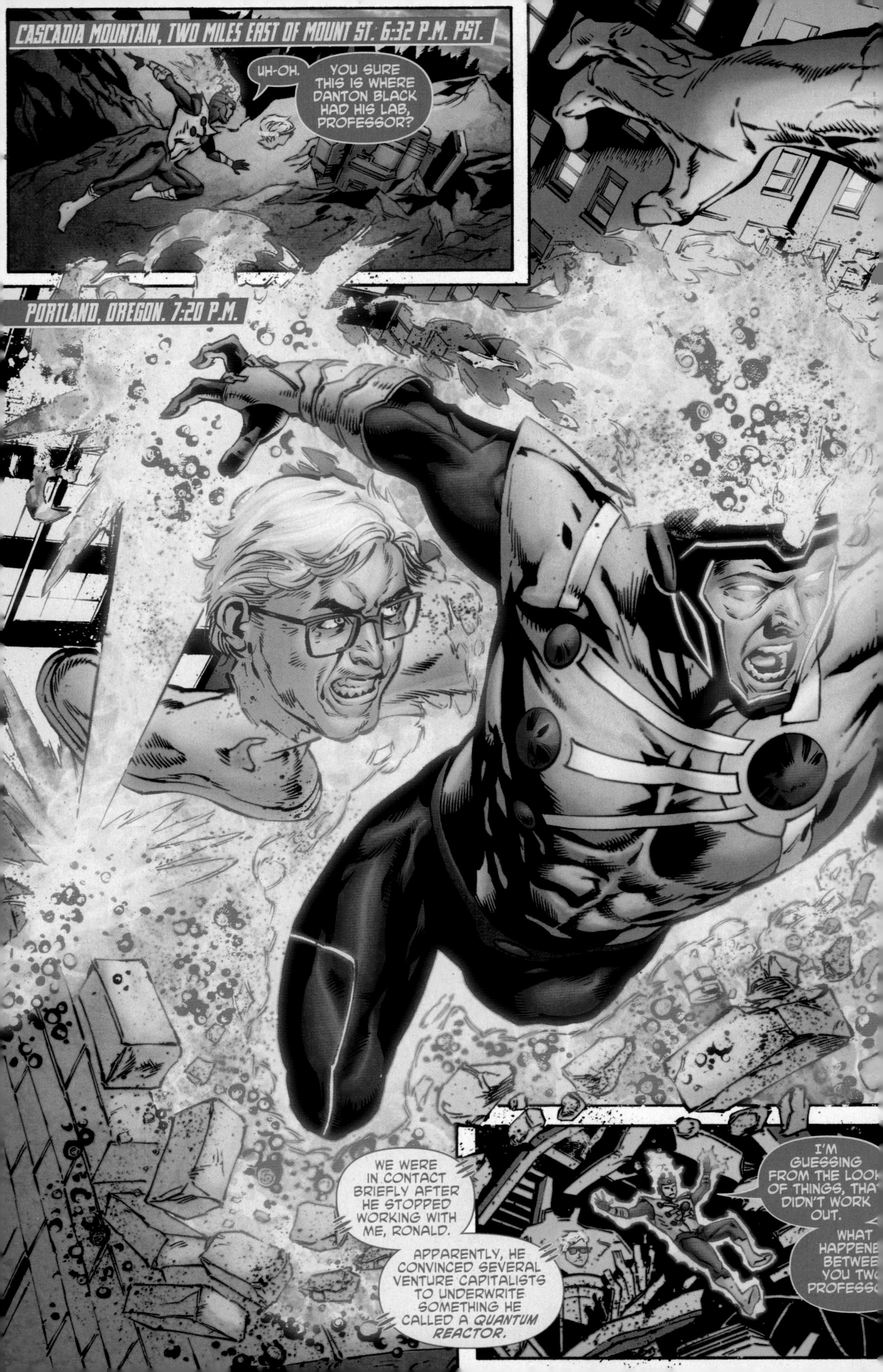
CASCADIA MOUNTAIN, TWO MILES EAST OF MOUNT ST. 6:32 P.M. PST.
UH-OH.
YOU SURE THIS IS WHERE DANTON BLACK HAD HIS LAB, PROFESSOR?
PORTLAND, OREGON. 7:20 P.M.
WE WERE IN CONTACT BRIEFLY AFTER HE STOPPED WORKING WITH ME, RONALD.
APPARENTLY, HE CONVINCED SEVERAL VENTURE CAPITALISTS TO UNDERWRITE SOMETHING HE CALLED A *QUANTUM REACTOR*.
I'M GUESSING FROM THE LOO OF THINGS, THA DIDN'T WORK OUT.
WHAT HAPPENE BETWEE YOU TW PROFESS

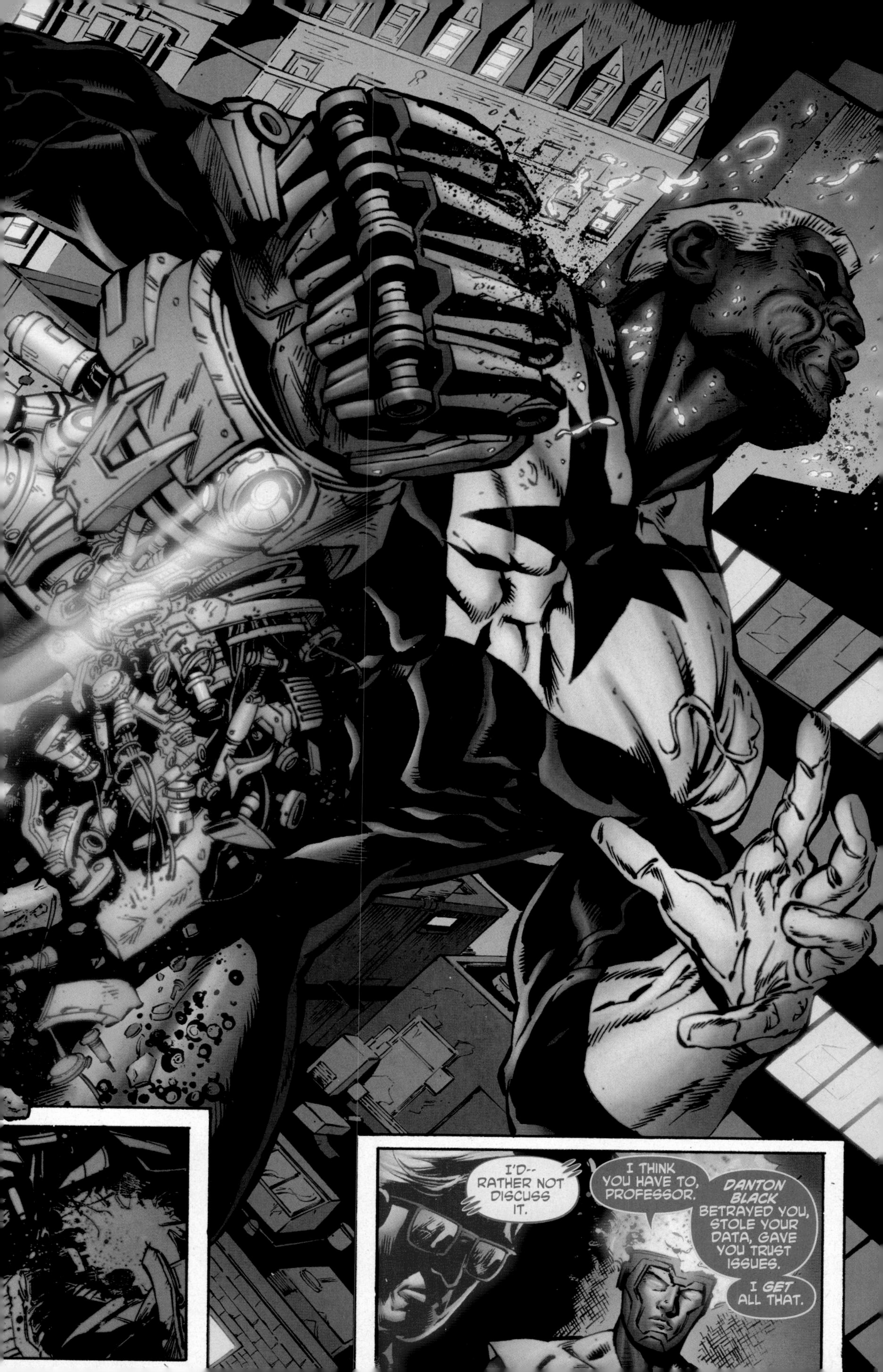
I'D--
RATHER NOT DISCUSS IT.
I THINK YOU HAVE TO, PROFESSOR.
DANTON BLACK BETRAYED YOU, STOLE YOUR DATA, GAVE YOU TRUST ISSUES.
I GET ALL THAT.

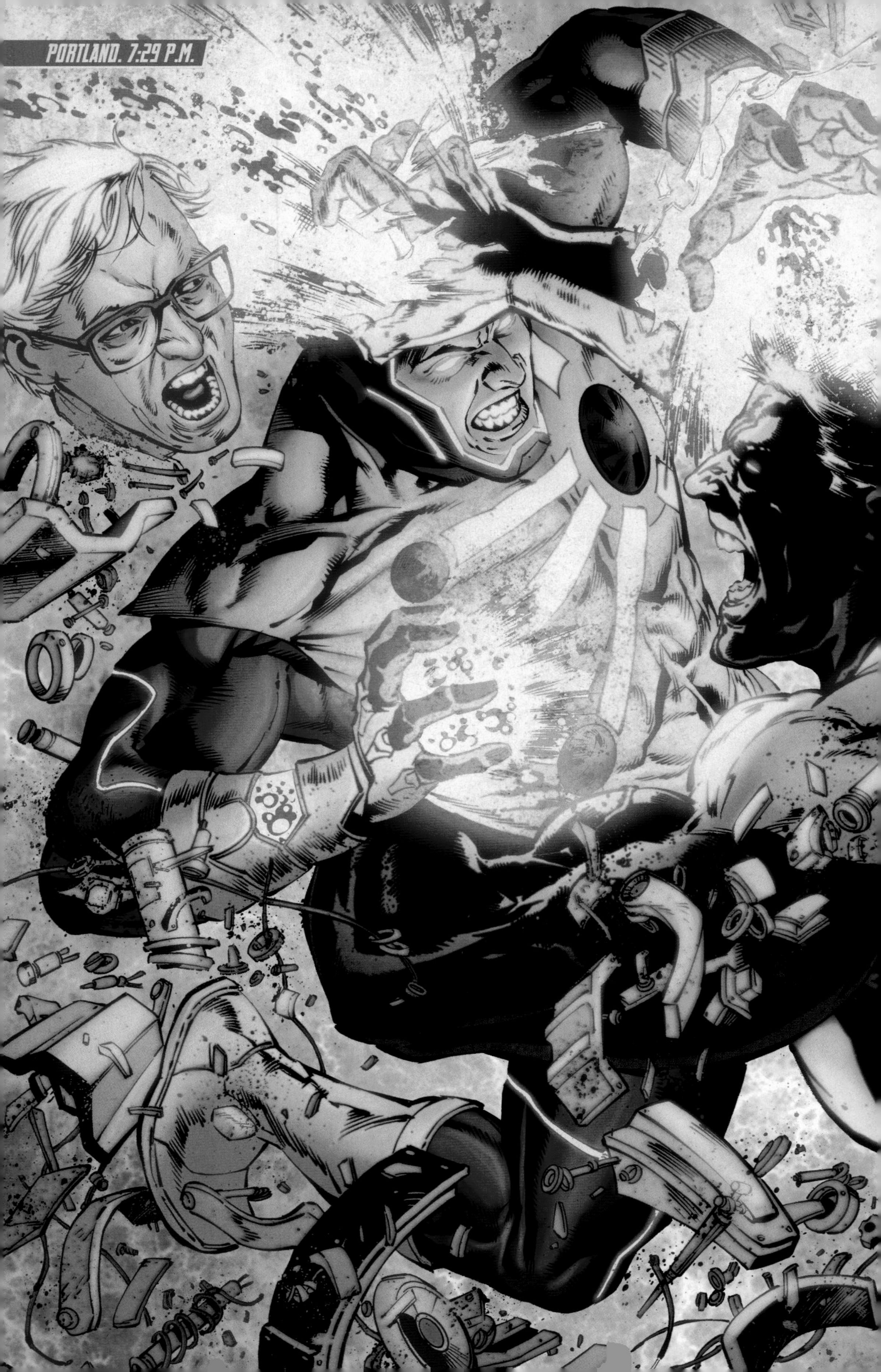
PORTLAND. 7:29 P.M.

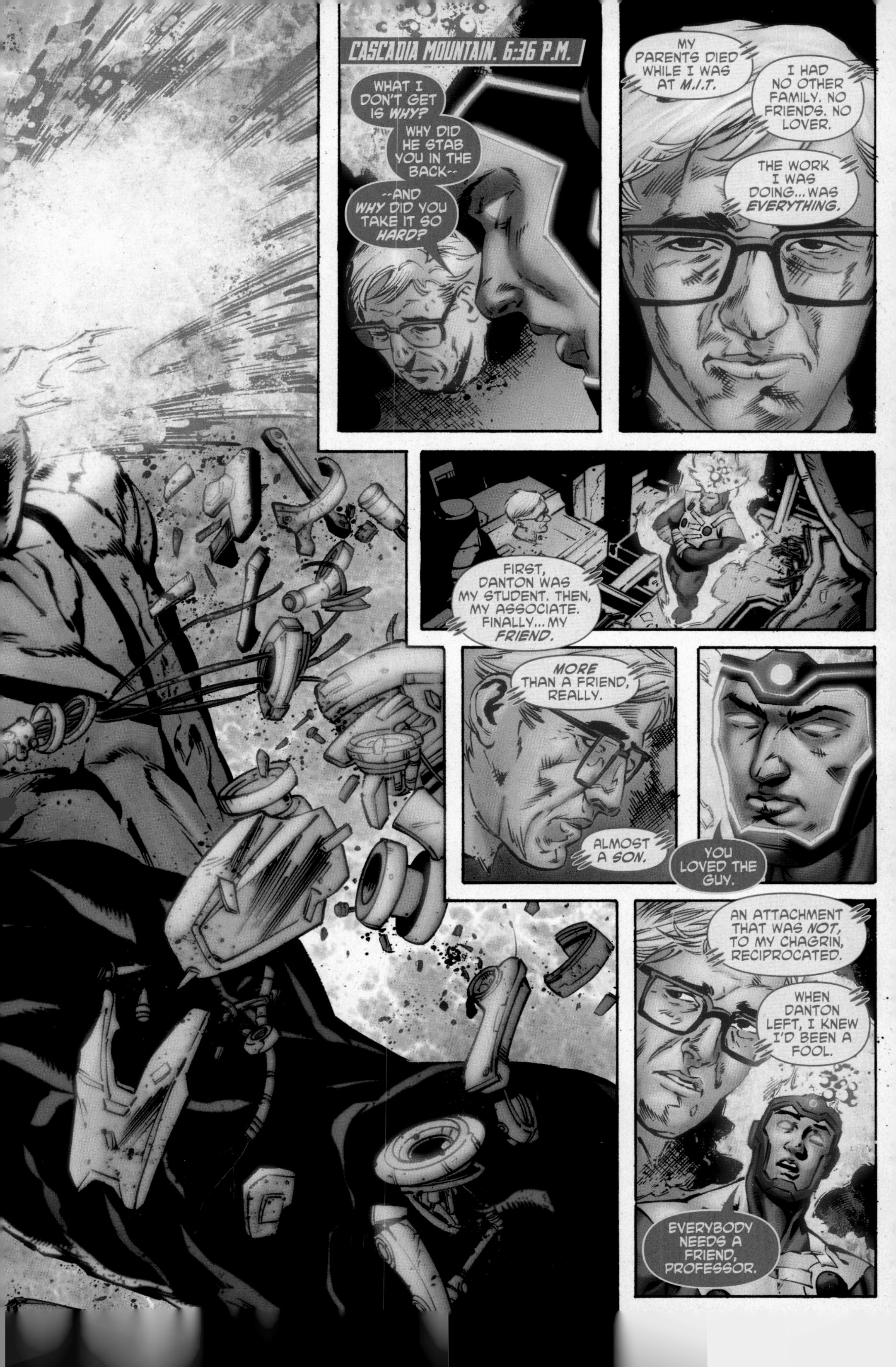

CASCADIA MOUNTAIN. 6:36 P.M.
WHAT I DON'T GET IS WHY?
WHY DID HE STAB YOU IN THE BACK--
--AND WHY DID YOU TAKE IT SO HARD?
MY PARENTS DIED WHILE I WAS AT M.I.T.
I HAD NO OTHER FAMILY. NO FRIENDS. NO LOVER.
THE WORK I WAS DOING...WAS EVERYTHING.
FIRST, DANTON WAS MY STUDENT. THEN, MY ASSOCIATE. FINALLY... MY FRIEND.
MORE THAN A FRIEND, REALLY.
ALMOST A SON.
YOU LOVED THE GUY.
AN ATTACHMENT THAT WAS NOT, TO MY CHAGRIN, RECIPROCATED.
WHEN DANTON LEFT, I KNEW I'D BEEN A FOOL.
EVERYBODY NEEDS A FRIEND, PROFESSOR.

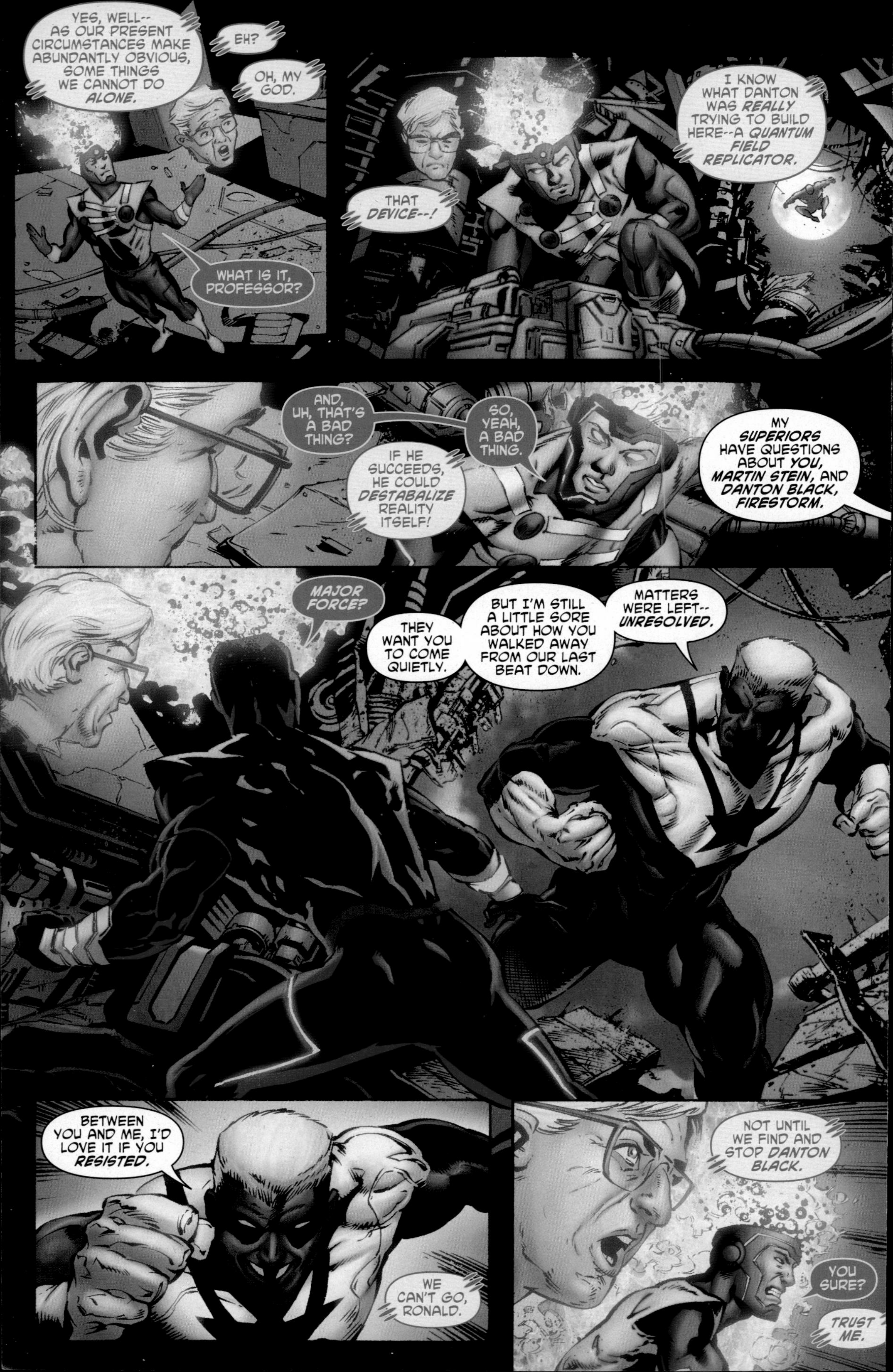

YES, WELL-- AS OUR PRESENT CIRCUMSTANCES MAKE ABUNDANTLY OBVIOUS, SOME THINGS WE CANNOT DO ALONE.
EH?
OH, MY GOD.
WHAT IS IT, PROFESSOR?
THAT DEVICE--!
I KNOW WHAT DANTON WAS REALLY TRYING TO BUILD HERE--A QUANTUM FIELD REPLICATOR.
AND, UH, THAT'S A BAD THING?
IF HE SUCCEEDS, HE COULD DESTABALIZE REALITY ITSELF!
SO, YEAH, A BAD THING.
MY SUPERIORS HAVE QUESTIONS ABOUT YOU, MARTIN STEIN, AND DANTON BLACK, FIRESTORM.
MAJOR FORCE?
THEY WANT YOU TO COME QUIETLY.
BUT I'M STILL A LITTLE SORE ABOUT HOW YOU WALKED AWAY FROM OUR LAST BEAT DOWN.
MATTERS WERE LEFT-- UNRESOLVED.
BETWEEN YOU AND ME, I'D LOVE IT IF YOU RESISTED.
WE CAN'T GO, RONALD.
NOT UNTIL WE FIND AND STOP DANTON BLACK.
YOU SURE?
TRUST ME.

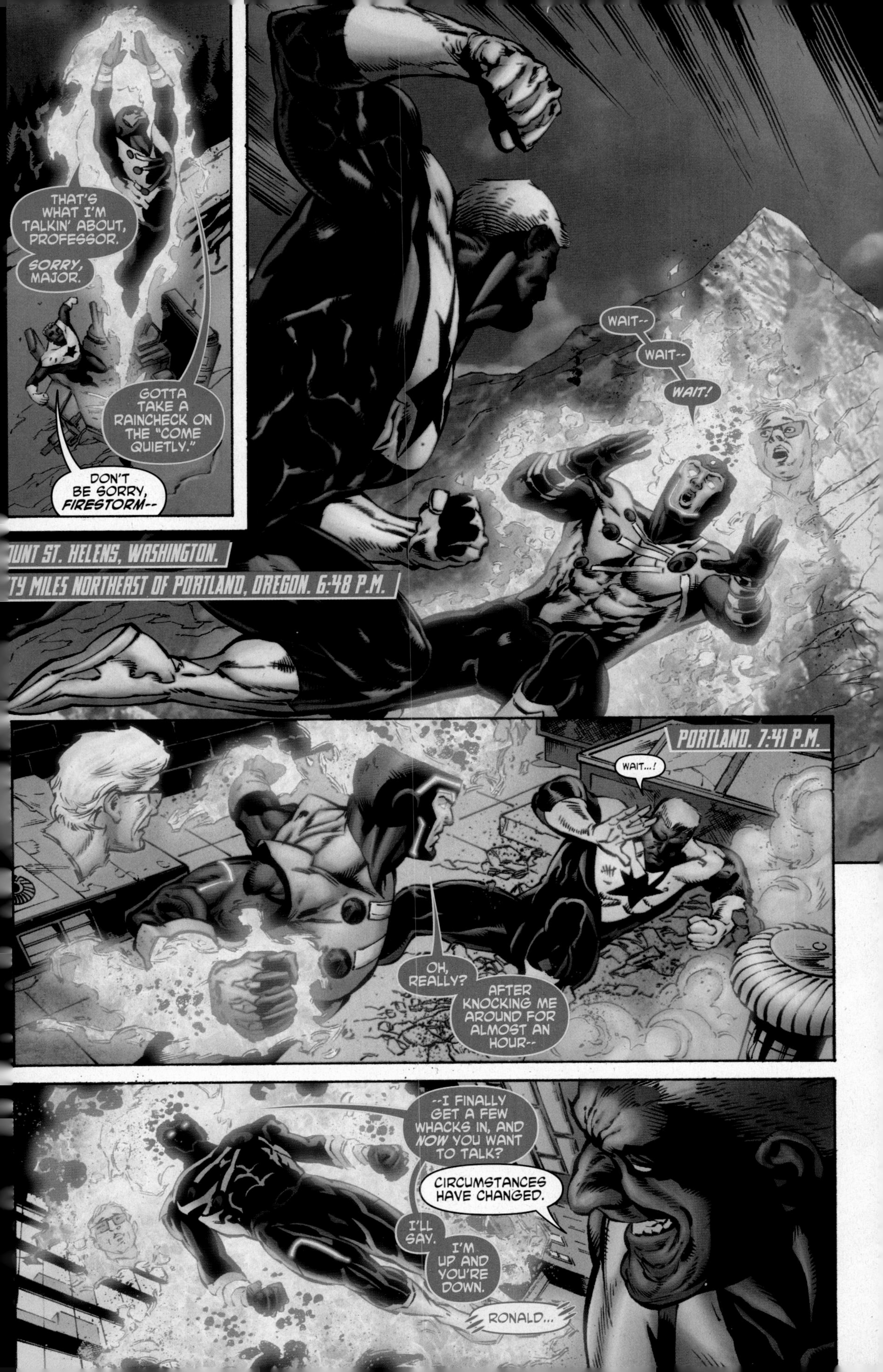
THAT'S WHAT I'M TALKIN' ABOUT, PROFESSOR.
SORRY, MAJOR.
GOTTA TAKE A RAINCHECK ON THE "COME QUIETLY."
DON'T BE SORRY, FIRESTORM--
OUNT ST. HELENS, WASHINGTON.
TY MILES NORTHEAST OF PORTLAND, OREGON. 6:48 P.M.
WAIT--
WAIT--
WAIT!
PORTLAND. 7:41 P.M.
WAIT...!
OH, REALLY?
AFTER KNOCKING ME AROUND FOR ALMOST AN HOUR--
--I FINALLY GET A FEW WHACKS IN, AND NOW YOU WANT TO TALK?
CIRCUMSTANCES HAVE CHANGED.
I'LL SAY.
I'M UP AND YOU'RE DOWN.
RONALD...

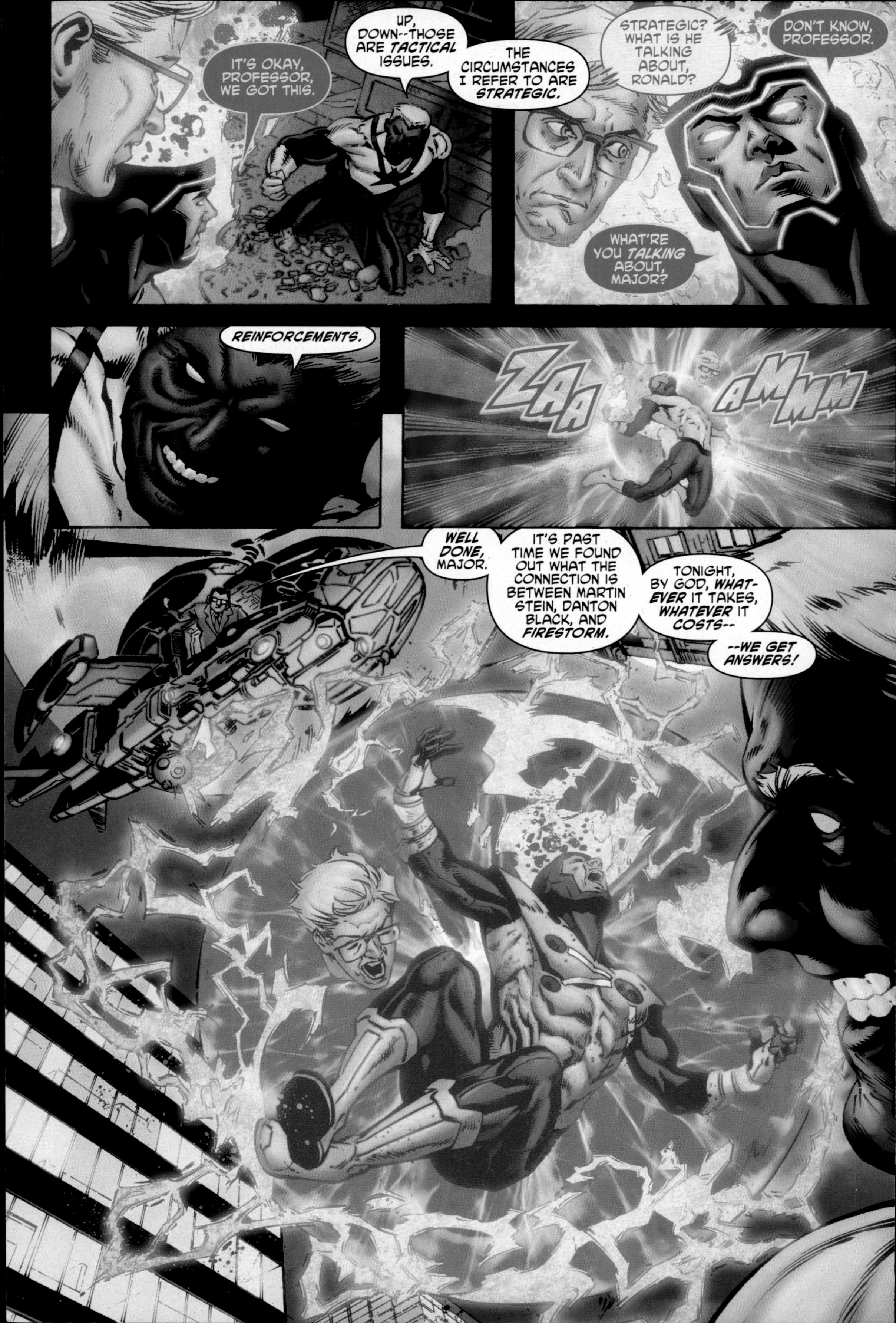
IT'S OKAY, PROFESSOR, WE GOT THIS.
UP, DOWN--THOSE ARE *TACTICAL* ISSUES.
THE CIRCUMSTANCES I REFER TO ARE *STRATEGIC.*
STRATEGIC? WHAT IS HE TALKING ABOUT, RONALD?
DON'T KNOW, PROFESSOR.
WHAT'RE YOU *TALKING* ABOUT, MAJOR?
REINFORCEMENTS.
ZAA
AMMMM
WELL DONE, MAJOR.
IT'S PAST TIME WE FOUND OUT WHAT THE CONNECTION IS BETWEEN MARTIN STEIN, DANTON BLACK, AND *FIRESTORM.*
TONIGHT, BY GOD, *WHATEVER* IT TAKES, *WHATEVER* IT COSTS--
--WE GET ANSWERS!

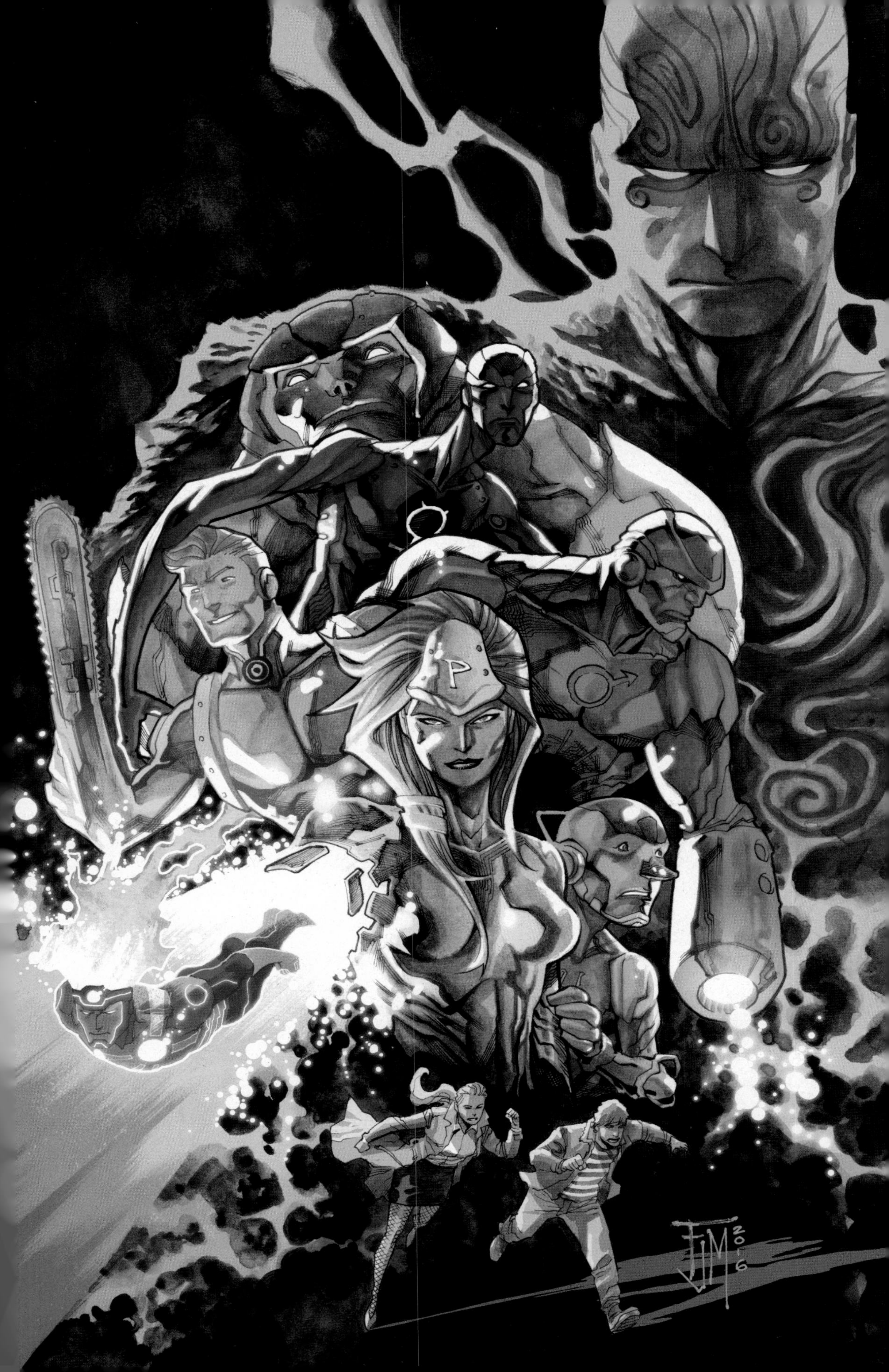

GERRY CONWAY writer **EDUARDO PANSICA** penciller **ROB HUNTER** inker **ANDREW DALHOUSE** colorist **COREY BREEN** letterer
FRANCIS MANAPUL cover

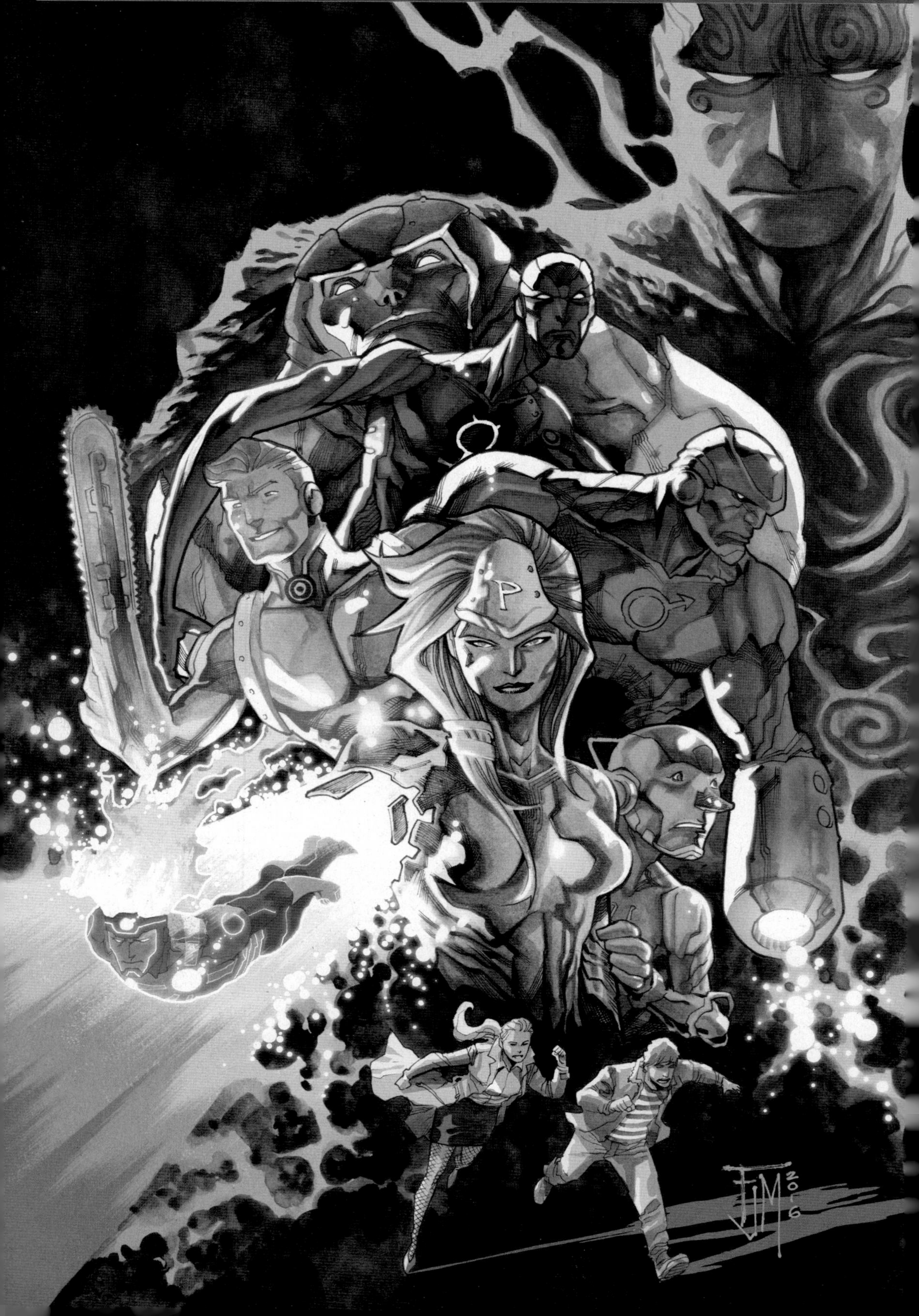
P

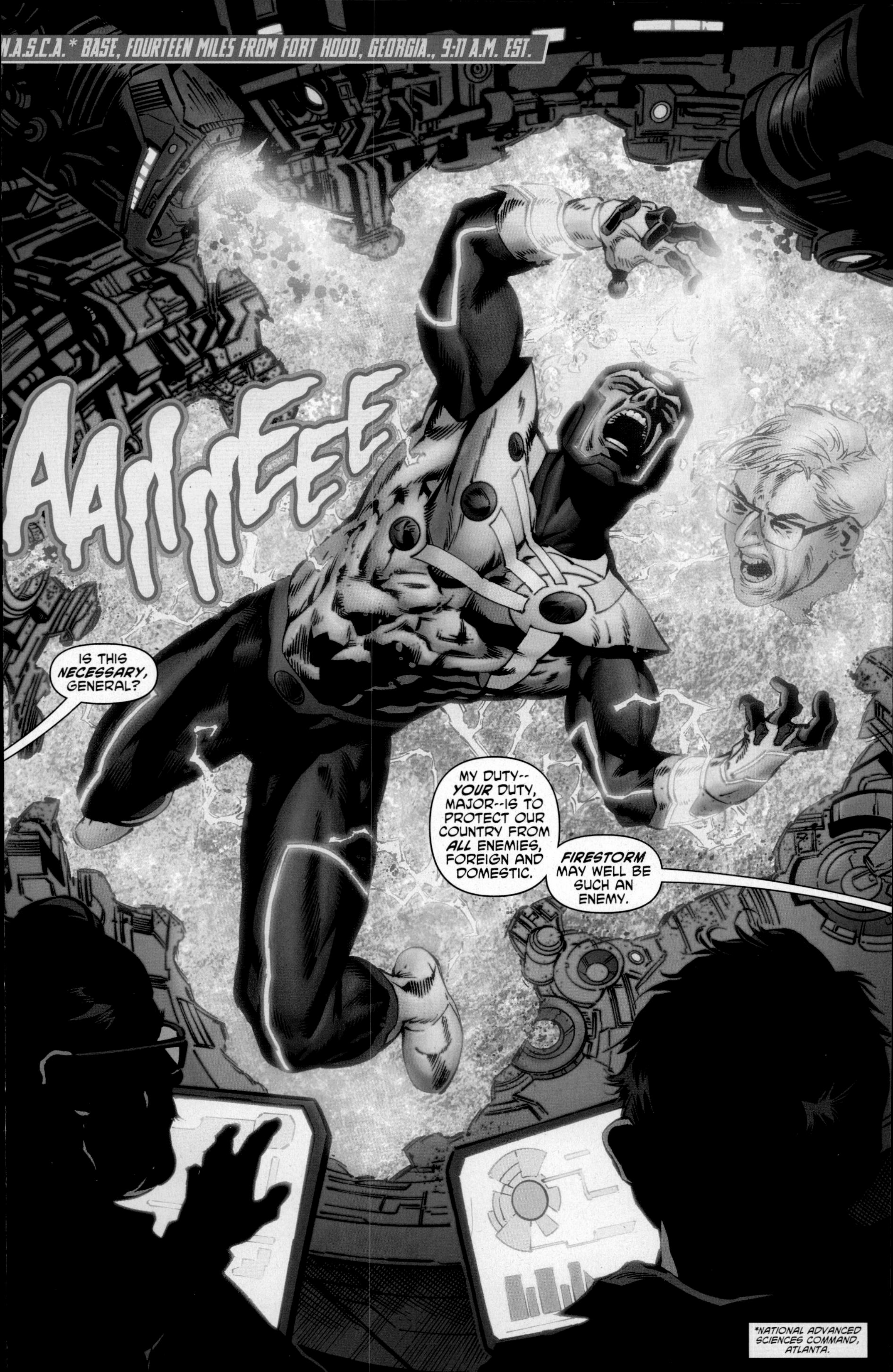
N.A.S.C.A.* BASE, FOURTEEN MILES FROM FORT HOOD, GEORGIA., 9:11 A.M. EST.
AAIIIEEE
IS THIS NECESSARY, GENERAL?
MY DUTY--YOUR DUTY, MAJOR--IS TO PROTECT OUR COUNTRY FROM ALL ENEMIES, FOREIGN AND DOMESTIC.
FIRESTORM MAY WELL BE SUCH AN ENEMY.
*NATIONAL ADVANCED SCIENCES COMMAND, ATLANTA.

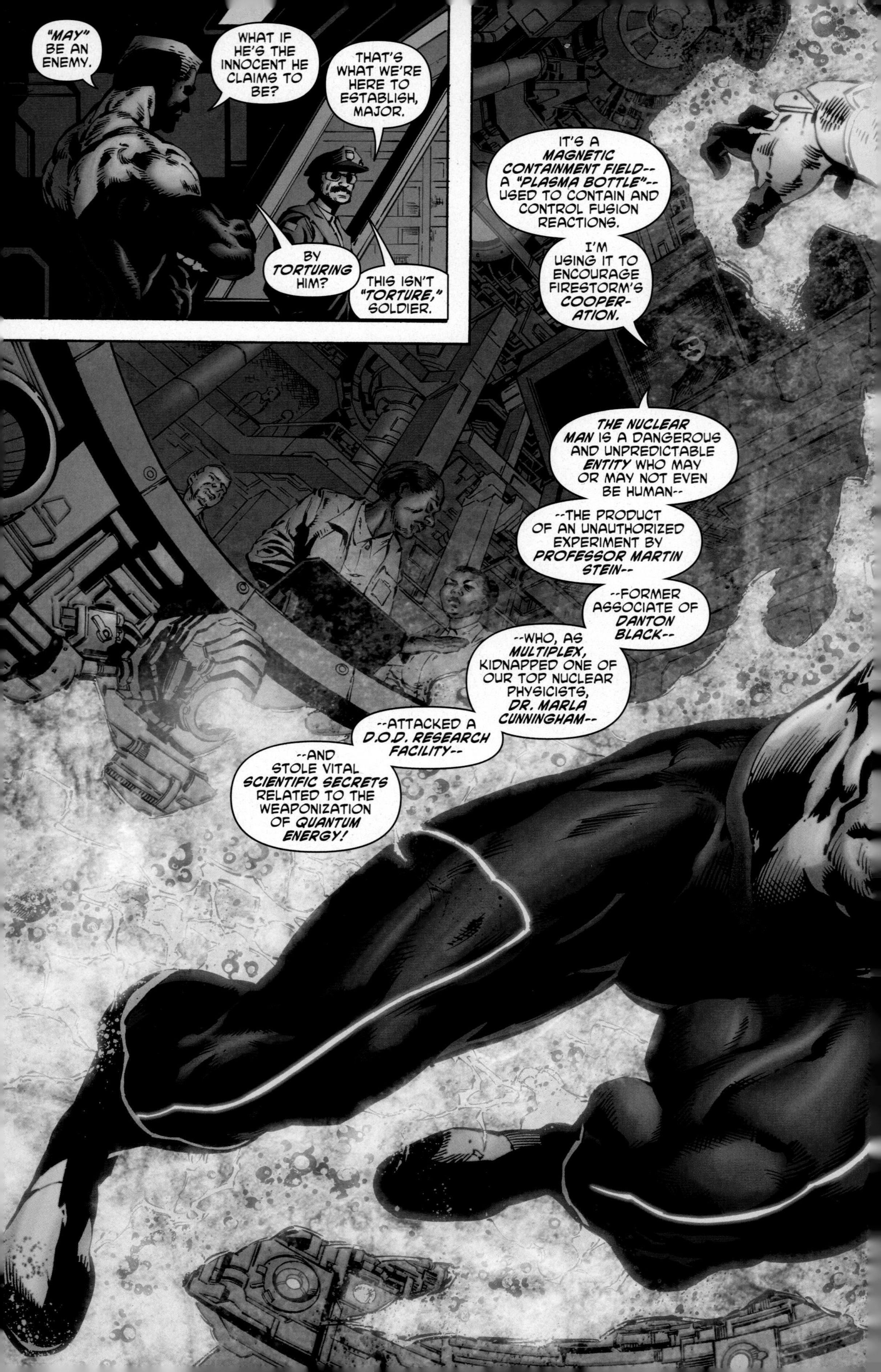
"MAY" BE AN ENEMY.
WHAT IF HE'S THE INNOCENT HE CLAIMS TO BE?
THAT'S WHAT WE'RE HERE TO ESTABLISH, MAJOR.
BY TORTURING HIM?
THIS ISN'T "TORTURE," SOLDIER.
IT'S A MAGNETIC CONTAINMENT FIELD-- A "PLASMA BOTTLE"-- USED TO CONTAIN AND CONTROL FUSION REACTIONS.
I'M USING IT TO ENCOURAGE FIRESTORM'S COOPERATION.
THE NUCLEAR MAN IS A DANGEROUS AND UNPREDICTABLE ENTITY WHO MAY OR MAY NOT EVEN BE HUMAN--
--THE PRODUCT OF AN UNAUTHORIZED EXPERIMENT BY PROFESSOR MARTIN STEIN--
--FORMER ASSOCIATE OF DANTON BLACK--
--WHO, AS MULTIPLEX, KIDNAPPED ONE OF OUR TOP NUCLEAR PHYSICISTS, DR. MARLA CUNNINGHAM--
--ATTACKED A D.O.D. RESEARCH FACILITY--
--AND STOLE VITAL SCIENTIFIC SECRETS RELATED TO THE WEAPONIZATION OF QUANTUM ENERGY!

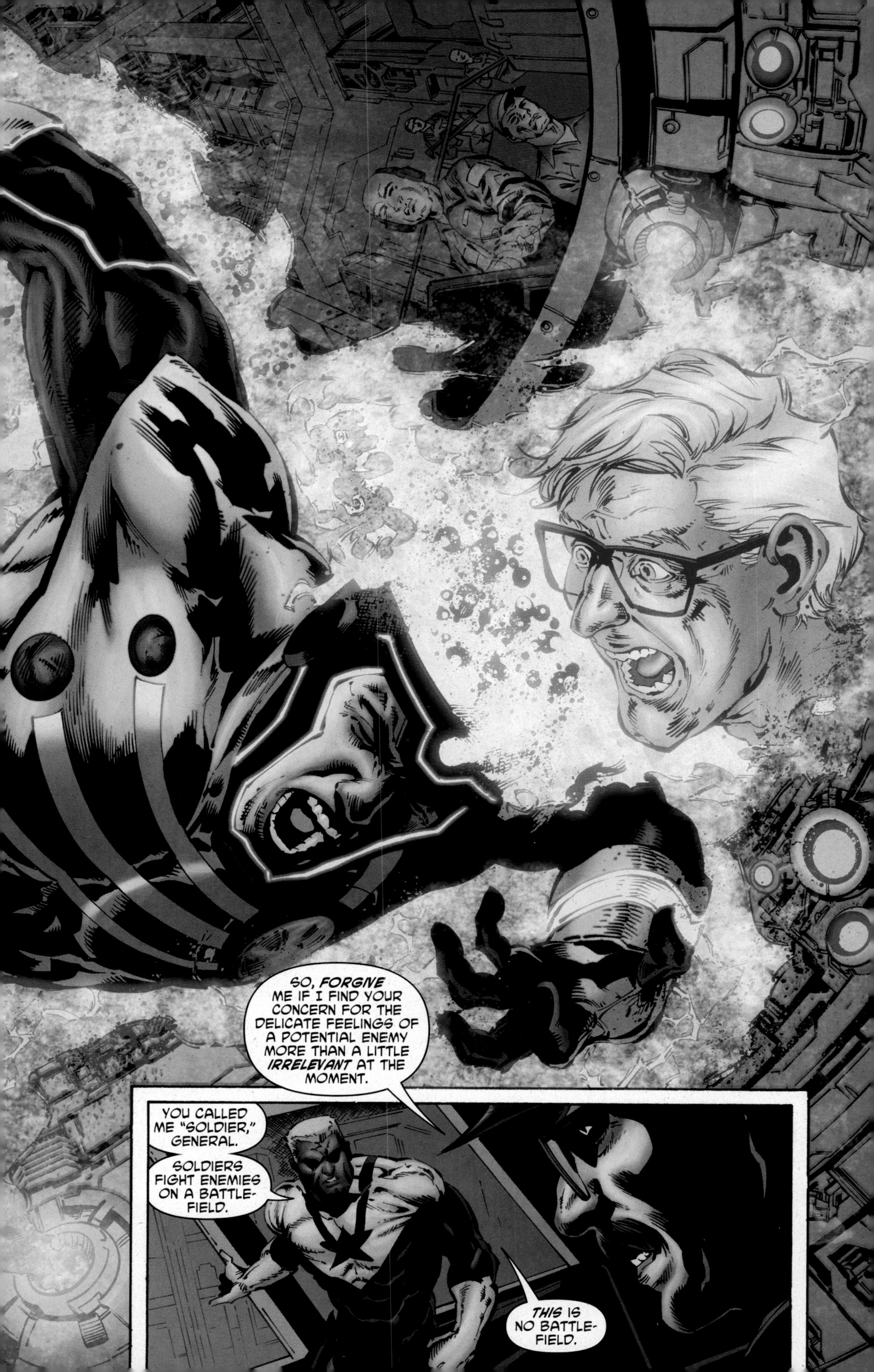
SO, FORGIVE ME IF I FIND YOUR CONCERN FOR THE DELICATE FEELINGS OF A POTENTIAL ENEMY MORE THAN A LITTLE IRRELEVANT AT THE MOMENT.
YOU CALLED ME "SOLDIER," GENERAL.
SOLDIERS FIGHT ENEMIES ON A BATTLE-FIELD.
THIS IS NO BATTLE-FIELD.

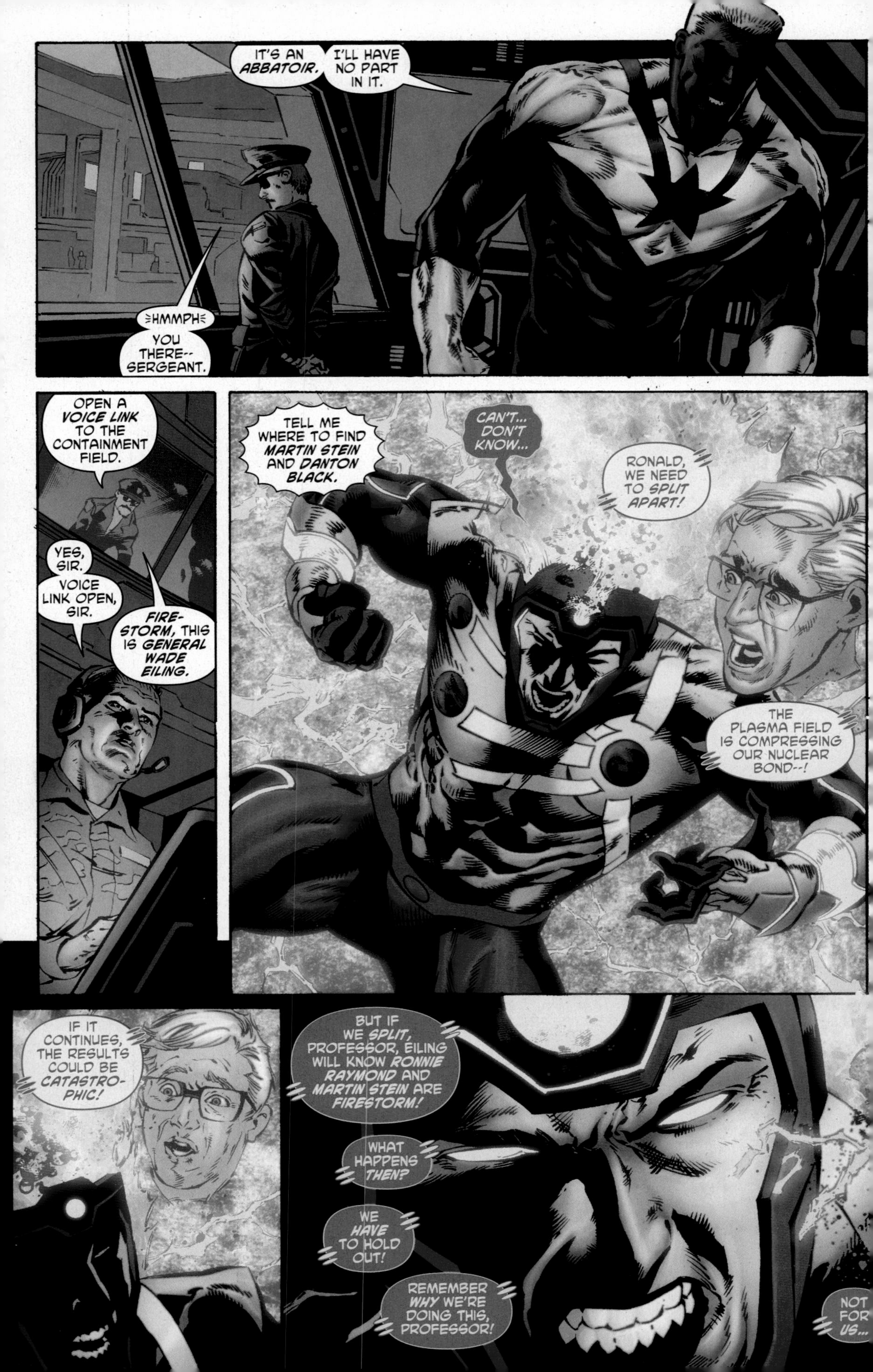
IT'S AN ABBATOIR.
I'LL HAVE NO PART IN IT.
HMMPH
YOU THERE-- SERGEANT.
OPEN A VOICE LINK TO THE CONTAINMENT FIELD.
YES, SIR.
VOICE LINK OPEN, SIR.
FIRE-STORM, THIS IS GENERAL WADE EILING.
TELL ME WHERE TO FIND MARTIN STEIN AND DANTON BLACK.
CAN'T... DON'T KNOW...
RONALD, WE NEED TO SPLIT APART!
THE PLASMA FIELD IS COMPRESSING OUR NUCLEAR BOND--!
IF IT CONTINUES, THE RESULTS COULD BE CATASTRO-PHIC!
BUT IF WE SPLIT, PROFESSOR, EILING WILL KNOW RONNIE RAYMOND AND MARTIN STEIN ARE FIRESTORM!
WHAT HAPPENS THEN?
WE HAVE TO HOLD OUT!
REMEMBER WHY WE'RE DOING THIS, PROFESSOR!
NOT FOR US...

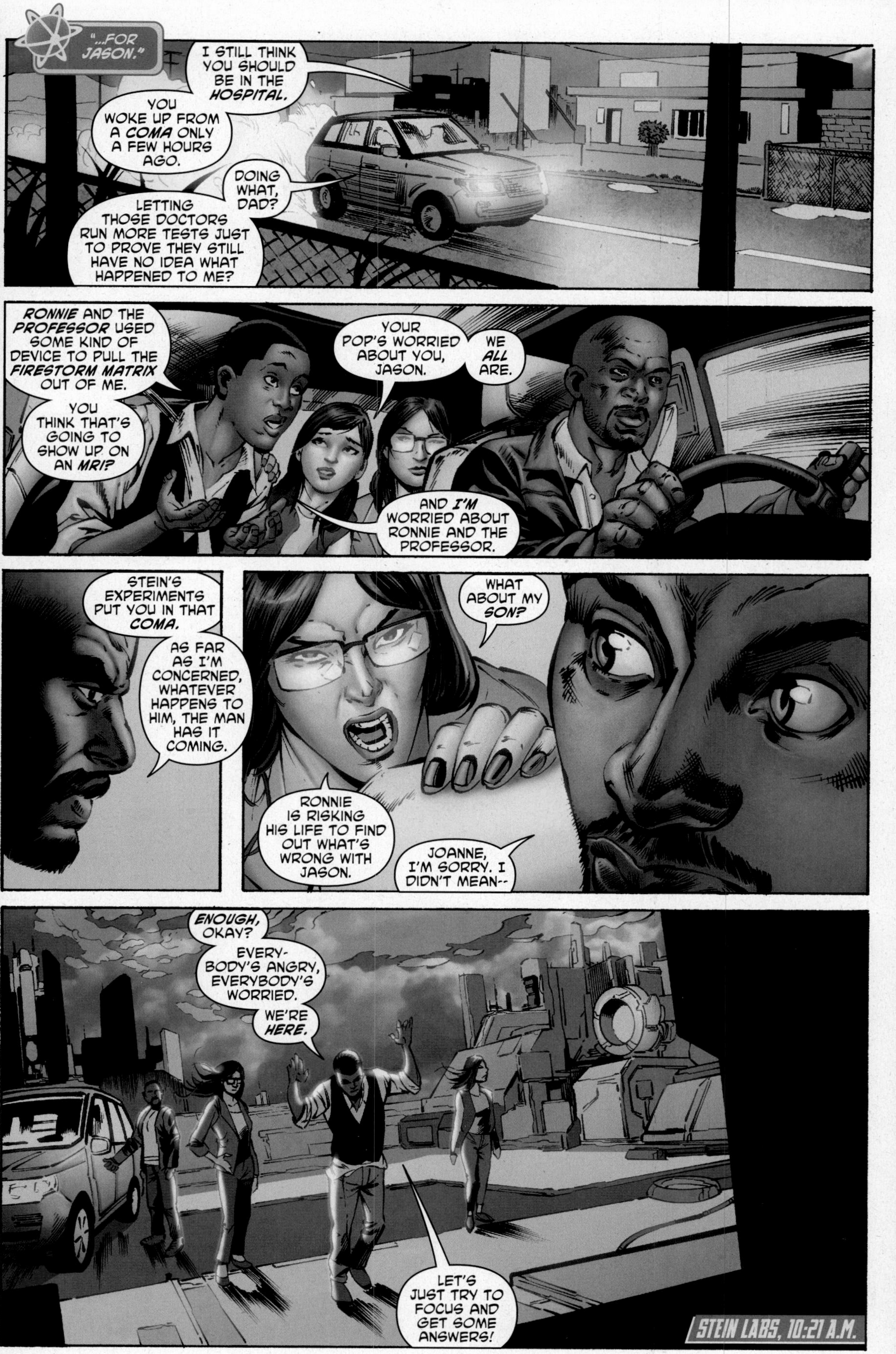
"...FOR JASON."
I STILL THINK YOU SHOULD BE IN THE HOSPITAL.
YOU WOKE UP FROM A COMA ONLY A FEW HOURS AGO.
DOING WHAT, DAD?
LETTING THOSE DOCTORS RUN MORE TESTS JUST TO PROVE THEY STILL HAVE NO IDEA WHAT HAPPENED TO ME?
RONNIE AND THE PROFESSOR USED SOME KIND OF DEVICE TO PULL THE FIRESTORM MATRIX OUT OF ME.
YOU THINK THAT'S GOING TO SHOW UP ON AN MRI?
YOUR POP'S WORRIED ABOUT YOU, JASON.
WE ALL ARE.
AND I'M WORRIED ABOUT RONNIE AND THE PROFESSOR.
STEIN'S EXPERIMENTS PUT YOU IN THAT COMA.
AS FAR AS I'M CONCERNED, WHATEVER HAPPENS TO HIM, THE MAN HAS IT COMING.
WHAT ABOUT MY SON?
RONNIE IS RISKING HIS LIFE TO FIND OUT WHAT'S WRONG WITH JASON.
JOANNE, I'M SORRY. I DIDN'T MEAN--
ENOUGH, OKAY?
EVERY-BODY'S ANGRY, EVERYBODY'S WORRIED.
WE'RE HERE.
LET'S JUST TRY TO FOCUS AND GET SOME ANSWERS!
STEIN LABS, 10:21 A.M.

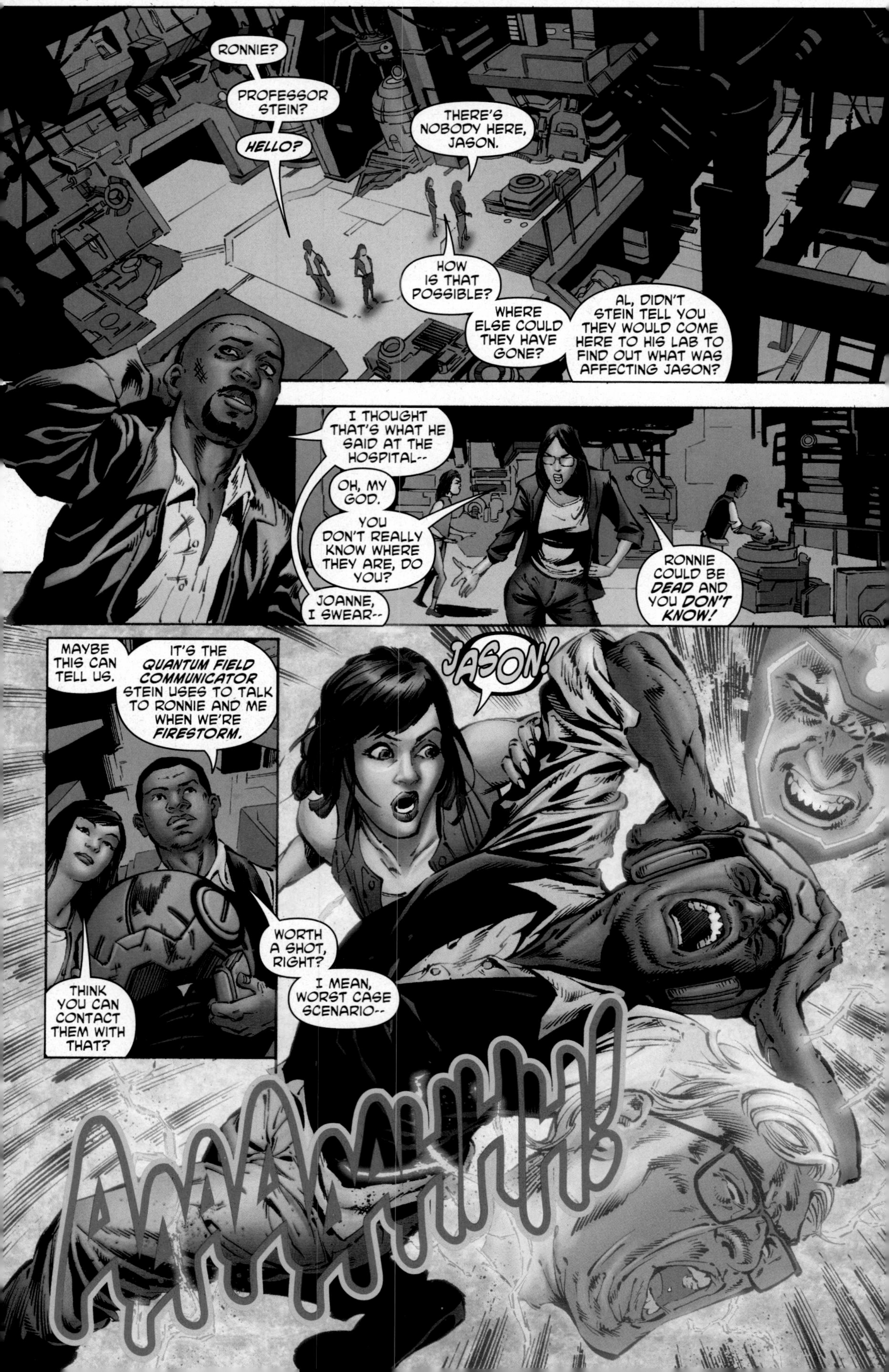
RONNIE?
PROFESSOR STEIN?
HELLO?
THERE'S NOBODY HERE, JASON.
HOW IS THAT POSSIBLE?
WHERE ELSE COULD THEY HAVE GONE?
AL, DIDN'T STEIN TELL YOU THEY WOULD COME HERE TO HIS LAB TO FIND OUT WHAT WAS AFFECTING JASON?
I THOUGHT THAT'S WHAT HE SAID AT THE HOSPITAL--
OH, MY GOD.
YOU DON'T REALLY KNOW WHERE THEY ARE, DO YOU?
JOANNE, I SWEAR--
RONNIE COULD BE DEAD AND YOU DON'T KNOW!
MAYBE THIS CAN TELL US.
IT'S THE QUANTUM FIELD COMMUNICATOR STEIN USES TO TALK TO RONNIE AND ME WHEN WE'RE FIRESTORM.
THINK YOU CAN CONTACT THEM WITH THAT?
WORTH A SHOT, RIGHT?
I MEAN, WORST CASE SCENARIO--
JASON!
AAAAAARRRRHH!

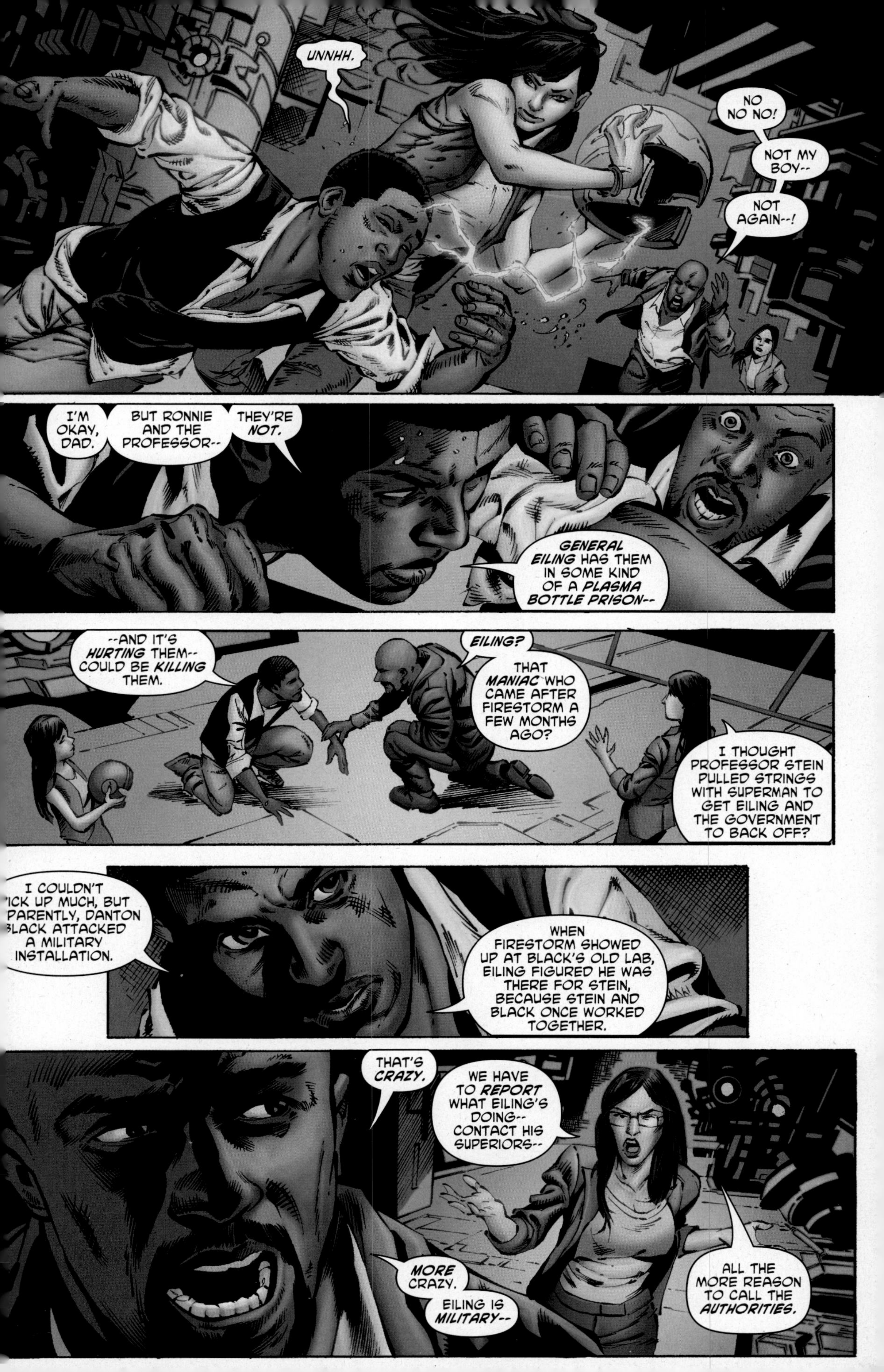
UNNHH.
NO NO NO!
NOT MY BOY--
NOT AGAIN--!
I'M OKAY, DAD.
BUT RONNIE AND THE PROFESSOR--
THEY'RE NOT.
GENERAL EILING HAS THEM IN SOME KIND OF A PLASMA BOTTLE PRISON--
--AND IT'S HURTING THEM-- COULD BE KILLING THEM.
EILING?
THAT MANIAC WHO CAME AFTER FIRESTORM A FEW MONTHS AGO?
I THOUGHT PROFESSOR STEIN PULLED STRINGS WITH SUPERMAN TO GET EILING AND THE GOVERNMENT TO BACK OFF?
I COULDN'T PICK UP MUCH, BUT APPARENTLY, DANTON BLACK ATTACKED A MILITARY INSTALLATION.
WHEN FIRESTORM SHOWED UP AT BLACK'S OLD LAB, EILING FIGURED HE WAS THERE FOR STEIN, BECAUSE STEIN AND BLACK ONCE WORKED TOGETHER.
THAT'S CRAZY.
WE HAVE TO REPORT WHAT EILING'S DOING-- CONTACT HIS SUPERIORS--
MORE CRAZY.
EILING IS MILITARY--
ALL THE MORE REASON TO CALL THE AUTHORITIES.

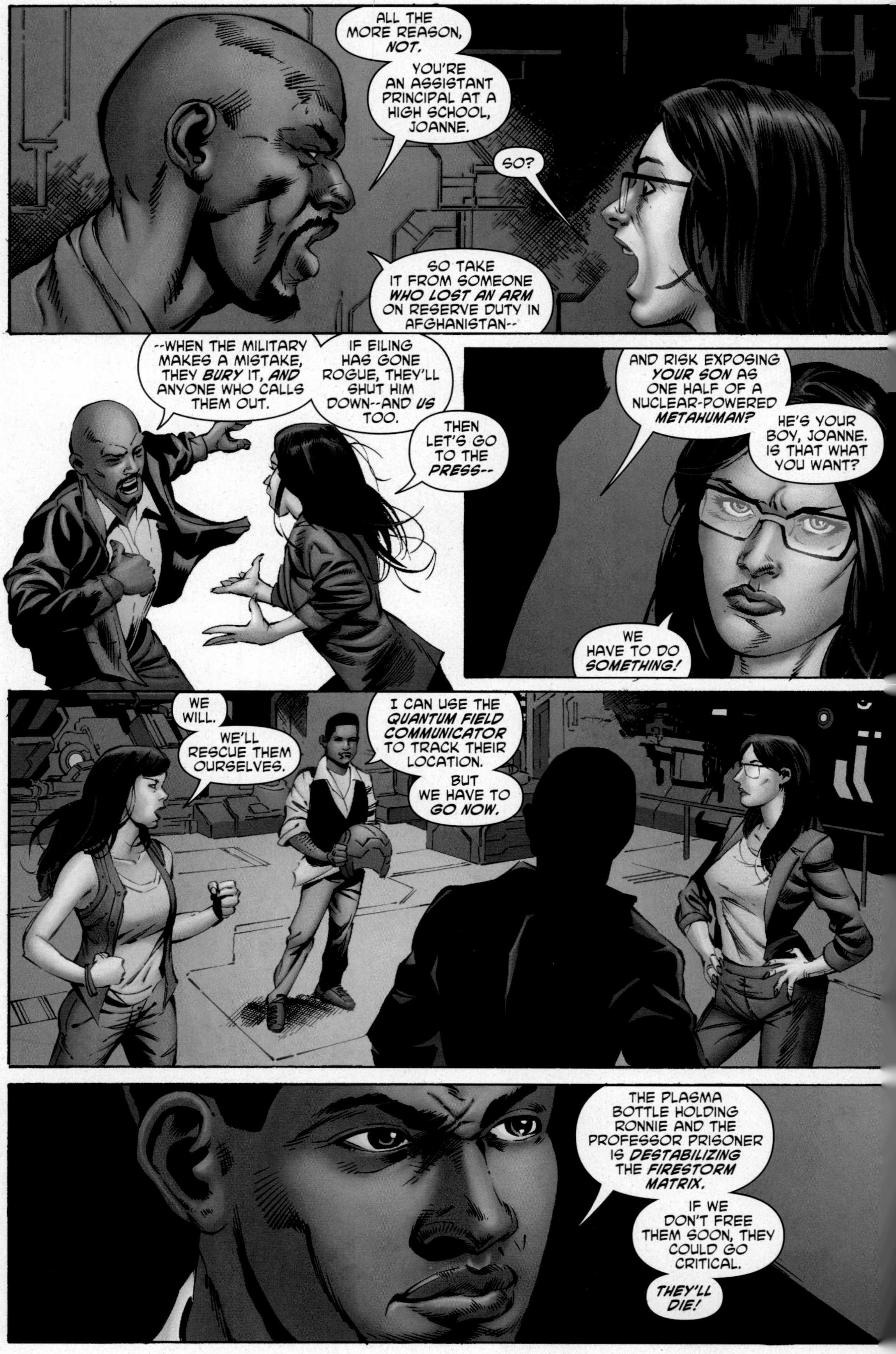
ALL THE MORE REASON, *NOT.*
YOU'RE AN ASSISTANT PRINCIPAL AT A HIGH SCHOOL, JOANNE.
SO?
SO TAKE IT FROM SOMEONE *WHO LOST AN ARM* ON RESERVE DUTY IN AFGHANISTAN--
--WHEN THE MILITARY MAKES A MISTAKE, THEY *BURY* IT, *AND* ANYONE WHO CALLS THEM OUT.
IF EILING HAS GONE ROGUE, THEY'LL SHUT HIM DOWN--AND *US* TOO.
THEN LET'S GO TO THE *PRESS*--
AND RISK EXPOSING *YOUR SON* AS ONE HALF OF A NUCLEAR-POWERED *METAHUMAN?*
HE'S YOUR BOY, JOANNE. IS THAT WHAT YOU WANT?
WE HAVE TO DO *SOMETHING!*
WE WILL.
WE'LL RESCUE THEM OURSELVES.
I CAN USE THE *QUANTUM FIELD COMMUNICATOR* TO TRACK THEIR LOCATION.
BUT WE HAVE TO *GO NOW.*
THE PLASMA BOTTLE HOLDING RONNIE AND THE PROFESSOR PRISONER IS *DESTABILIZING* THE *FIRESTORM MATRIX.*
IF WE DON'T FREE THEM SOON, THEY COULD GO CRITICAL.
THEY'LL DIE!

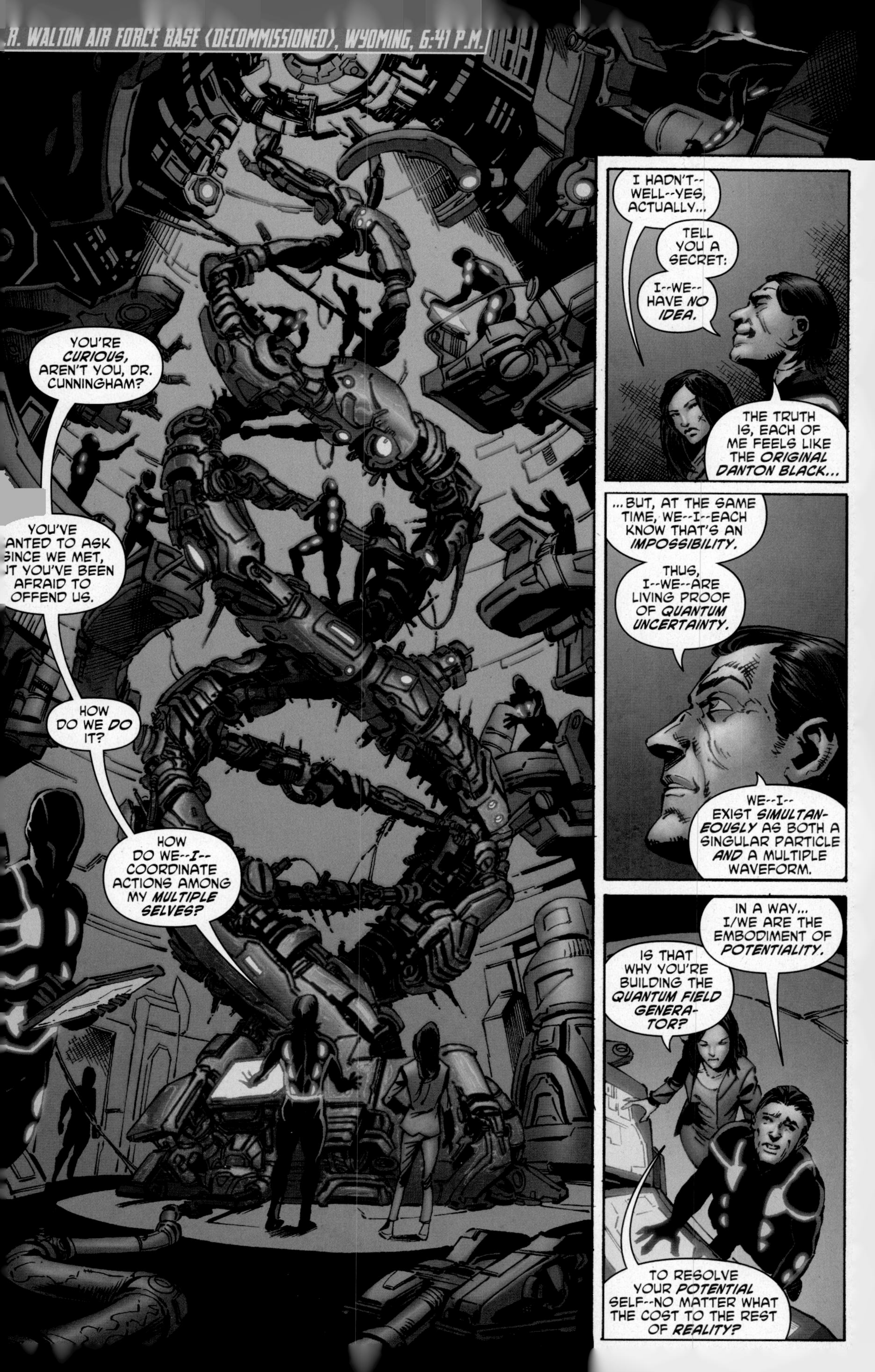
.R. WALTON AIR FORCE BASE (DECOMMISSIONED), WYOMING, 6:41 P.M.
YOU'RE CURIOUS, AREN'T YOU, DR. CUNNINGHAM?
YOU'VE ANTED TO ASK SINCE WE MET, UT YOU'VE BEEN AFRAID TO OFFEND US.
HOW DO WE DO IT?
HOW DO WE--I-- COORDINATE ACTIONS AMONG MY MULTIPLE SELVES?
I HADN'T-- WELL--YES, ACTUALLY...
TELL YOU A SECRET:
I--WE-- HAVE NO IDEA.
THE TRUTH IS, EACH OF ME FEELS LIKE THE ORIGINAL DANTON BLACK...
...BUT, AT THE SAME TIME, WE--I--EACH KNOW THAT'S AN IMPOSSIBILITY.
THUS, I--WE--ARE LIVING PROOF OF QUANTUM UNCERTAINTY.
WE--I-- EXIST SIMULTAN-EOUSLY AS BOTH A SINGULAR PARTICLE AND A MULTIPLE WAVEFORM.
IN A WAY... I/WE ARE THE EMBODIMENT OF POTENTIALITY.
IS THAT WHY YOU'RE BUILDING THE QUANTUM FIELD GENERA-TOR?
TO RESOLVE YOUR POTENTIAL SELF--NO MATTER WHAT THE COST TO THE REST OF REALITY?

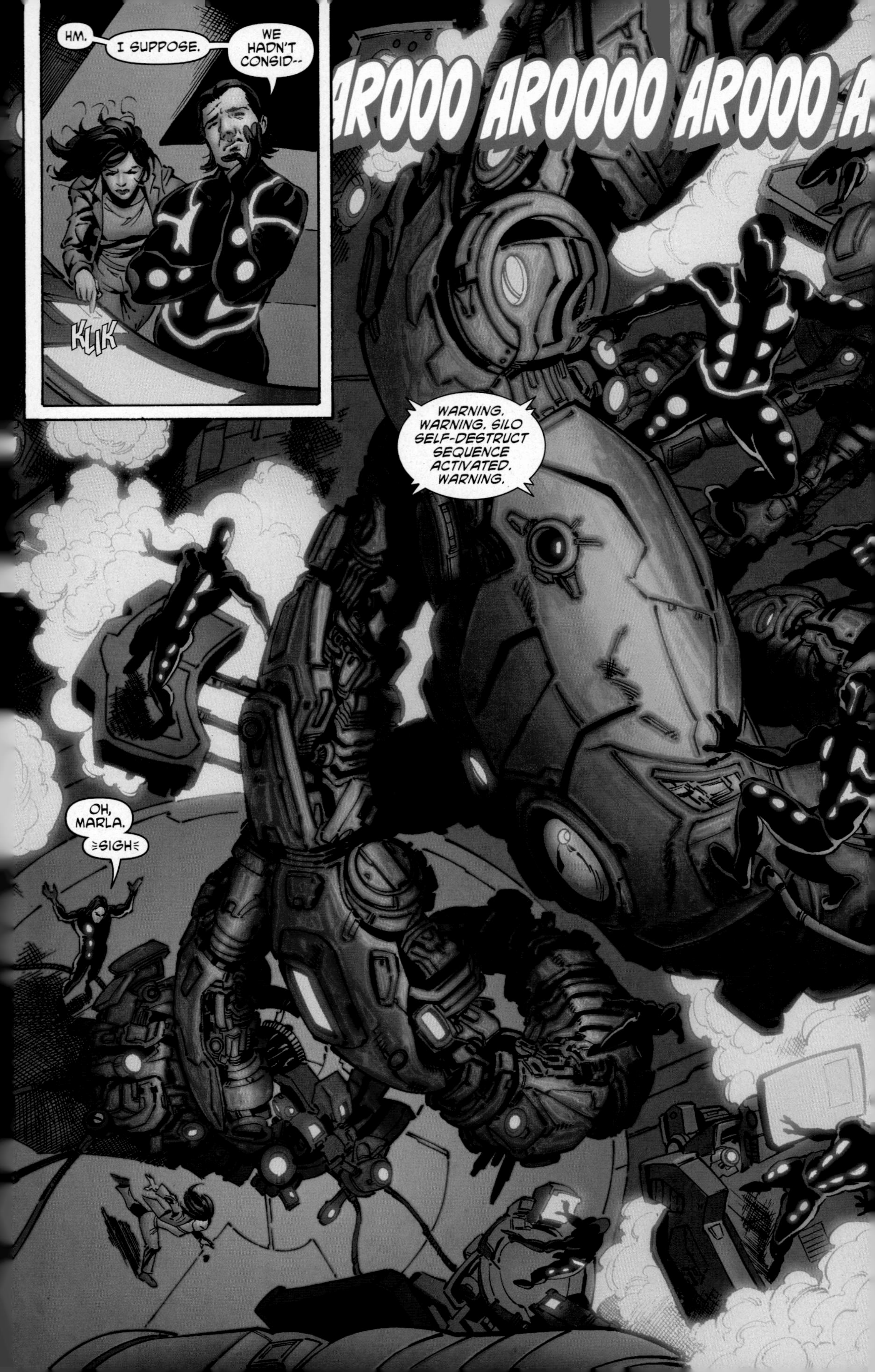
HM.
I SUPPOSE.
WE HADN'T CONSID--
KLIK
AROOO AROOOO AROOO A
WARNING. WARNING. SILO SELF-DESTRUCT SEQUENCE ACTIVATED. WARNING.
OH, MARLA.
SIGH

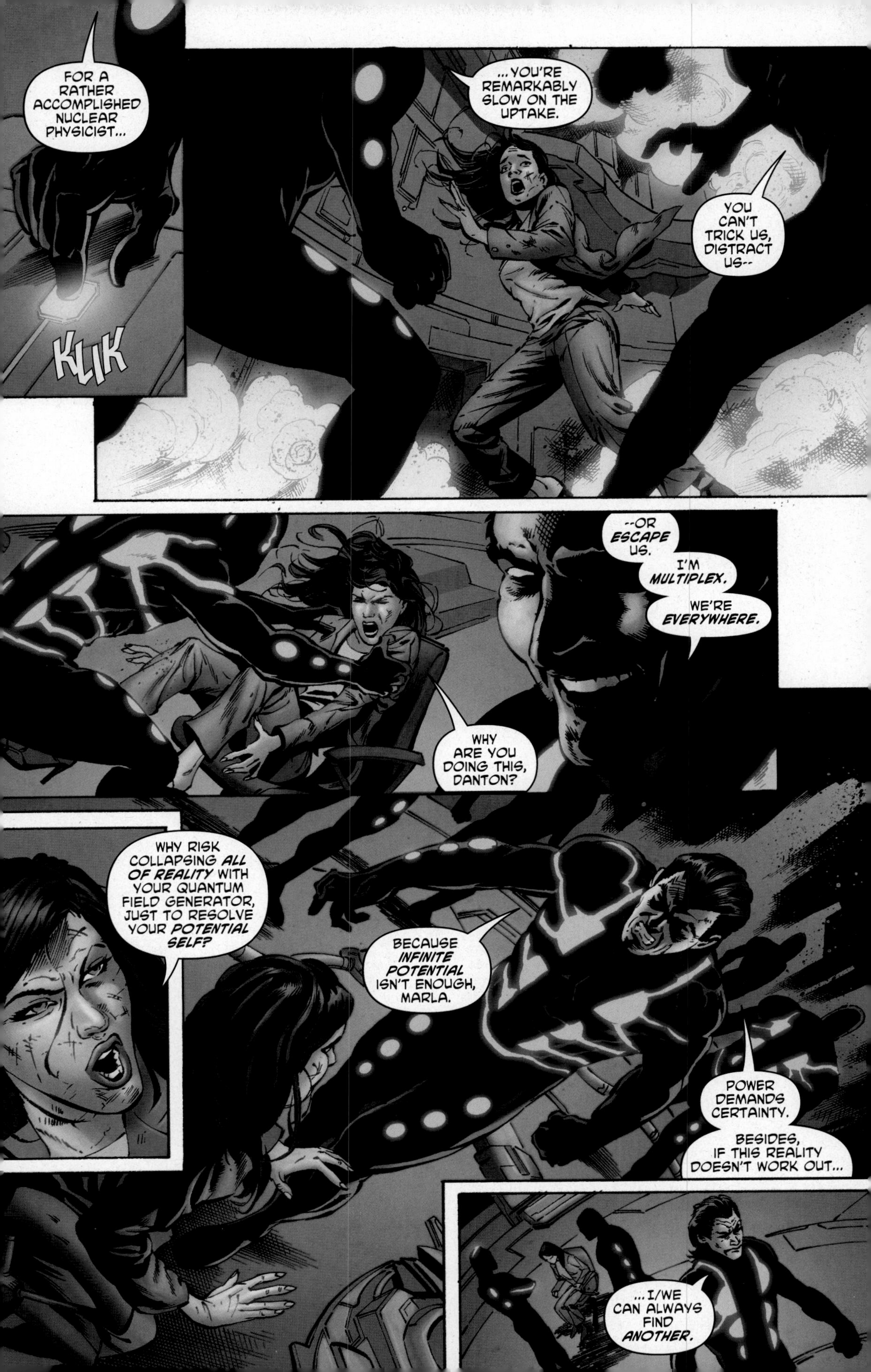
FOR A RATHER ACCOMPLISHED NUCLEAR PHYSICIST...
KLIK
...YOU'RE REMARKABLY SLOW ON THE UPTAKE.
YOU CAN'T TRICK US, DISTRACT US--
--OR ESCAPE US.
I'M MULTIPLEX.
WE'RE EVERYWHERE.
WHY ARE YOU DOING THIS, DANTON?
WHY RISK COLLAPSING ALL OF REALITY WITH YOUR QUANTUM FIELD GENERATOR, JUST TO RESOLVE YOUR POTENTIAL SELF?
BECAUSE INFINITE POTENTIAL ISN'T ENOUGH, MARLA.
POWER DEMANDS CERTAINTY.
BESIDES, IF THIS REALITY DOESN'T WORK OUT...
...I/WE CAN ALWAYS FIND ANOTHER.

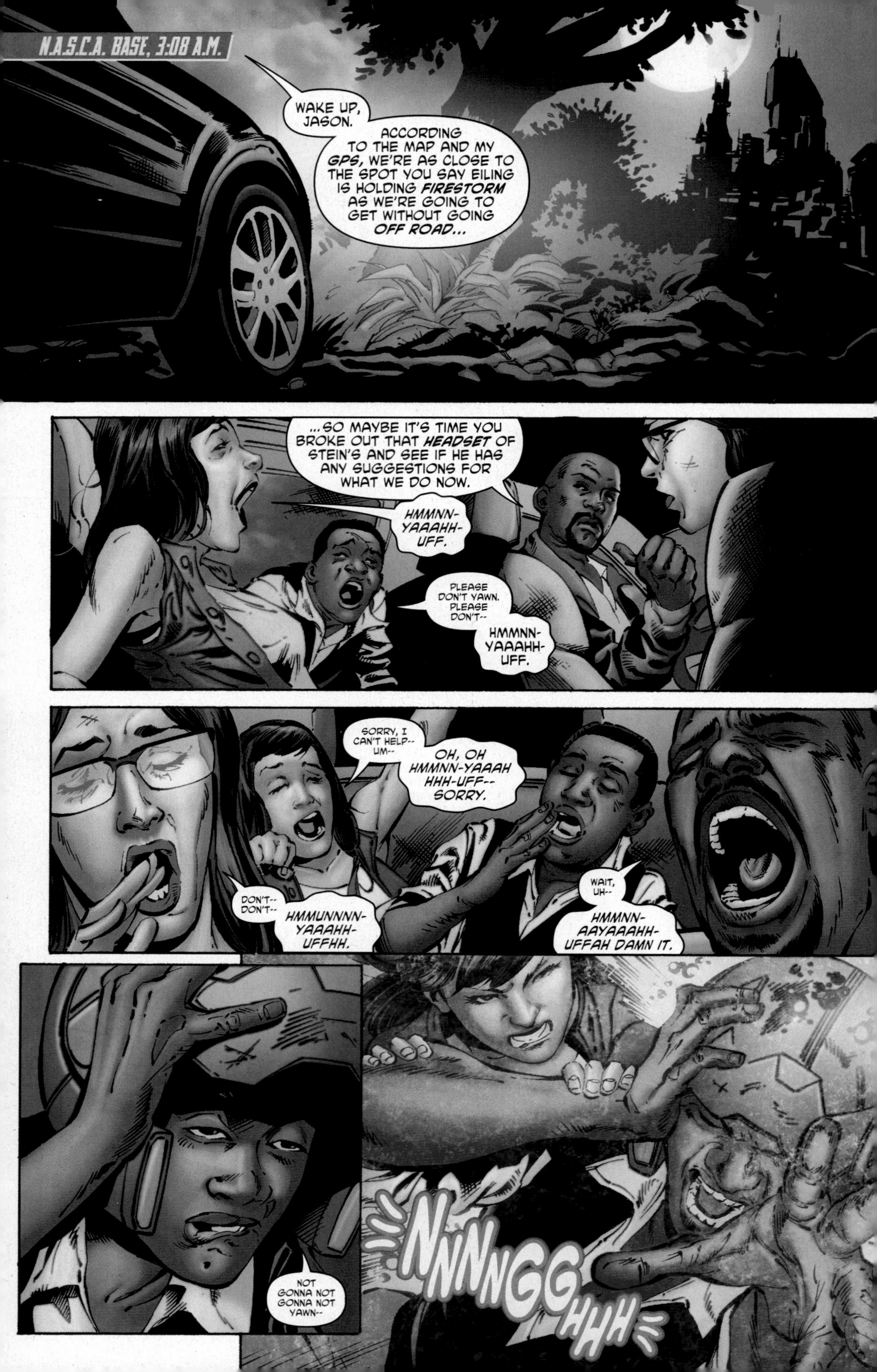
N.A.S.C.A. BASE, 3:08 A.M.
WAKE UP, JASON.
ACCORDING TO THE MAP AND MY GPS, WE'RE AS CLOSE TO THE SPOT YOU SAY EILING IS HOLDING FIRESTORM AS WE'RE GOING TO GET WITHOUT GOING OFF ROAD...
...SO MAYBE IT'S TIME YOU BROKE OUT THAT HEADSET OF STEIN'S AND SEE IF HE HAS ANY SUGGESTIONS FOR WHAT WE DO NOW.
HMMNN-YAAAHH-UFF.
PLEASE DON'T YAWN. PLEASE DON'T--
HMMNN-YAAAHH-UFF.
SORRY, I CAN'T HELP-- UM--
OH, OH HMMNN-YAAAH HHH-UFF-- SORRY.
DON'T-- DON'T--
HMMUNNNN-YAAAHH-UFFHH.
WAIT, UH--
HMMNN-AAYAAAHH-UFFAH DAMN IT.
NOT GONNA NOT GONNA NOT YAWN--
NNNNGGHHH

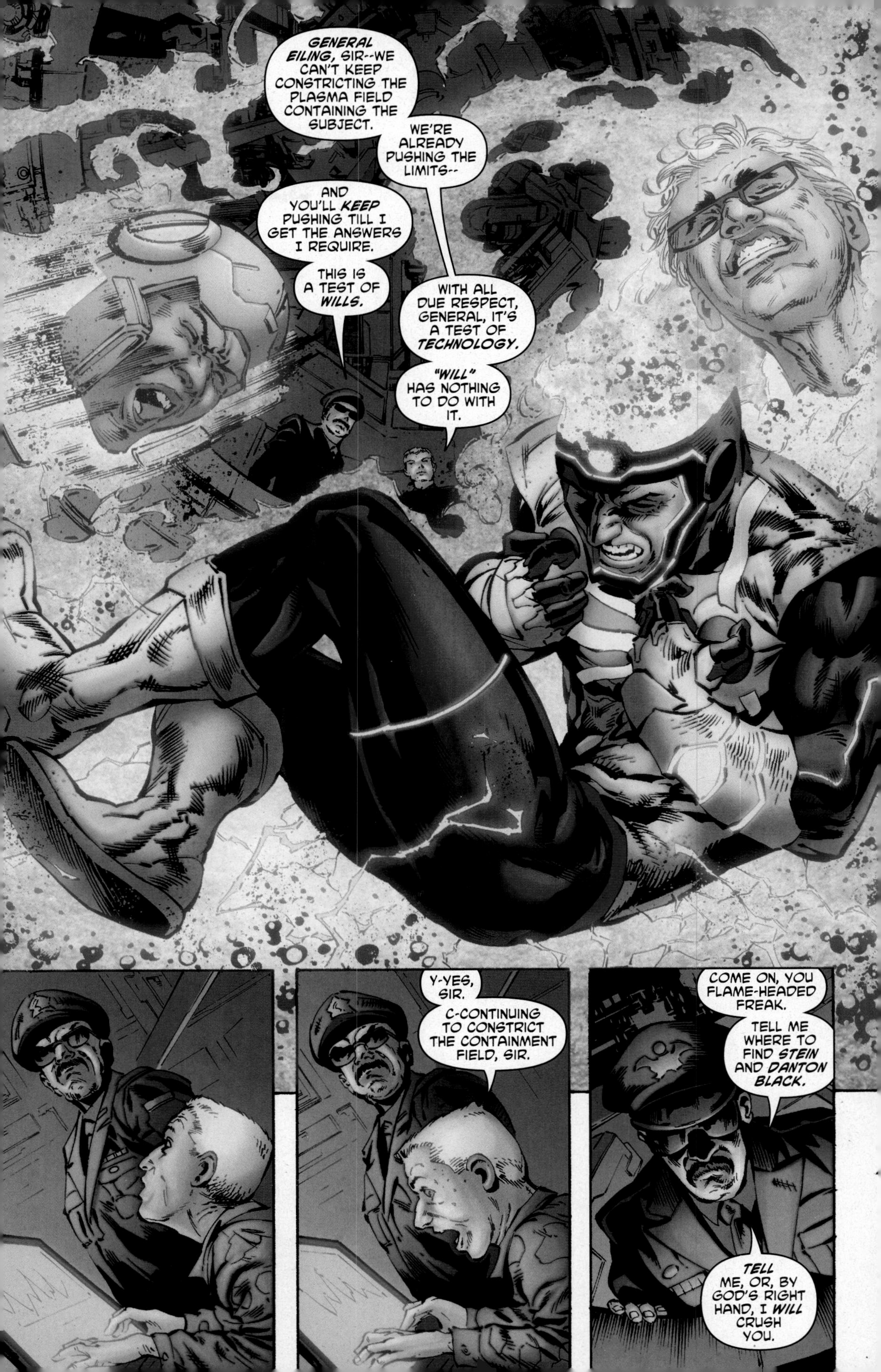
GENERAL EILING, SIR--WE CAN'T KEEP CONSTRICTING THE PLASMA FIELD CONTAINING THE SUBJECT.
WE'RE ALREADY PUSHING THE LIMITS--
AND YOU'LL KEEP PUSHING TILL I GET THE ANSWERS I REQUIRE.
THIS IS A TEST OF WILLS.
WITH ALL DUE RESPECT, GENERAL, IT'S A TEST OF TECHNOLOGY.
"WILL" HAS NOTHING TO DO WITH IT.
Y-YES, SIR.
C-CONTINUING TO CONSTRICT THE CONTAINMENT FIELD, SIR.
COME ON, YOU FLAME-HEADED FREAK.
TELL ME WHERE TO FIND STEIN AND DANTON BLACK.
TELL ME, OR, BY GOD'S RIGHT HAND, I WILL CRUSH YOU.

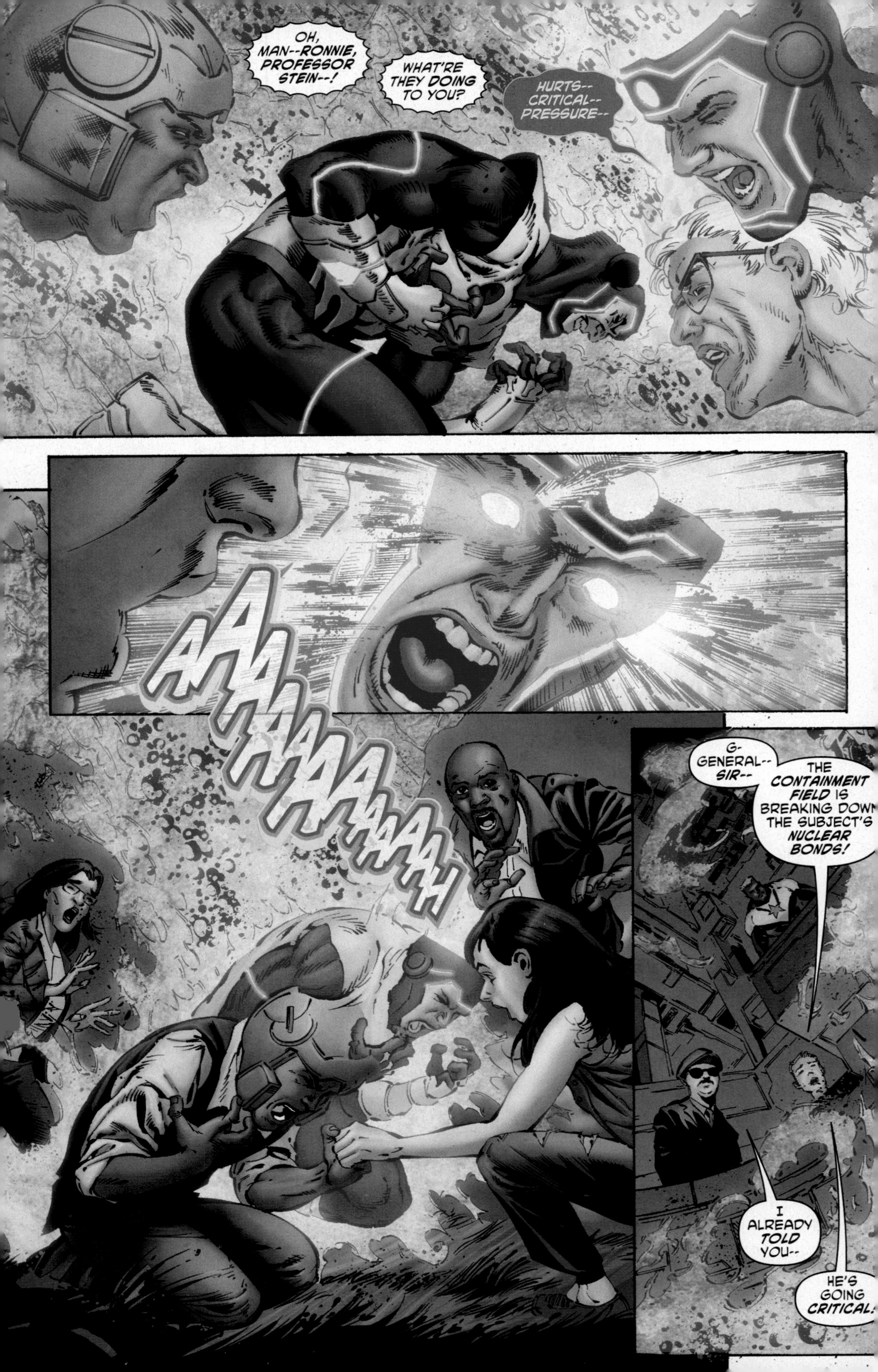

OH, MAN--RONNIE, PROFESSOR STEIN--!
WHAT'RE THEY DOING TO YOU?
HURTS-- CRITICAL-- PRESSURE--
AAAAAAAAAAAAAAH
G-GENERAL-- SIR--
THE CONTAINMENT FIELD IS BREAKING DOWN THE SUBJECT'S NUCLEAR BONDS!
I ALREADY TOLD YOU--
HE'S GOING CRITICAL.

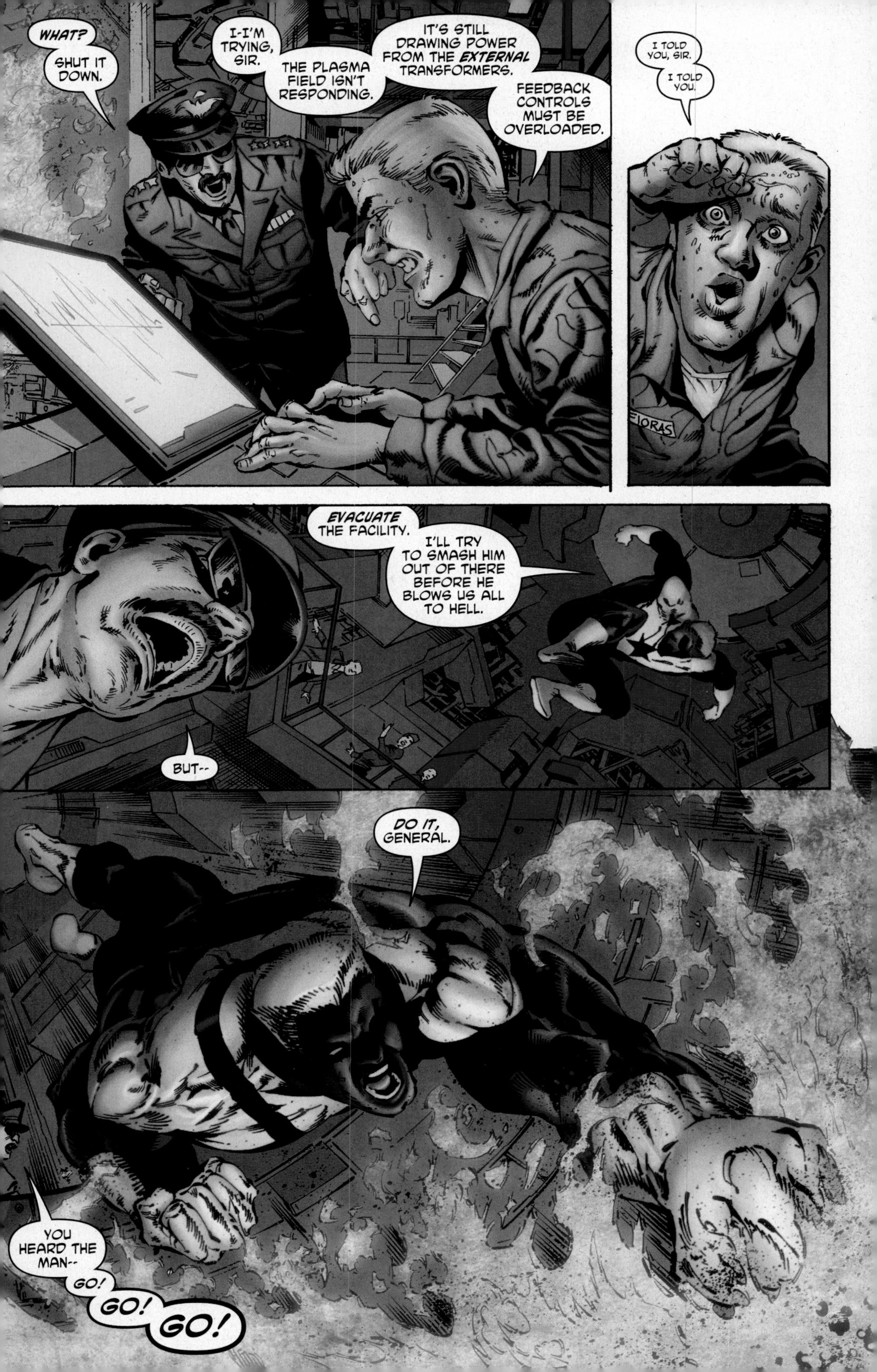
WHAT?
SHUT IT DOWN.
I-I'M TRYING, SIR.
THE PLASMA FIELD ISN'T RESPONDING.
IT'S STILL DRAWING POWER FROM THE EXTERNAL TRANSFORMERS.
FEEDBACK CONTROLS MUST BE OVERLOADED.
I TOLD YOU, SIR.
I TOLD YOU.
FIORAS
EVACUATE THE FACILITY.
I'LL TRY TO SMASH HIM OUT OF THERE BEFORE HE BLOWS US ALL TO HELL.
BUT--
DO IT, GENERAL.
YOU HEARD THE MAN--
GO!
GO!
GO!

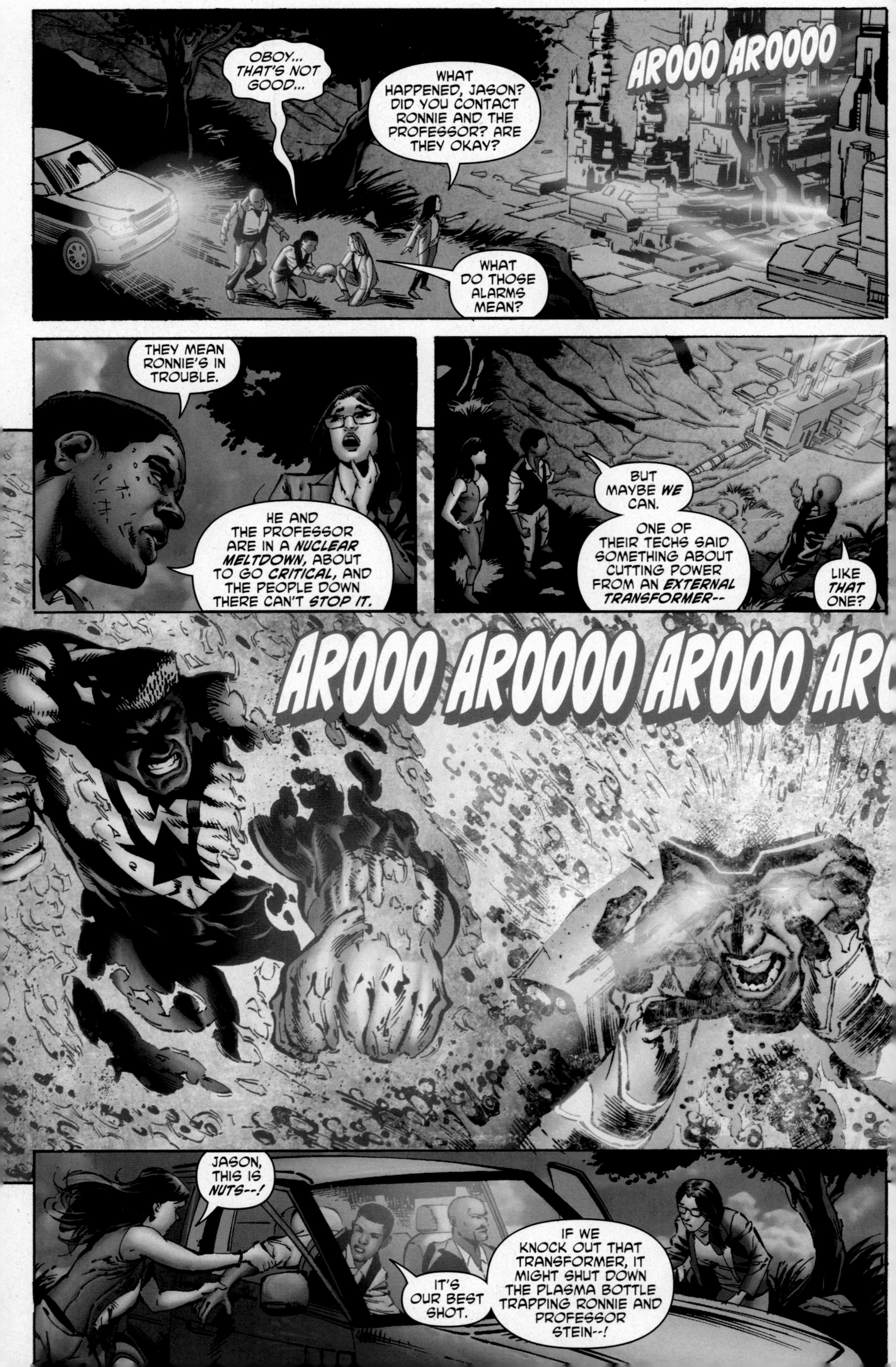
OBOY... THAT'S NOT GOOD...
WHAT HAPPENED, JASON? DID YOU CONTACT RONNIE AND THE PROFESSOR? ARE THEY OKAY?
AROOO AROOOO
WHAT DO THOSE ALARMS MEAN?
THEY MEAN RONNIE'S IN TROUBLE.
HE AND THE PROFESSOR ARE IN A NUCLEAR MELTDOWN, ABOUT TO GO CRITICAL, AND THE PEOPLE DOWN THERE CAN'T STOP IT.
BUT MAYBE WE CAN.
ONE OF THEIR TECHS SAID SOMETHING ABOUT CUTTING POWER FROM AN EXTERNAL TRANSFORMER--
LIKE THAT ONE?
AROOO AROOOO AROOO AR
JASON, THIS IS NUTS--!
IT'S OUR BEST SHOT.
IF WE KNOCK OUT THAT TRANSFORMER, IT MIGHT SHUT DOWN THE PLASMA BOTTLE TRAPPING RONNIE AND PROFESSOR STEIN--!

LOOK AT YOU, MR. SCIENCE NERD, BEING ALL BRAVE.

I WISH.

YOU DON'T HAVE TO DO THIS.

THAT'S WHAT MY DAD SAID.

BUT RONNIE AND--MARTIN--ARE IN THIS BECAUSE THEY'RE TRYING TO HELP ME.

SO, YEAH, THIS IS EXACTLY WHAT I HAVE TO DO.

READY, SON?

SURE YOU WON'T LET ME DRIVE?

WITHOUT EVEN A LEARNER'S PERMIT?

YOU WANT ME TO LOSE MY LICENSE?

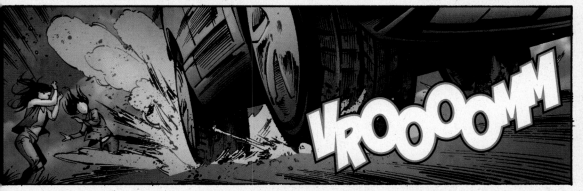

VROOOOMM

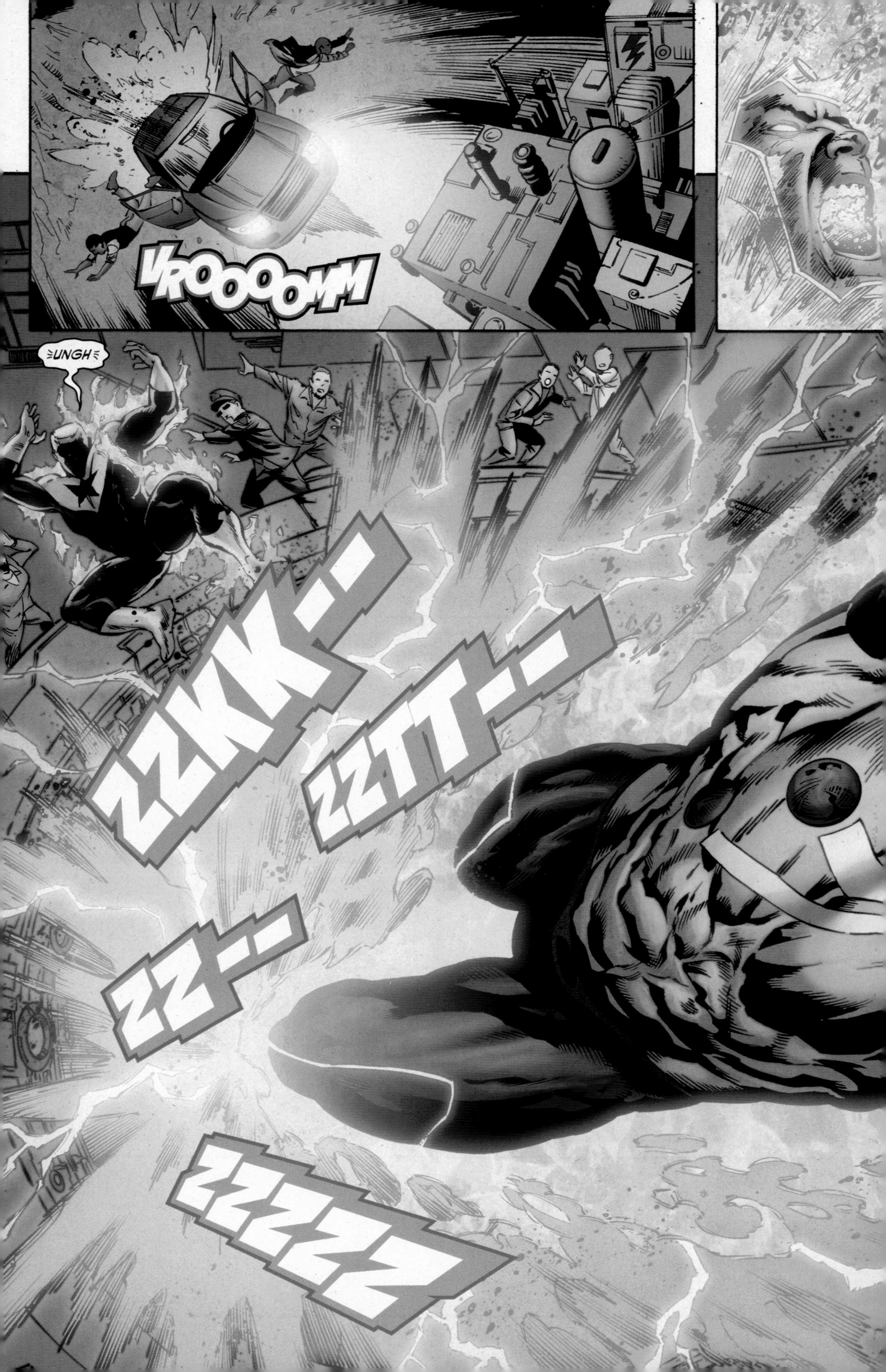
VROOOOOMM
UNGH
ZZKK--
ZZTT--
ZZ--
ZZZZ

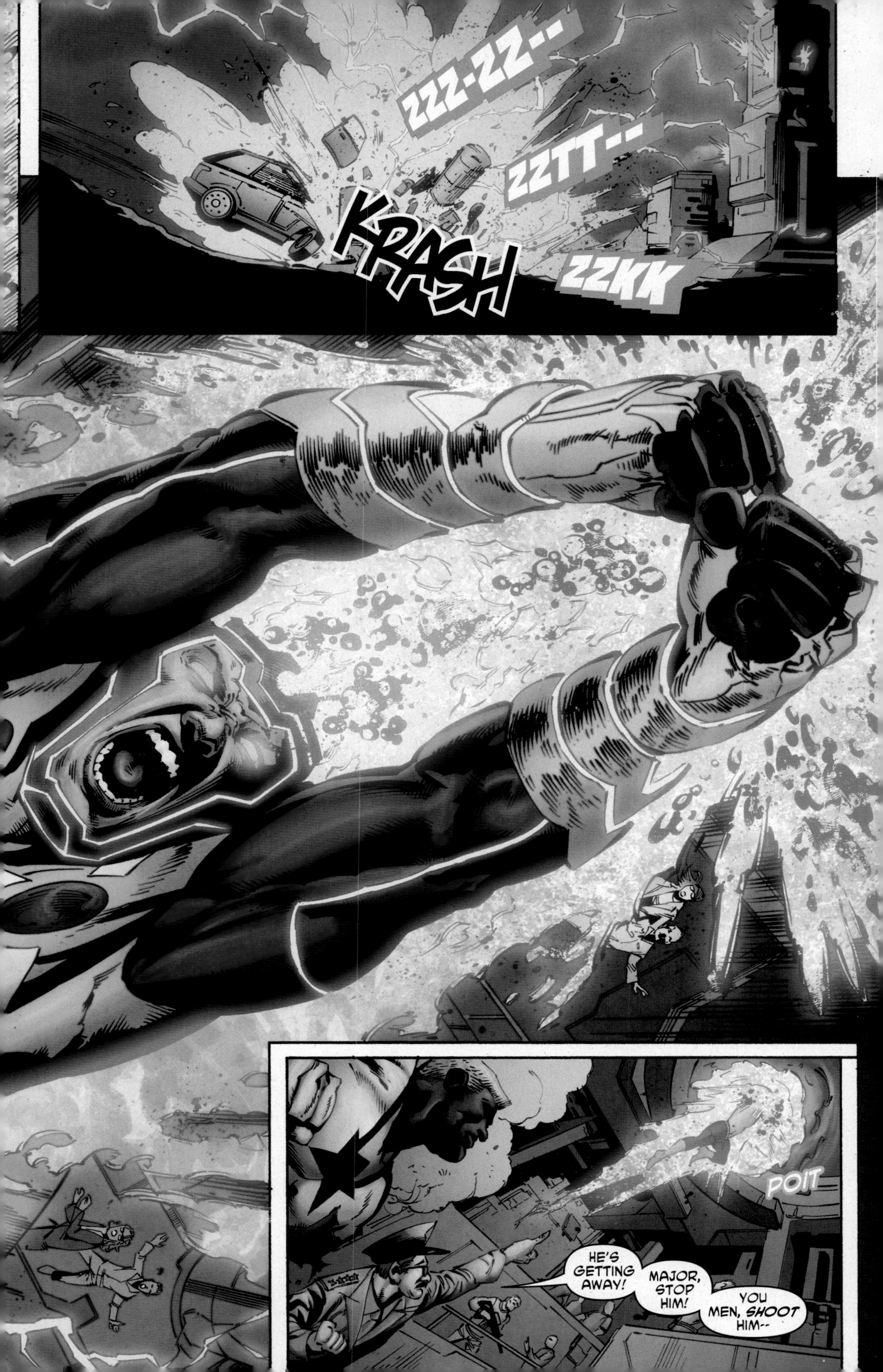
ZZZ-ZZ--
ZZTT--
KRASH
ZZKK
POIT
HE'S GETTING AWAY!
MAJOR, STOP HIM!
YOU MEN, SHOOT HIM--

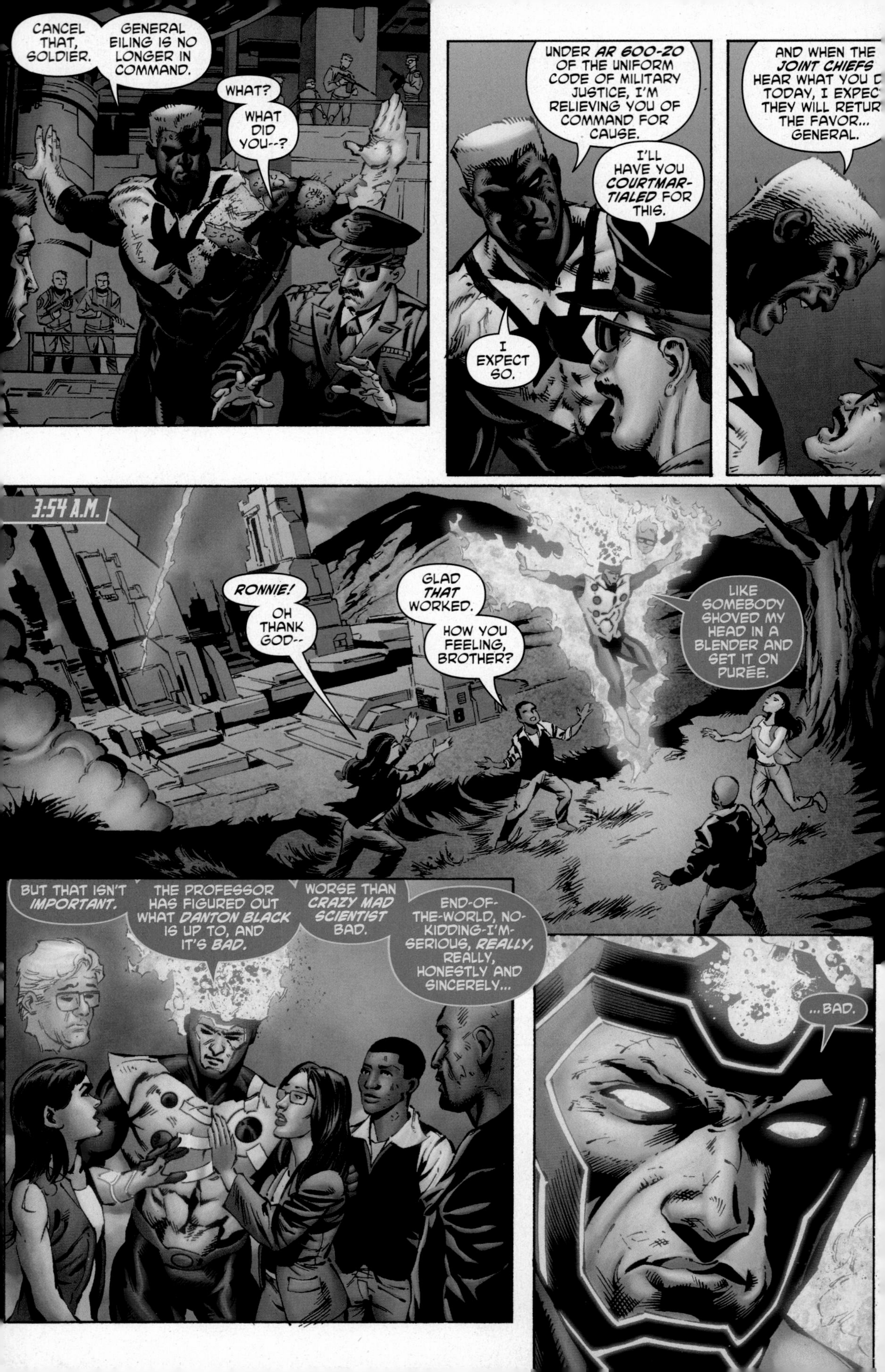

CANCEL THAT, SOLDIER.
GENERAL EILING IS NO LONGER IN COMMAND.
WHAT?
WHAT DID YOU--?
UNDER AR 600-20 OF THE UNIFORM CODE OF MILITARY JUSTICE, I'M RELIEVING YOU OF COMMAND FOR CAUSE.
I'LL HAVE YOU COURTMAR-TIALED FOR THIS.
I EXPECT SO.
AND WHEN THE JOINT CHIEFS HEAR WHAT YOU D TODAY, I EXPEC THEY WILL RETUR THE FAVOR... GENERAL.
3:54 A.M.
RONNIE!
OH THANK GOD--
GLAD THAT WORKED.
HOW YOU FEELING, BROTHER?
LIKE SOMEBODY SHOVED MY HEAD IN A BLENDER AND SET IT ON PURÉE.
BUT THAT ISN'T IMPORTANT.
THE PROFESSOR HAS FIGURED OUT WHAT DANTON BLACK IS UP TO, AND IT'S BAD.
WORSE THAN CRAZY MAD SCIENTIST BAD.
END-OF-THE-WORLD, NO-KIDDING-I'M-SERIOUS, REALLY, REALLY, HONESTLY AND SINCERELY...
...BAD.

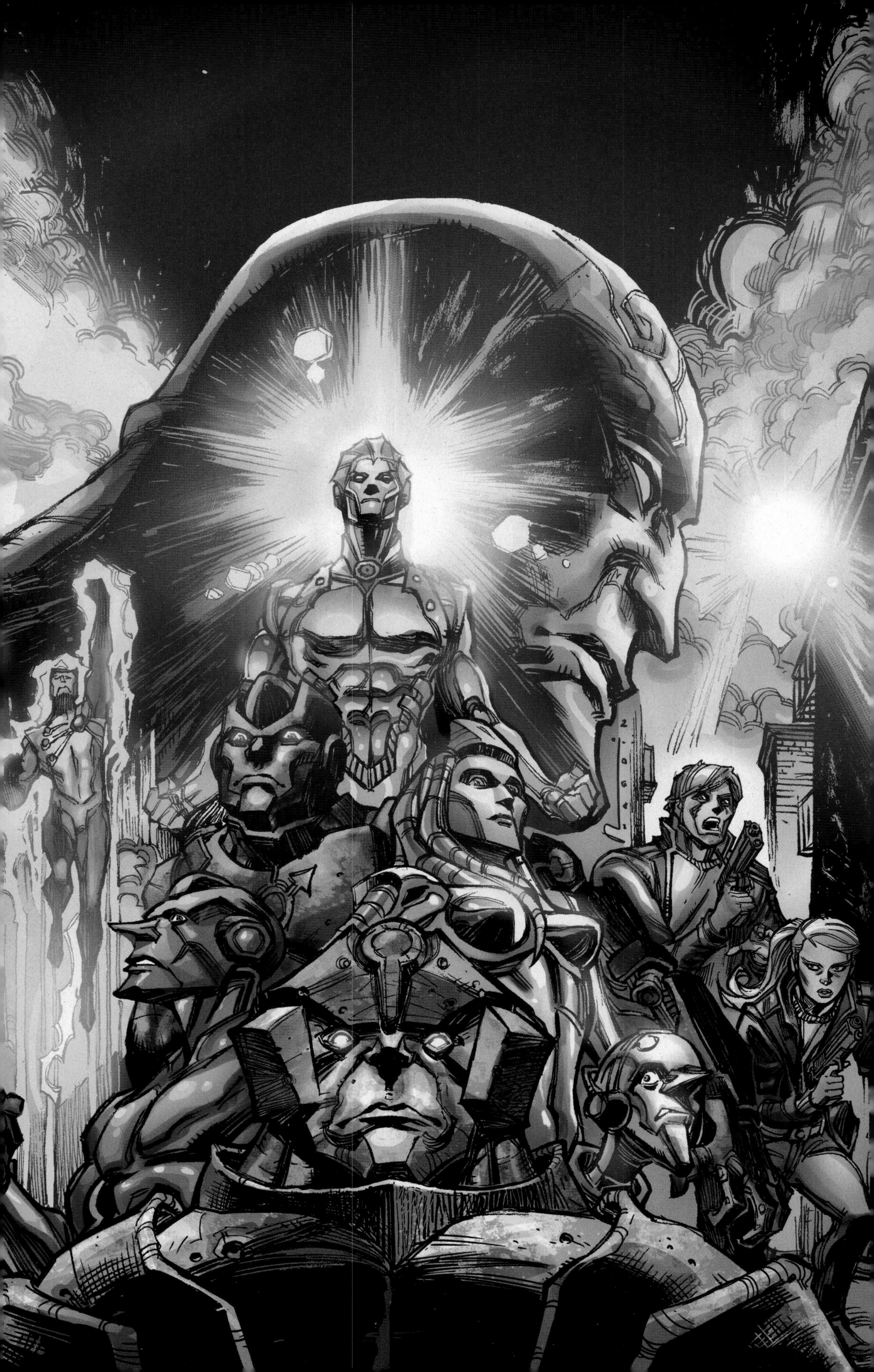

GERRY CONWAY writer **EDUARDO PANSICA** penciller **ROB HUNTER** inker **ANDREW DALHOUSE** colorist **COREY BREEN** letterer
CHAD HARDIN with **PAUL MOUNTS** cover

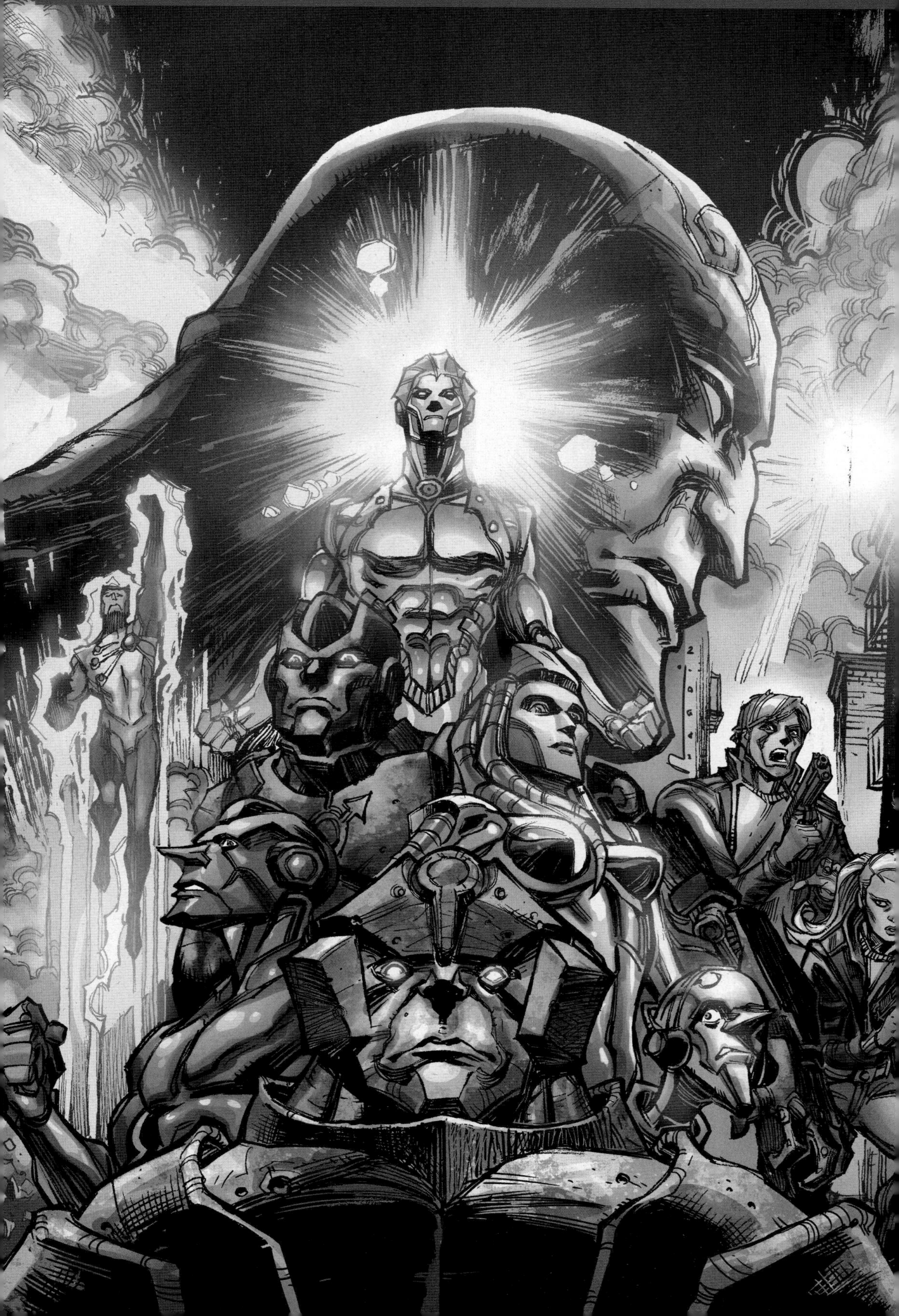

LABORATORIES OF PROFESSOR MARTIN STEIN, ON THE OUTSKIRTS OF WALTON MILLS, 5:19 A.M.
SEE, PROFESSOR?
TOLD YOU WE COULD FLY EVERYBODY BACK HOME IN ONE PIECE.
THIS IS SO COOL!
EASY THERE, MRS. RAYMOND.
ARE WE ON THE GROUND YET?
PLEASE TELL ME WE'RE ON THE GROUND.
ALMOST, JOANNE.
YOU CAN LET GO OF MY ARM NOW.
I'M PRETTY SURE I'VE LOST ALL FEELING IN MY REMAINING HAND.
WOULDN'T HAVE BEEN SO BAD IF YOU'D GRABBED MY PROSTHETIC.

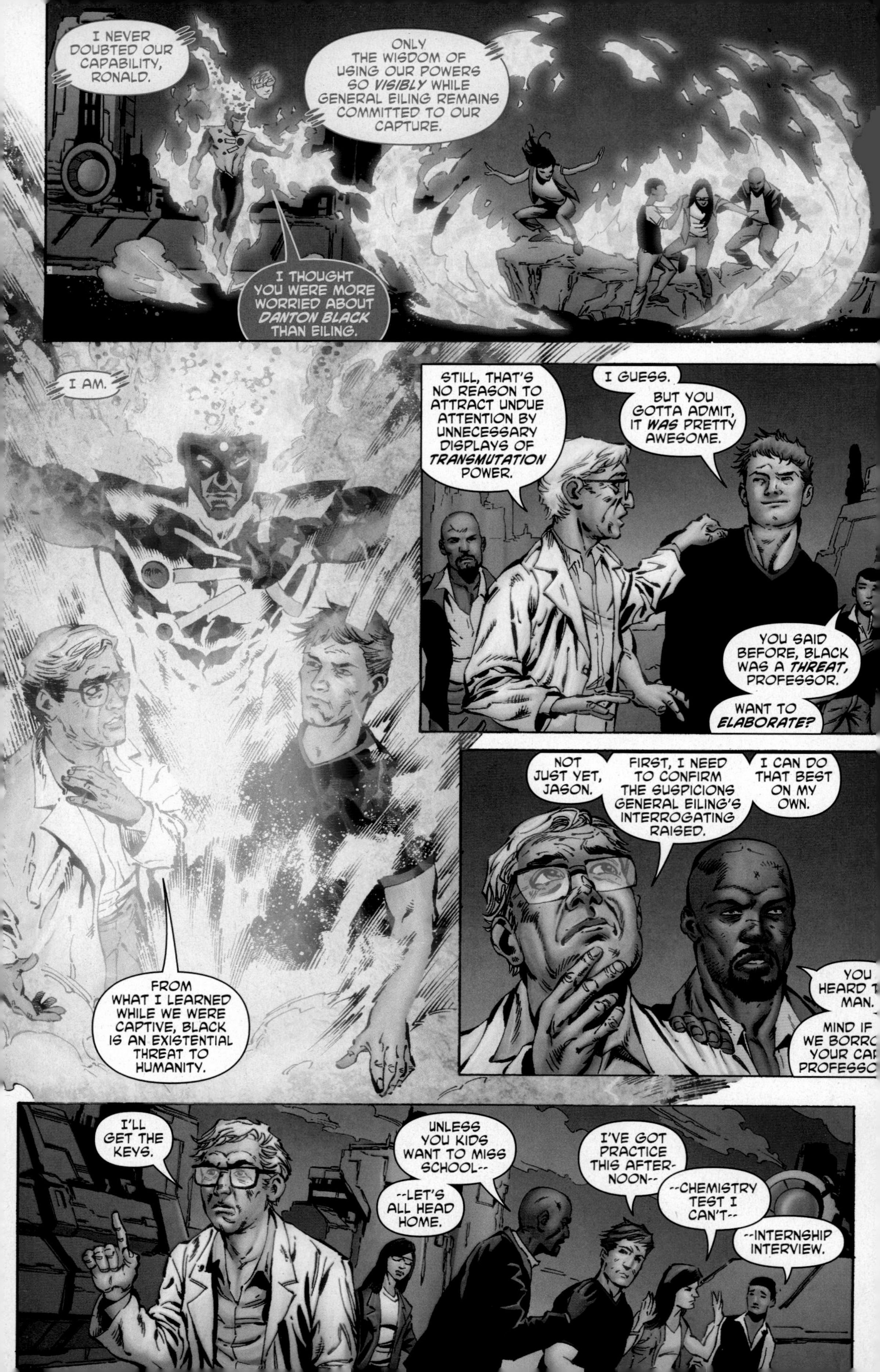
I NEVER DOUBTED OUR CAPABILITY, RONALD.
ONLY THE WISDOM OF USING OUR POWERS SO *VISIBLY* WHILE GENERAL EILING REMAINS COMMITTED TO OUR CAPTURE.
I THOUGHT YOU WERE MORE WORRIED ABOUT *DANTON BLACK* THAN EILING.
I AM.
FROM WHAT I LEARNED WHILE WE WERE CAPTIVE, BLACK IS AN EXISTENTIAL THREAT TO HUMANITY.
STILL, THAT'S NO REASON TO ATTRACT UNDUE ATTENTION BY UNNECESSARY DISPLAYS OF *TRANSMUTATION* POWER.
I GUESS.
BUT YOU GOTTA ADMIT, IT *WAS* PRETTY AWESOME.
YOU SAID BEFORE, BLACK WAS A *THREAT,* PROFESSOR.
WANT TO *ELABORATE?*
NOT JUST YET, JASON.
FIRST, I NEED TO CONFIRM THE SUSPICIONS GENERAL EILING'S INTERROGATING RAISED.
I CAN DO THAT BEST ON MY OWN.
I'LL GET THE KEYS.
UNLESS YOU KIDS WANT TO MISS SCHOOL--
--LET'S ALL HEAD HOME.
I'VE GOT PRACTICE THIS AFTER-NOON--
--CHEMISTRY TEST I CAN'T--
--INTERNSHIP INTERVIEW.

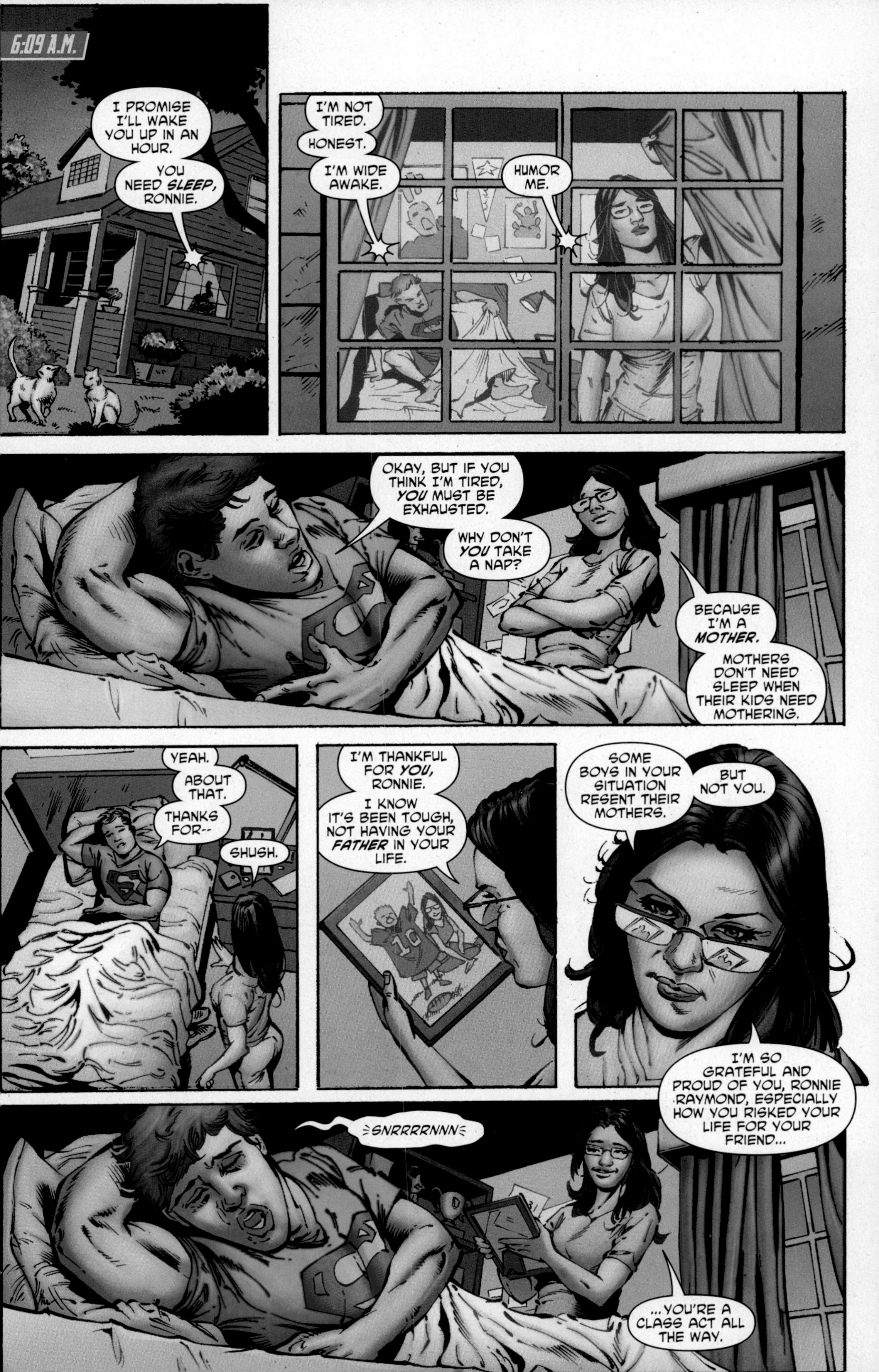
6:09 A.M.
I PROMISE I'LL WAKE YOU UP IN AN HOUR.
YOU NEED *SLEEP,* RONNIE.
I'M NOT TIRED.
HONEST.
I'M WIDE AWAKE.
HUMOR ME.
OKAY, BUT IF YOU THINK I'M TIRED, *YOU* MUST BE EXHAUSTED.
WHY DON'T *YOU* TAKE A NAP?
BECAUSE I'M A *MOTHER.*
MOTHERS DON'T NEED SLEEP WHEN THEIR KIDS NEED MOTHERING.
YEAH.
ABOUT THAT.
THANKS FOR--
SHUSH.
I'M THANKFUL FOR *YOU,* RONNIE.
I KNOW IT'S BEEN TOUGH, NOT HAVING YOUR *FATHER* IN YOUR LIFE.
SOME BOYS IN YOUR SITUATION RESENT THEIR MOTHERS.
BUT NOT YOU.
I'M SO GRATEFUL AND PROUD OF YOU, RONNIE RAYMOND, ESPECIALLY HOW YOU RISKED YOUR LIFE FOR YOUR FRIEND...
SNRRRRNNN
...YOU'RE A CLASS ACT ALL THE WAY.

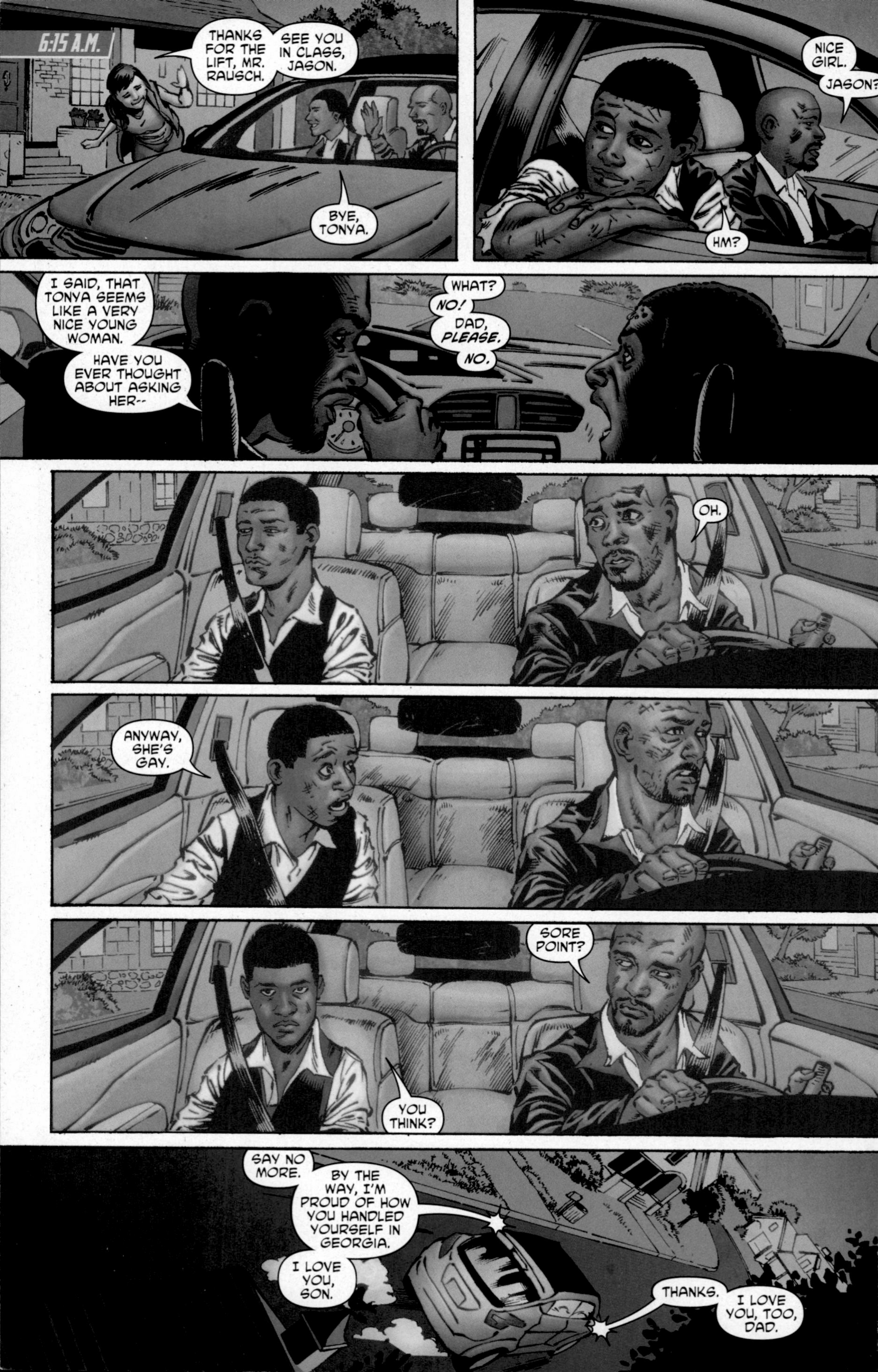
6:15 A.M.
THANKS FOR THE LIFT, MR. RAUSCH.
SEE YOU IN CLASS, JASON.
BYE, TONYA.
NICE GIRL.
JASON?
HM?
I SAID, THAT TONYA SEEMS LIKE A VERY NICE YOUNG WOMAN.
HAVE YOU EVER THOUGHT ABOUT ASKING HER--
WHAT?
NO!
DAD, PLEASE.
NO.
OH.
ANYWAY, SHE'S GAY.
SORE POINT?
YOU THINK?
SAY NO MORE.
BY THE WAY, I'M PROUD OF HOW YOU HANDLED YOURSELF IN GEORGIA.
I LOVE YOU, SON.
THANKS.
I LOVE YOU, TOO, DAD.

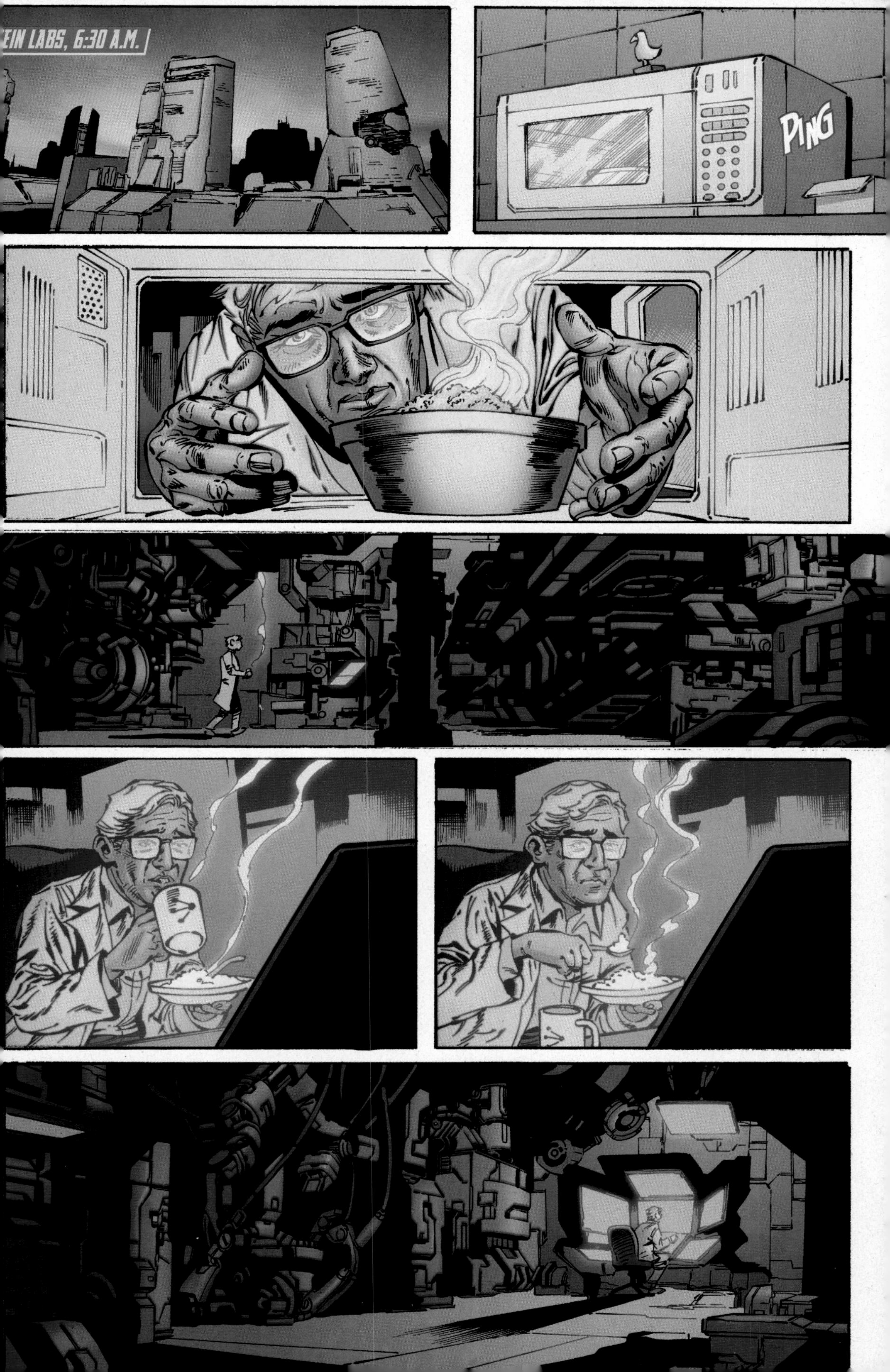

EIN LABS, 6:30 A.M.
PING

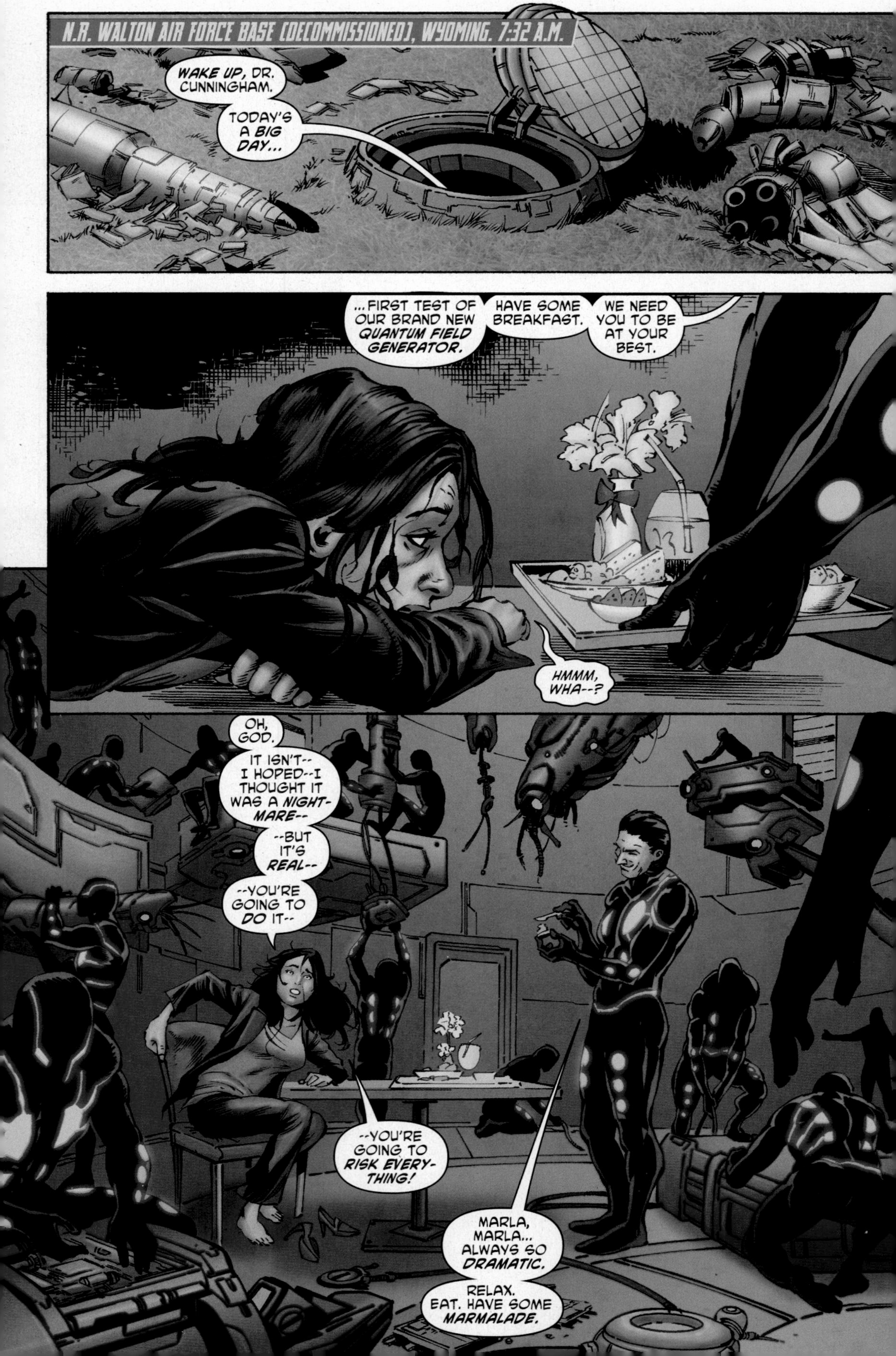
N.R. WALTON AIR FORCE BASE (DECOMMISSIONED), WYOMING. 7:32 A.M.
WAKE UP, DR. CUNNINGHAM.
TODAY'S A BIG DAY...
...FIRST TEST OF OUR BRAND NEW QUANTUM FIELD GENERATOR.
HAVE SOME BREAKFAST.
WE NEED YOU TO BE AT YOUR BEST.
HMMM, WHA--?
OH, GOD.
IT ISN'T-- I HOPED--I THOUGHT IT WAS A NIGHT-MARE--
--BUT IT'S REAL--
--YOU'RE GOING TO DO IT--
--YOU'RE GOING TO RISK EVERY-THING!
MARLA, MARLA... ALWAYS SO DRAMATIC.
RELAX. EAT. HAVE SOME MARMALADE.

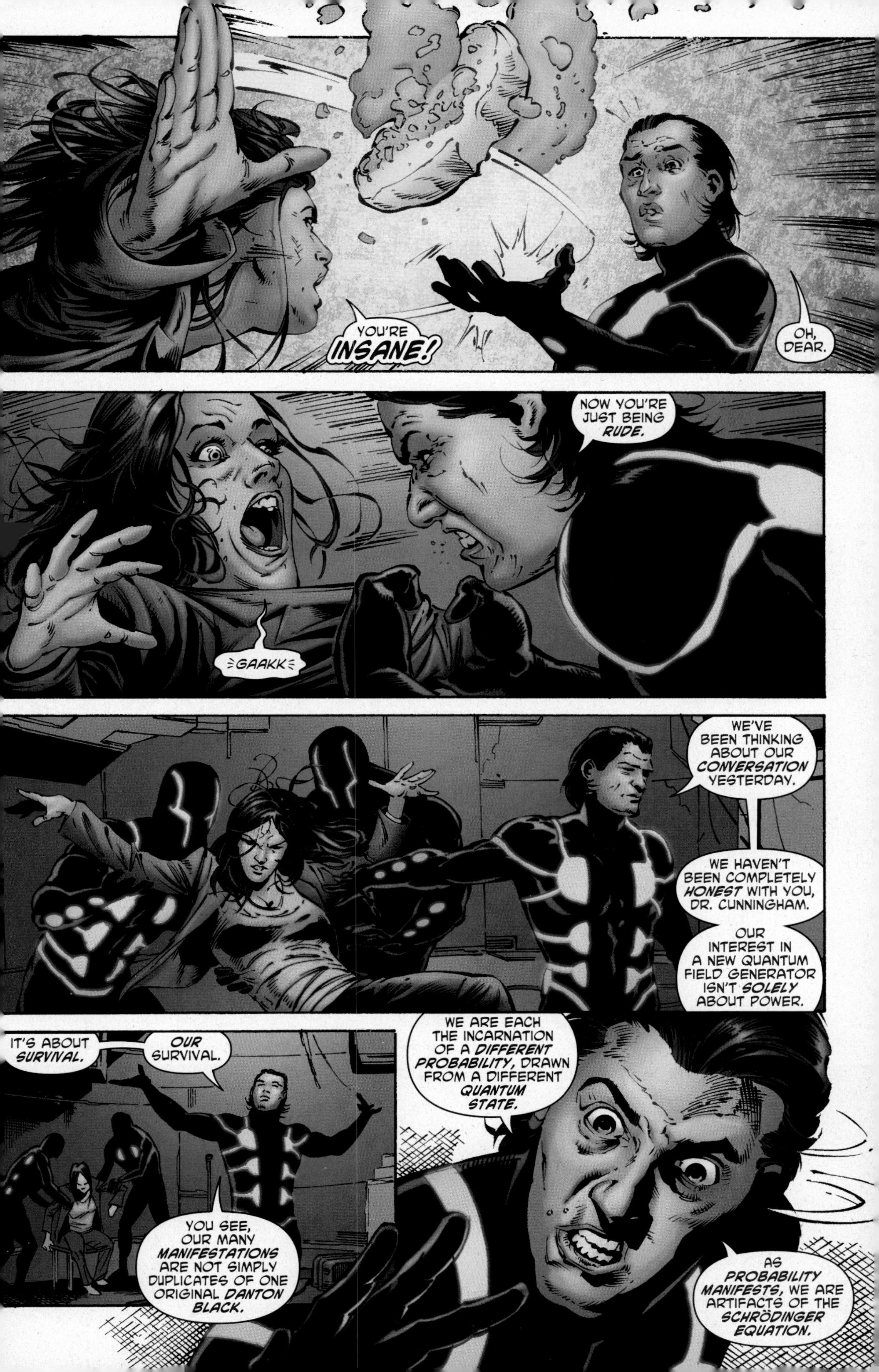
YOU'RE INSANE!
OH, DEAR.
NOW YOU'RE JUST BEING RUDE.
GAAKK
WE'VE BEEN THINKING ABOUT OUR CONVERSATION YESTERDAY.
WE HAVEN'T BEEN COMPLETELY HONEST WITH YOU, DR. CUNNINGHAM.
OUR INTEREST IN A NEW QUANTUM FIELD GENERATOR ISN'T SOLELY ABOUT POWER.
IT'S ABOUT SURVIVAL.
OUR SURVIVAL.
YOU SEE, OUR MANY MANIFESTATIONS ARE NOT SIMPLY DUPLICATES OF ONE ORIGINAL DANTON BLACK.
WE ARE EACH THE INCARNATION OF A DIFFERENT PROBABILITY, DRAWN FROM A DIFFERENT QUANTUM STATE.
AS PROBABILITY MANIFESTS, WE ARE ARTIFACTS OF THE SCHRÖDINGER EQUATION.

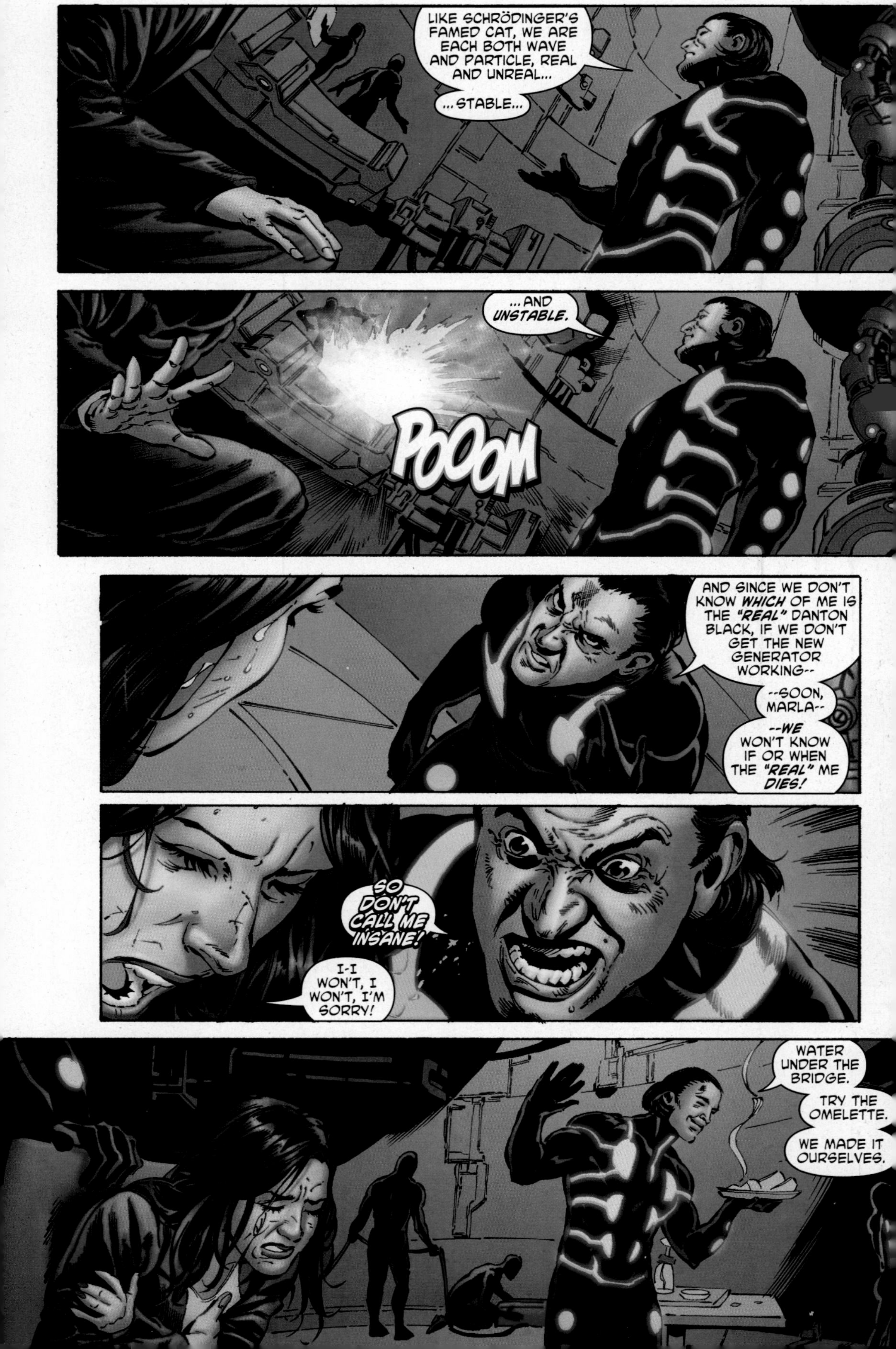
LIKE SCHRÖDINGER'S FAMED CAT, WE ARE EACH BOTH WAVE AND PARTICLE, REAL AND UNREAL...
...STABLE...
...AND UNSTABLE.
POOOM
AND SINCE WE DON'T KNOW WHICH OF ME IS THE "REAL" DANTON BLACK, IF WE DON'T GET THE NEW GENERATOR WORKING--
--SOON, MARLA--
--WE WON'T KNOW IF OR WHEN THE "REAL" ME DIES!
SO DON'T CALL ME INSANE!
I-I WON'T, I WON'T, I'M SORRY!
WATER UNDER THE BRIDGE.
TRY THE OMELETTE.
WE MADE IT OURSELVES.

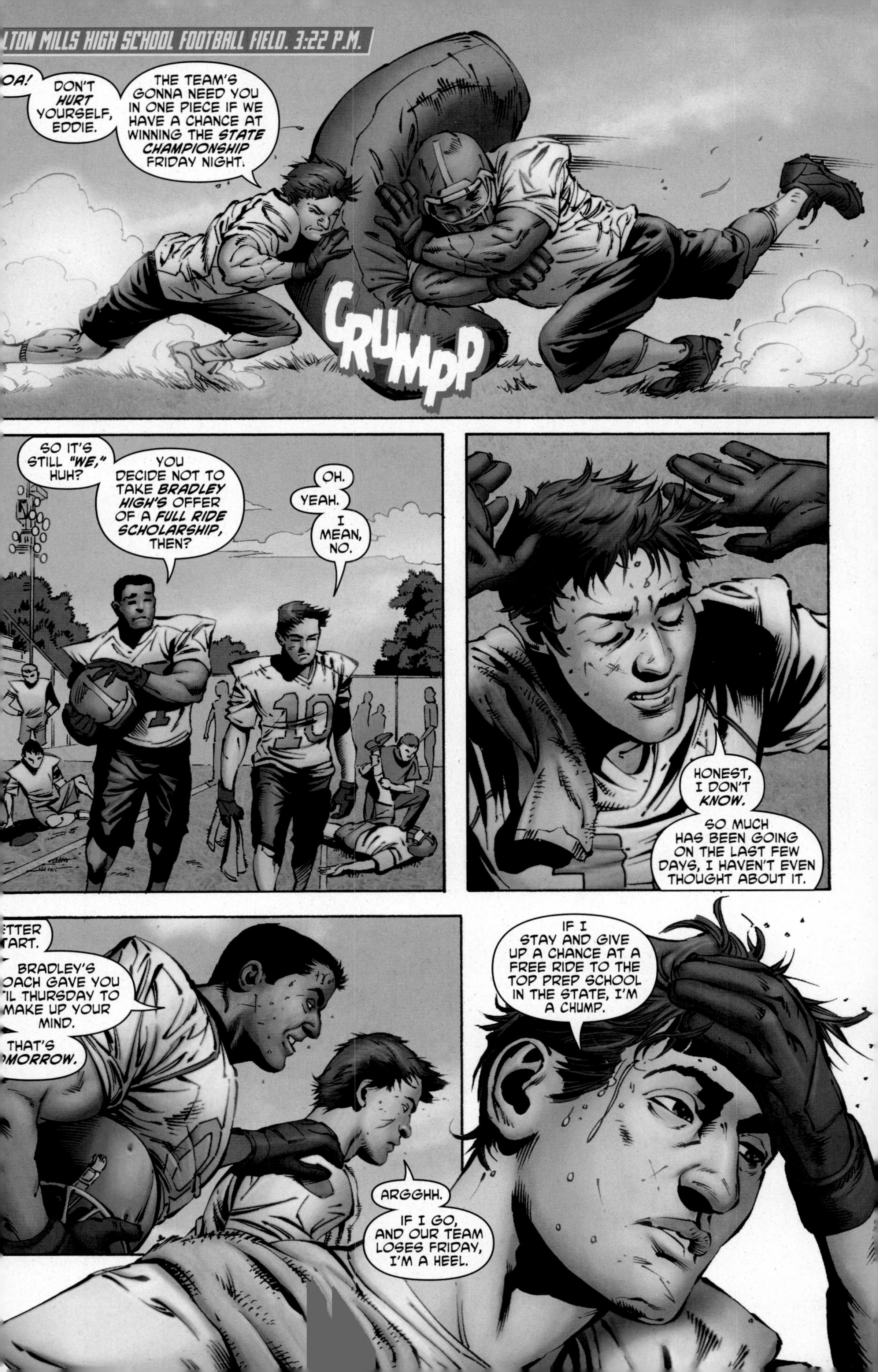
LTON MILLS HIGH SCHOOL FOOTBALL FIELD. 3:22 P.M.
OA!
DON'T HURT YOURSELF, EDDIE.
THE TEAM'S GONNA NEED YOU IN ONE PIECE IF WE HAVE A CHANCE AT WINNING THE STATE CHAMPIONSHIP FRIDAY NIGHT.
CRUMPP
SO IT'S STILL "WE," HUH?
YOU DECIDE NOT TO TAKE BRADLEY HIGH'S OFFER OF A FULL RIDE SCHOLARSHIP, THEN?
OH.
YEAH.
I MEAN, NO.
HONEST, I DON'T KNOW.
SO MUCH HAS BEEN GOING ON THE LAST FEW DAYS, I HAVEN'T EVEN THOUGHT ABOUT IT.
ETTER TART.
BRADLEY'S OACH GAVE YOU TIL THURSDAY TO MAKE UP YOUR MIND.
THAT'S OMORROW.
ARGGHH.
IF I GO, AND OUR TEAM LOSES FRIDAY, I'M A HEEL.
IF I STAY AND GIVE UP A CHANCE AT A FREE RIDE TO THE TOP PREP SCHOOL IN THE STATE, I'M A CHUMP.

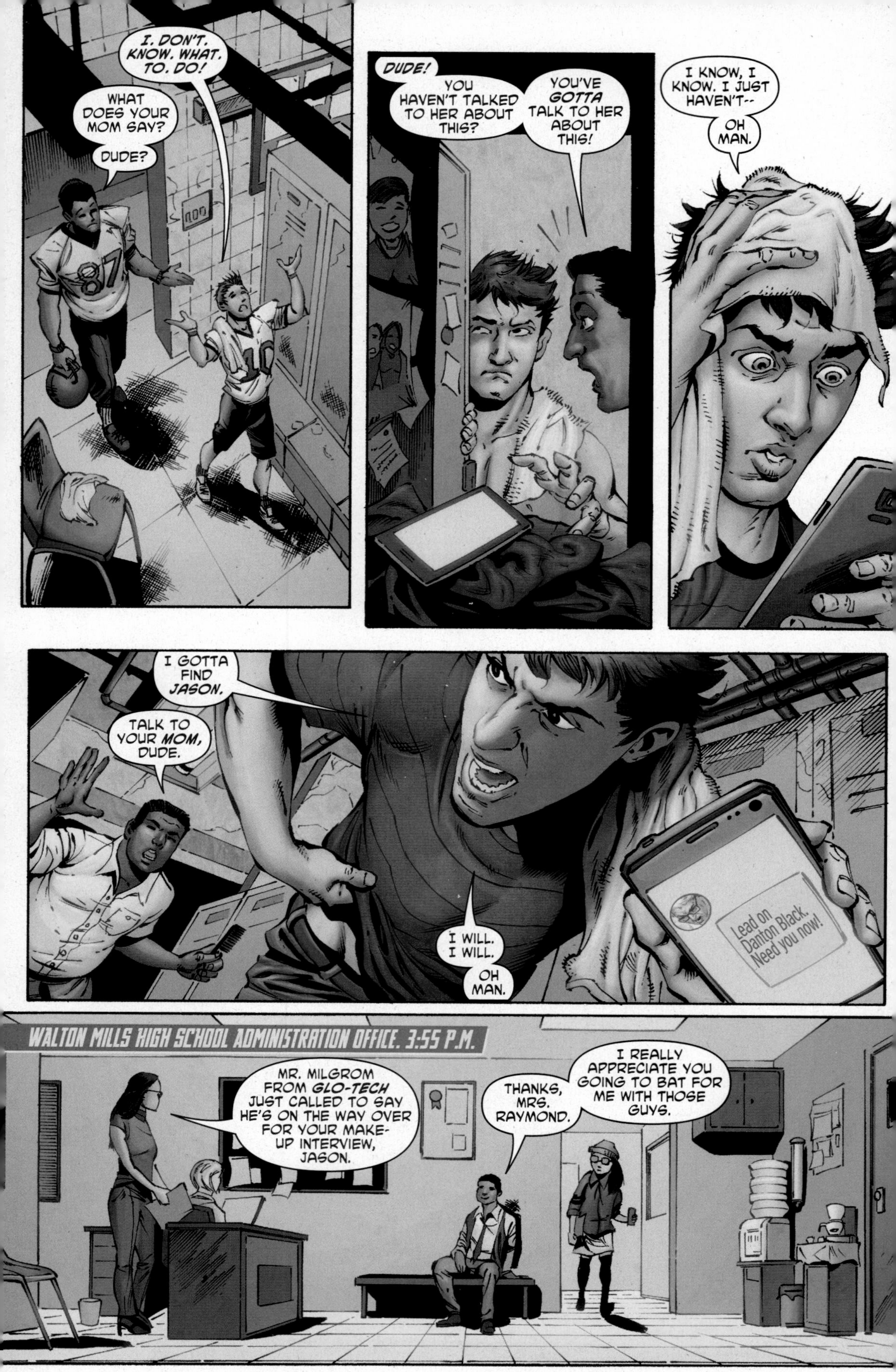

I. DON'T. KNOW. WHAT. TO. DO!
WHAT DOES YOUR MOM SAY?
DUDE?
DUDE!
YOU HAVEN'T TALKED TO HER ABOUT THIS?
YOU'VE GOTTA TALK TO HER ABOUT THIS!
I KNOW, I KNOW. I JUST HAVEN'T--
OH MAN.
I GOTTA FIND JASON.
TALK TO YOUR MOM, DUDE.
I WILL. I WILL.
OH MAN.
Lead on Danton Black. Need you now!
WALTON MILLS HIGH SCHOOL ADMINISTRATION OFFICE. 3:55 P.M.
MR. MILGROM FROM GLO-TECH JUST CALLED TO SAY HE'S ON THE WAY OVER FOR YOUR MAKE-UP INTERVIEW, JASON.
THANKS, MRS. RAYMOND.
I REALLY APPRECIATE YOU GOING TO BAT FOR ME WITH THOSE GUYS.

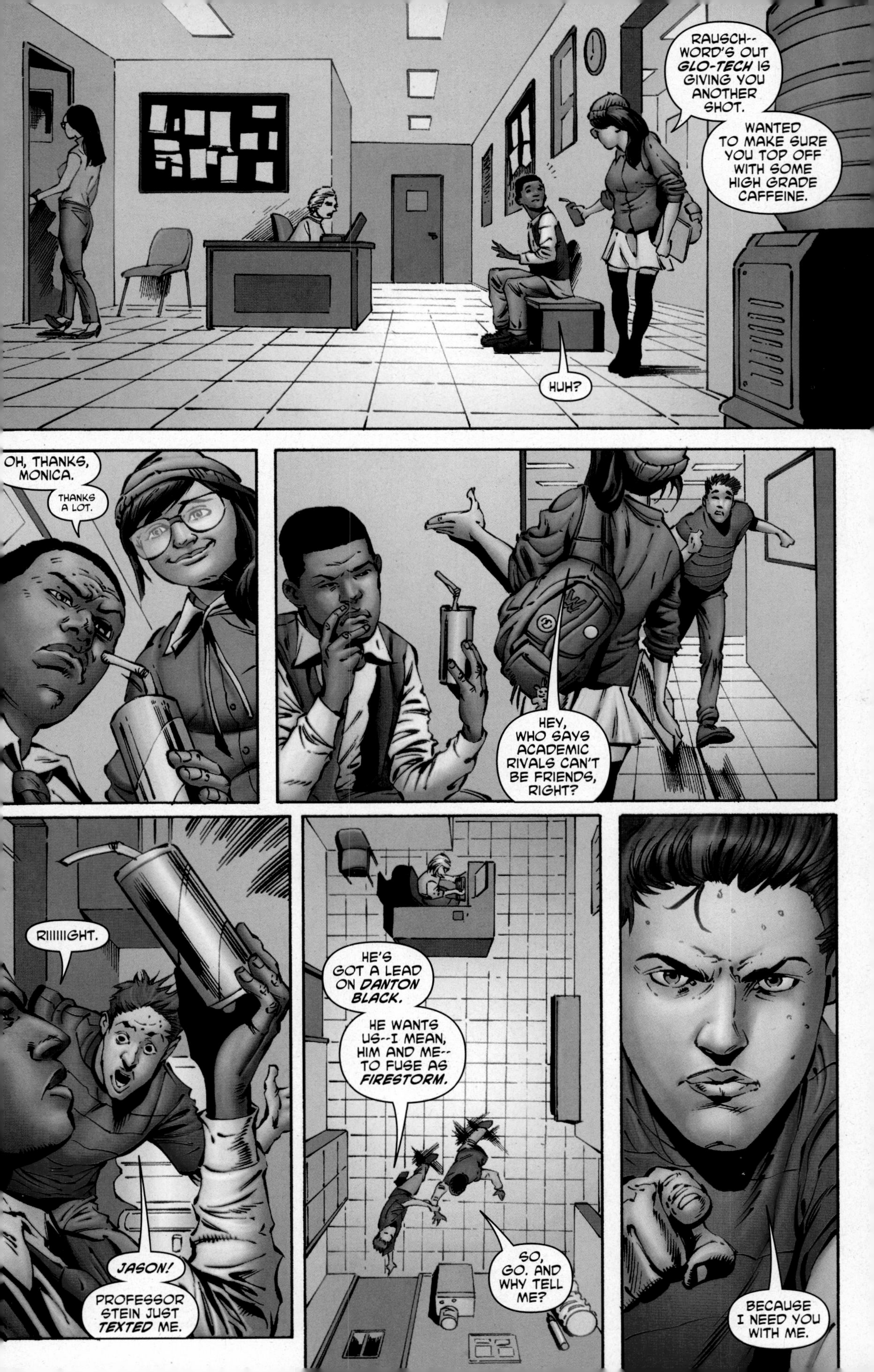
RAUSCH--WORD'S OUT GLO-TECH IS GIVING YOU ANOTHER SHOT.
WANTED TO MAKE SURE YOU TOP OFF WITH SOME HIGH GRADE CAFFEINE.
HUH?
OH, THANKS, MONICA.
THANKS A LOT.
HEY, WHO SAYS ACADEMIC RIVALS CAN'T BE FRIENDS, RIGHT?
RIIIIIIGHT.
JASON!
PROFESSOR STEIN JUST TEXTED ME.
HE'S GOT A LEAD ON DANTON BLACK.
HE WANTS US--I MEAN, HIM AND ME--TO FUSE AS FIRESTORM.
SO, GO. AND WHY TELL ME?
BECAUSE I NEED YOU WITH ME.

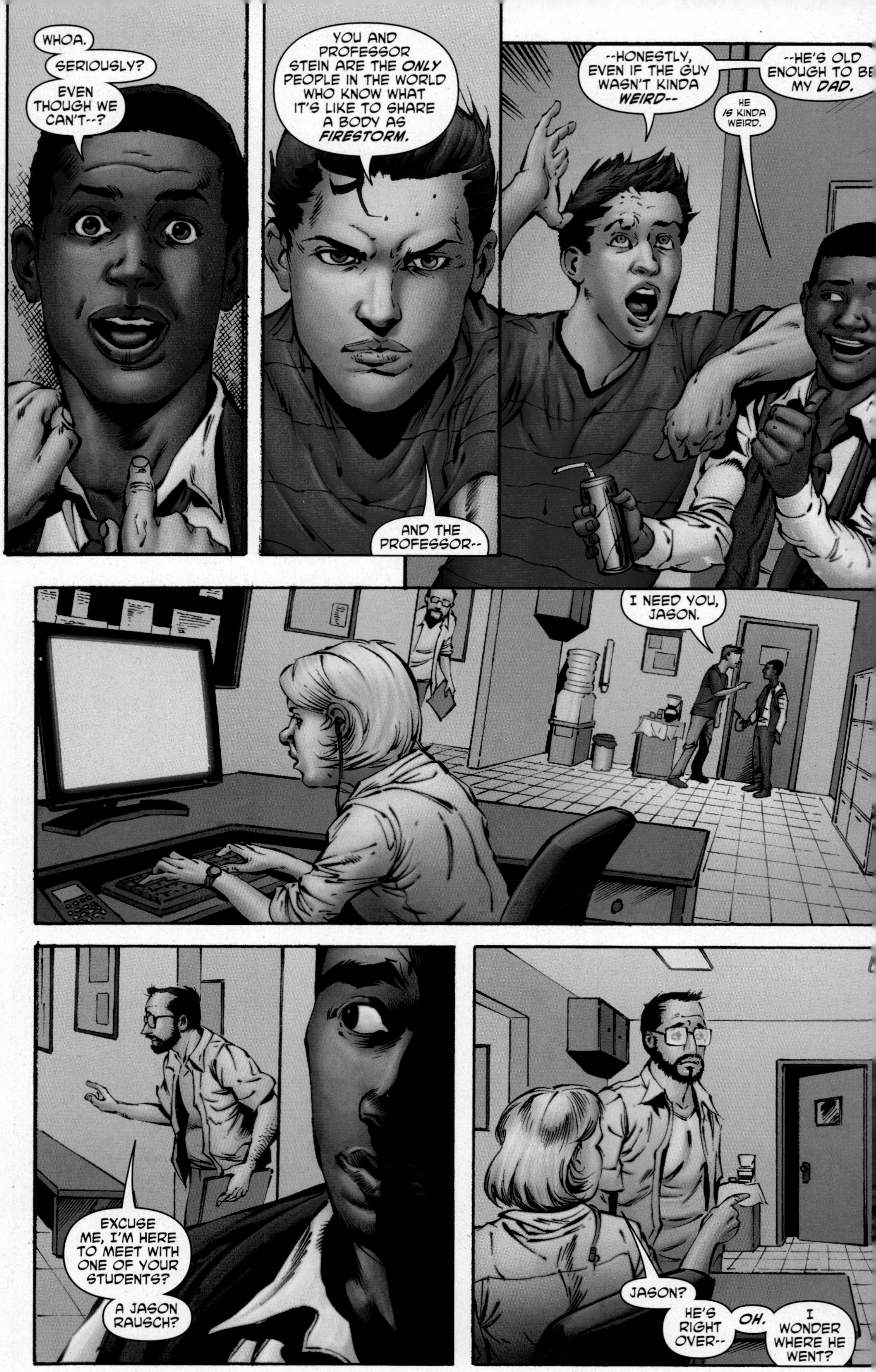
WHOA.
SERIOUSLY?
EVEN THOUGH WE CAN'T--?
YOU AND PROFESSOR STEIN ARE THE *ONLY* PEOPLE IN THE WORLD WHO KNOW WHAT IT'S LIKE TO SHARE A BODY AS *FIRESTORM.*
AND THE PROFESSOR--
--HONESTLY, EVEN IF THE GUY WASN'T KINDA *WEIRD*--
--HE'S OLD ENOUGH TO BE MY *DAD.*
HE *IS* KINDA WEIRD.
I NEED YOU, JASON.
EXCUSE ME, I'M HERE TO MEET WITH ONE OF YOUR STUDENTS?
A JASON RAUSCH?
JASON?
HE'S RIGHT OVER--
OH.
I WONDER WHERE HE WENT?

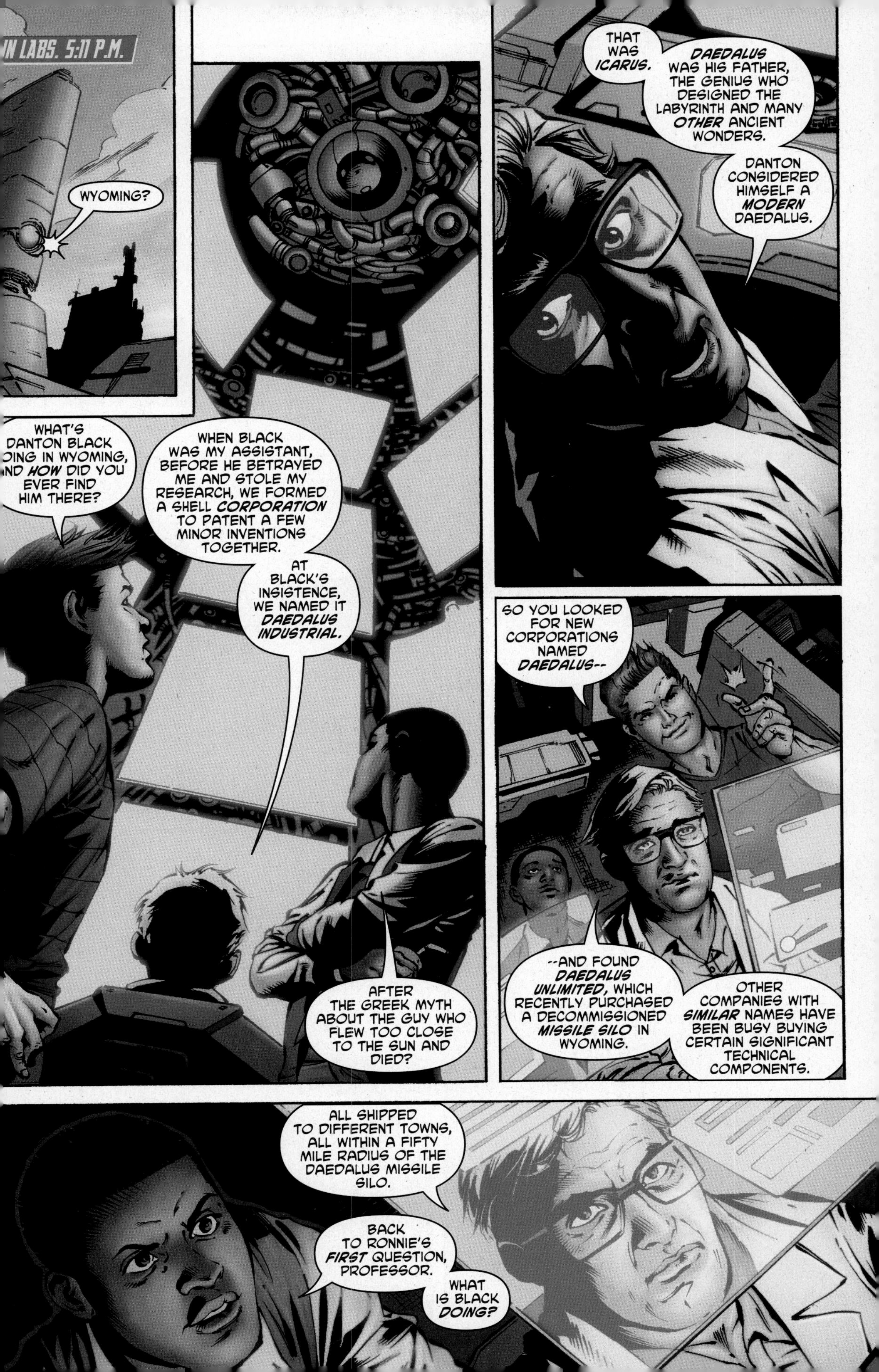

...N LABS. 5:11 P.M.
WYOMING?
THAT WAS ICARUS.
DAEDALUS WAS HIS FATHER, THE GENIUS WHO DESIGNED THE LABYRINTH AND MANY OTHER ANCIENT WONDERS.
DANTON CONSIDERED HIMSELF A MODERN DAEDALUS.
WHAT'S DANTON BLACK ...OING IN WYOMING, ...ND HOW DID YOU EVER FIND HIM THERE?
WHEN BLACK WAS MY ASSISTANT, BEFORE HE BETRAYED ME AND STOLE MY RESEARCH, WE FORMED A SHELL CORPORATION TO PATENT A FEW MINOR INVENTIONS TOGETHER.
AT BLACK'S INSISTENCE, WE NAMED IT DAEDALUS INDUSTRIAL.
AFTER THE GREEK MYTH ABOUT THE GUY WHO FLEW TOO CLOSE TO THE SUN AND DIED?
SO YOU LOOKED FOR NEW CORPORATIONS NAMED DAEDALUS--
--AND FOUND DAEDALUS UNLIMITED, WHICH RECENTLY PURCHASED A DECOMMISSIONED MISSILE SILO IN WYOMING.
OTHER COMPANIES WITH SIMILAR NAMES HAVE BEEN BUSY BUYING CERTAIN SIGNIFICANT TECHNICAL COMPONENTS.
ALL SHIPPED TO DIFFERENT TOWNS, ALL WITHIN A FIFTY MILE RADIUS OF THE DAEDALUS MISSILE SILO.
BACK TO RONNIE'S FIRST QUESTION, PROFESSOR.
WHAT IS BLACK DOING?

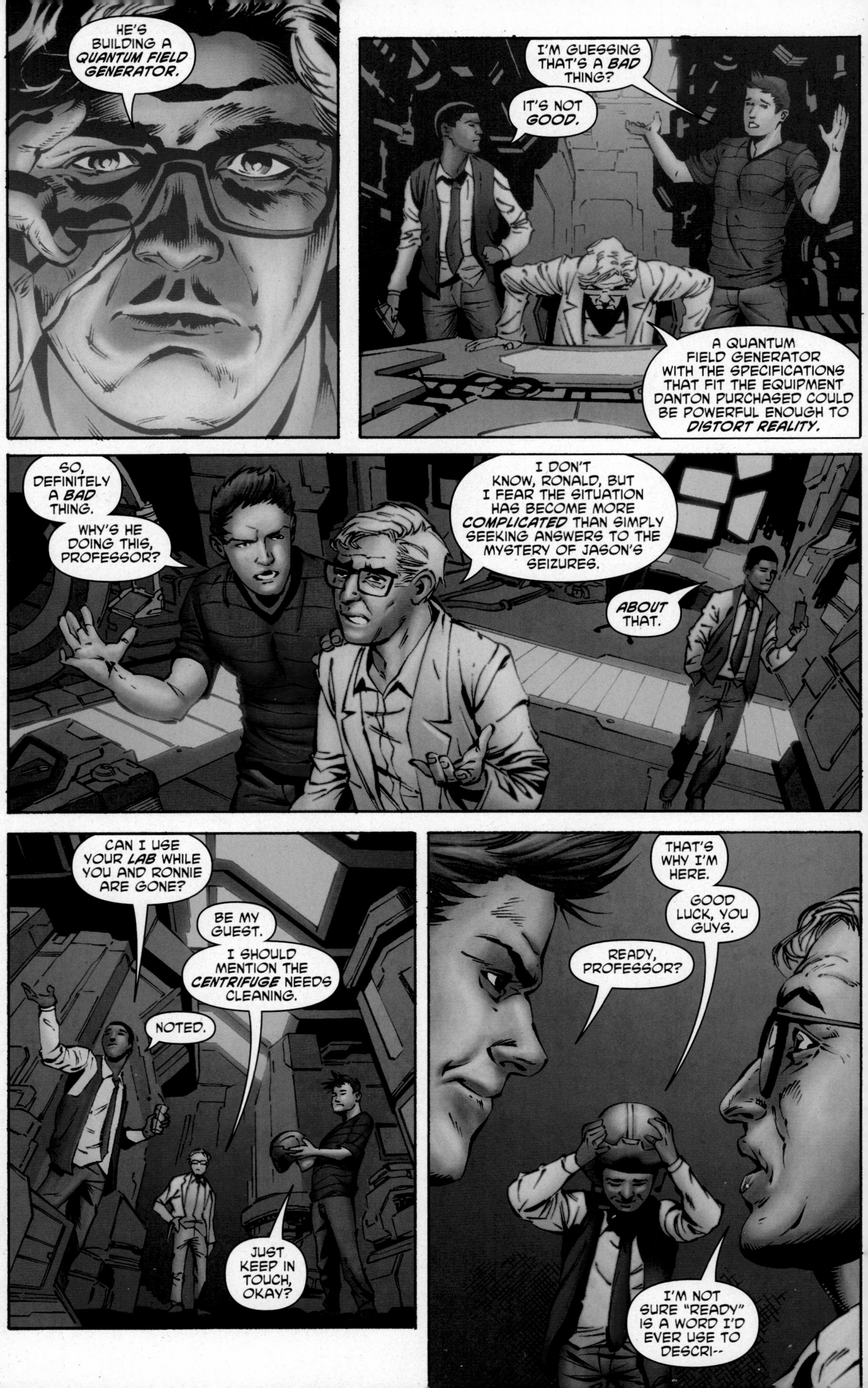
HE'S BUILDING A *QUANTUM FIELD GENERATOR.*
I'M GUESSING THAT'S A *BAD* THING?
IT'S NOT *GOOD.*
A QUANTUM FIELD GENERATOR WITH THE SPECIFICATIONS THAT FIT THE EQUIPMENT DANTON PURCHASED COULD BE POWERFUL ENOUGH TO *DISTORT REALITY.*
SO, DEFINITELY A *BAD* THING.
WHY'S HE DOING THIS, PROFESSOR?
I DON'T KNOW, RONALD, BUT I FEAR THE SITUATION HAS BECOME MORE *COMPLICATED* THAN SIMPLY SEEKING ANSWERS TO THE MYSTERY OF JASON'S SEIZURES.
ABOUT THAT.
CAN I USE YOUR *LAB* WHILE YOU AND RONNIE ARE GONE?
BE MY GUEST.
I SHOULD MENTION THE *CENTRIFUGE* NEEDS CLEANING.
NOTED.
JUST KEEP IN TOUCH, OKAY?
THAT'S WHY I'M HERE.
GOOD LUCK, YOU GUYS.
READY, PROFESSOR?
I'M NOT SURE "READY" IS A WORD I'D EVER USE TO DESCRI--

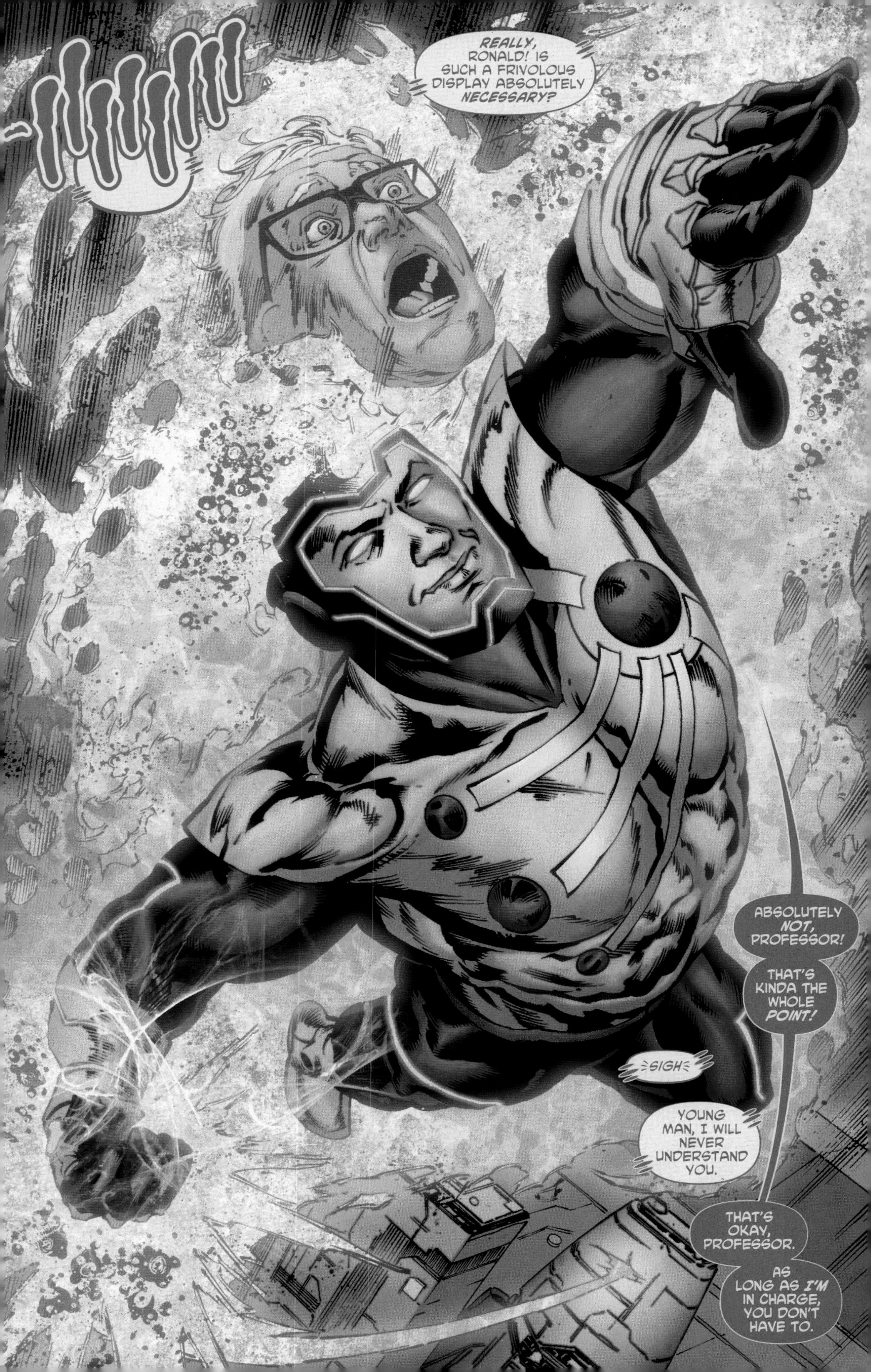

-fffffff
REALLY, RONALD! IS SUCH A FRIVOLOUS DISPLAY ABSOLUTELY NECESSARY?
ABSOLUTELY NOT, PROFESSOR!
THAT'S KINDA THE WHOLE POINT!
SIGH
YOUNG MAN, I WILL NEVER UNDERSTAND YOU.
THAT'S OKAY, PROFESSOR.
AS LONG AS I'M IN CHARGE, YOU DON'T HAVE TO.

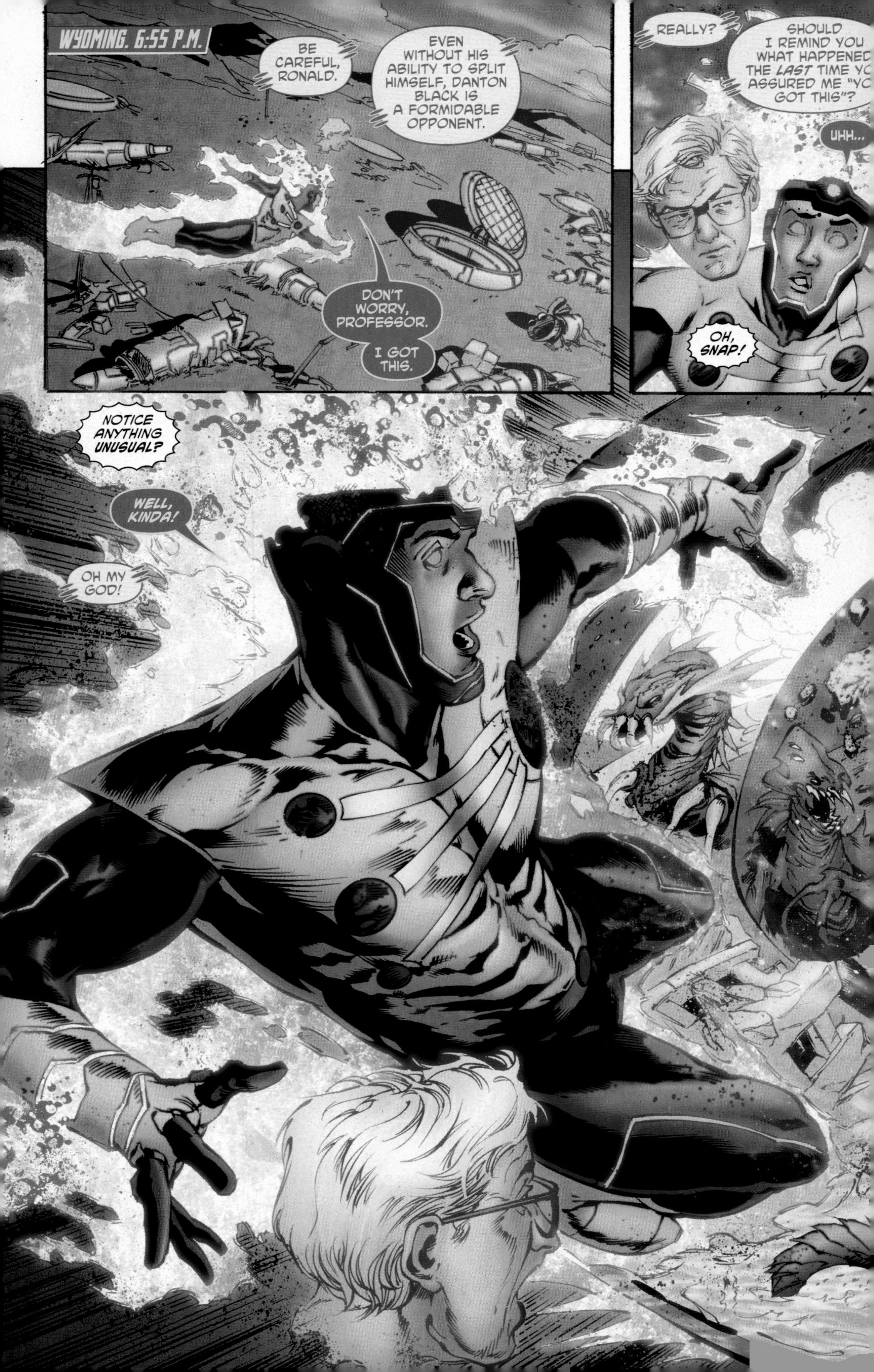
WYOMING. 6:55 P.M.
BE CAREFUL, RONALD.
EVEN WITHOUT HIS ABILITY TO SPLIT HIMSELF, DANTON BLACK IS A FORMIDABLE OPPONENT.
DON'T WORRY, PROFESSOR.
I GOT THIS.
REALLY?
SHOULD I REMIND YOU WHAT HAPPENED THE LAST TIME YO ASSURED ME "YO GOT THIS"?
UHH...
OH, SNAP!
NOTICE ANYTHING UNUSUAL?
WELL, KINDA!
OH MY GOD!

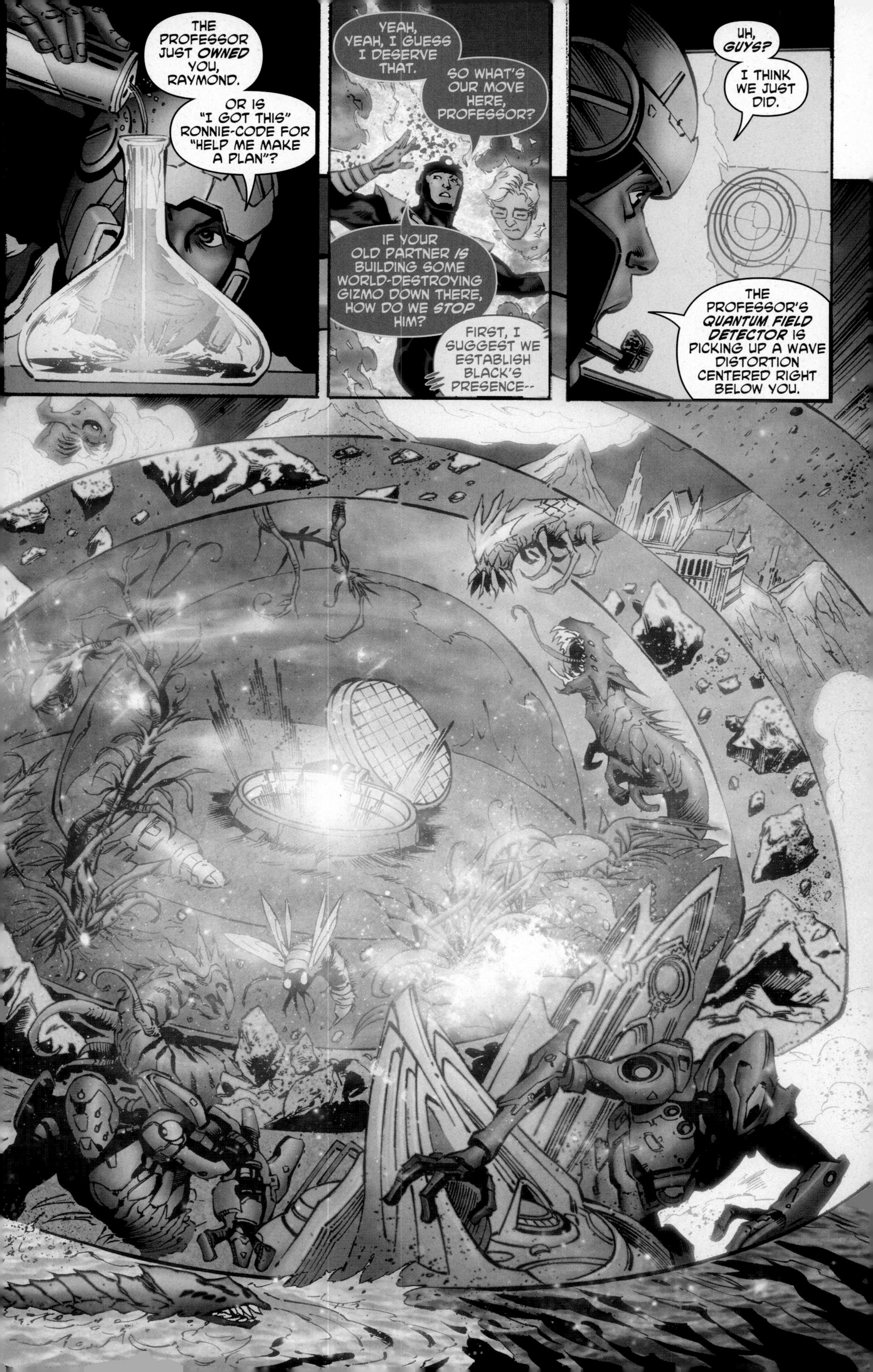
THE PROFESSOR JUST OWNED YOU, RAYMOND.
OR IS "I GOT THIS" RONNIE-CODE FOR "HELP ME MAKE A PLAN"?
YEAH, YEAH, I GUESS I DESERVE THAT.
SO WHAT'S OUR MOVE HERE, PROFESSOR?
IF YOUR OLD PARTNER IS BUILDING SOME WORLD-DESTROYING GIZMO DOWN THERE, HOW DO WE STOP HIM?
FIRST, I SUGGEST WE ESTABLISH BLACK'S PRESENCE--
UH, GUYS?
I THINK WE JUST DID.
THE PROFESSOR'S QUANTUM FIELD DETECTOR IS PICKING UP A WAVE DISTORTION CENTERED RIGHT BELOW YOU.

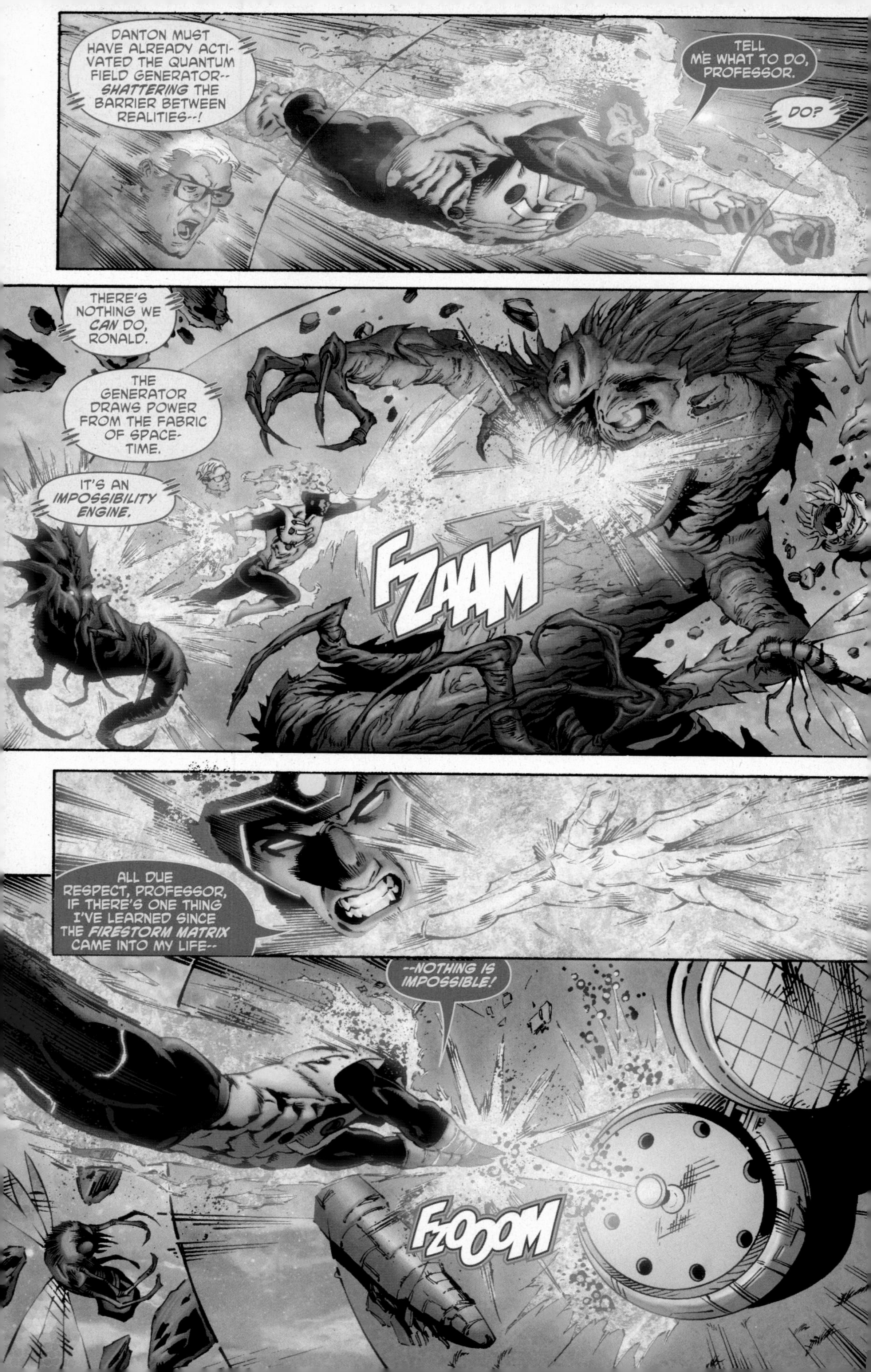
DANTON MUST HAVE ALREADY ACTIVATED THE QUANTUM FIELD GENERATOR-- *SHATTERING* THE BARRIER BETWEEN REALITIES--!
TELL ME WHAT TO DO, PROFESSOR.
DO?
THERE'S NOTHING WE *CAN* DO, RONALD.
THE GENERATOR DRAWS POWER FROM THE FABRIC OF SPACE-TIME.
IT'S AN *IMPOSSIBILITY ENGINE.*
FZAAM
ALL DUE RESPECT, PROFESSOR, IF THERE'S ONE THING I'VE LEARNED SINCE THE *FIRESTORM MATRIX* CAME INTO MY LIFE--
--NOTHING IS IMPOSSIBLE!
FZOOOM

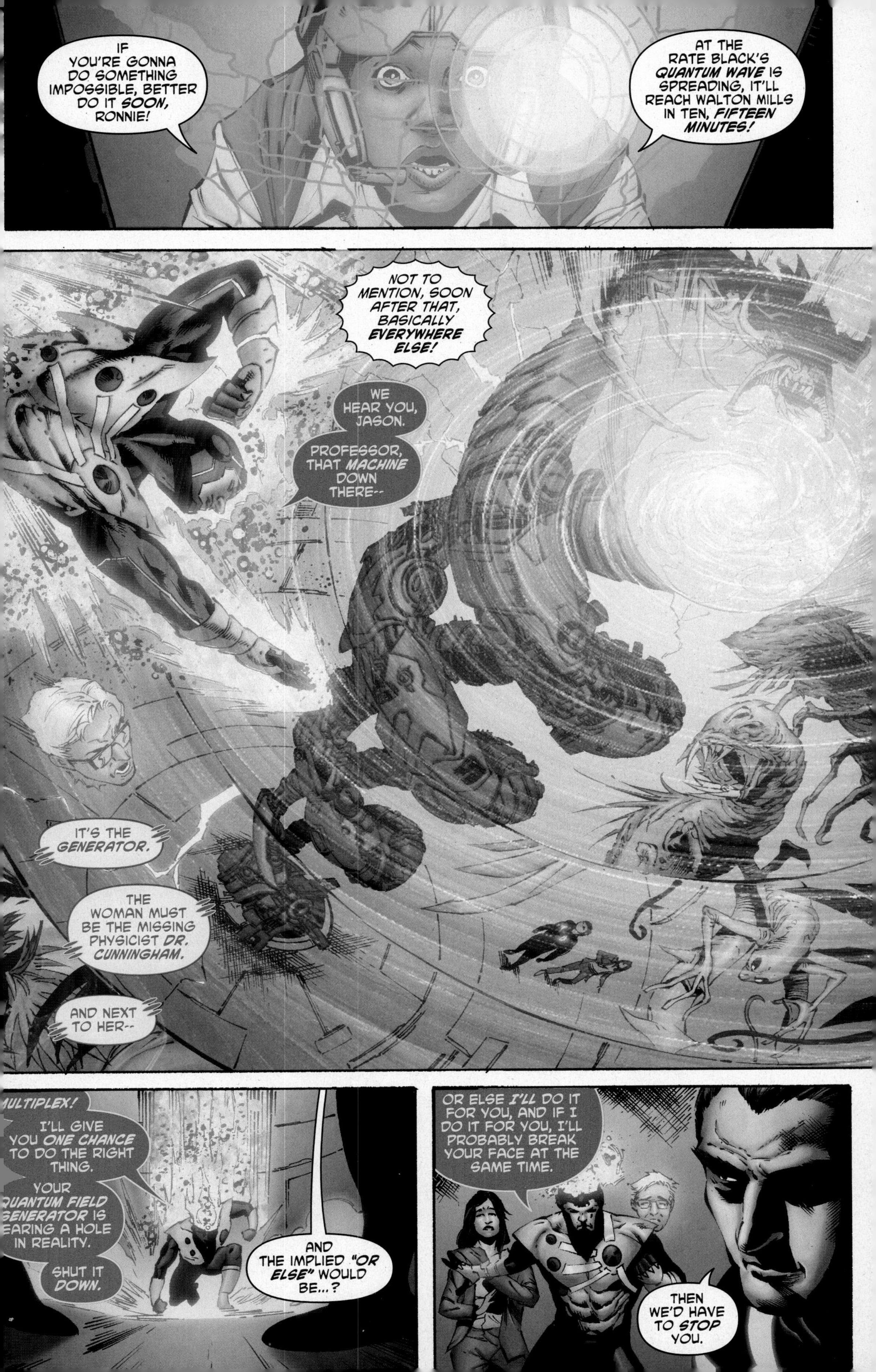

IF YOU'RE GONNA DO SOMETHING IMPOSSIBLE, BETTER DO IT SOON, RONNIE!
AT THE RATE BLACK'S QUANTUM WAVE IS SPREADING, IT'LL REACH WALTON MILLS IN TEN, FIFTEEN MINUTES!
NOT TO MENTION, SOON AFTER THAT, BASICALLY EVERYWHERE ELSE!
WE HEAR YOU, JASON.
PROFESSOR, THAT MACHINE DOWN THERE--
IT'S THE GENERATOR.
THE WOMAN MUST BE THE MISSING PHYSICIST DR. CUNNINGHAM.
AND NEXT TO HER--
MULTIPLEX!
I'LL GIVE YOU ONE CHANCE TO DO THE RIGHT THING.
YOUR QUANTUM FIELD GENERATOR IS TEARING A HOLE IN REALITY.
SHUT IT DOWN.
AND THE IMPLIED "OR ELSE" WOULD BE...?
OR ELSE I'LL DO IT FOR YOU, AND IF I DO IT FOR YOU, I'LL PROBABLY BREAK YOUR FACE AT THE SAME TIME.
THEN WE'D HAVE TO STOP YOU.

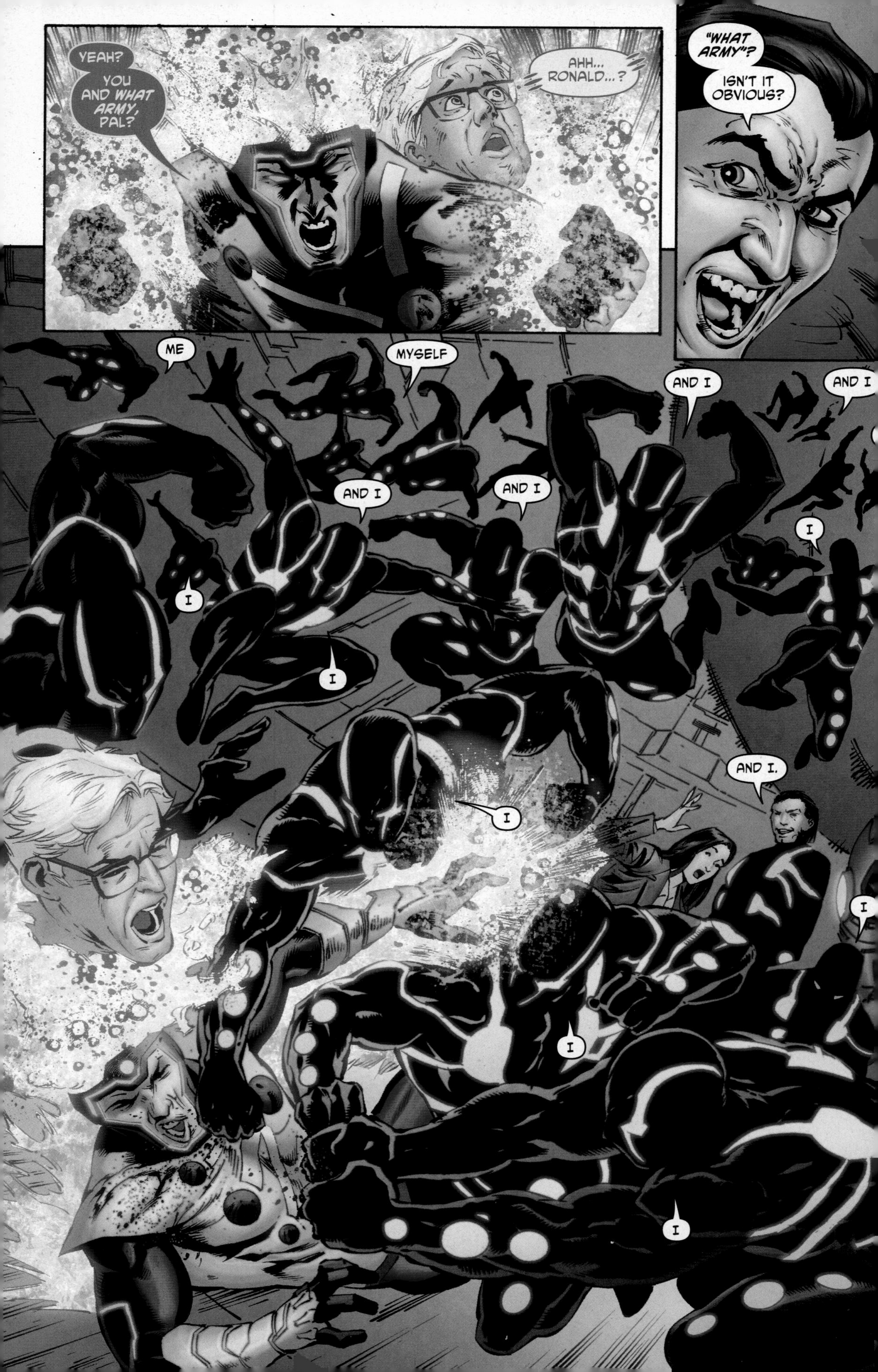

YEAH? YOU AND WHAT ARMY, PAL?
AHH... RONALD...?
"WHAT ARMY"? ISN'T IT OBVIOUS?
ME
MYSELF
AND I
AND I
AND I
AND I
I
I
I
AND I.
I
I
I
I

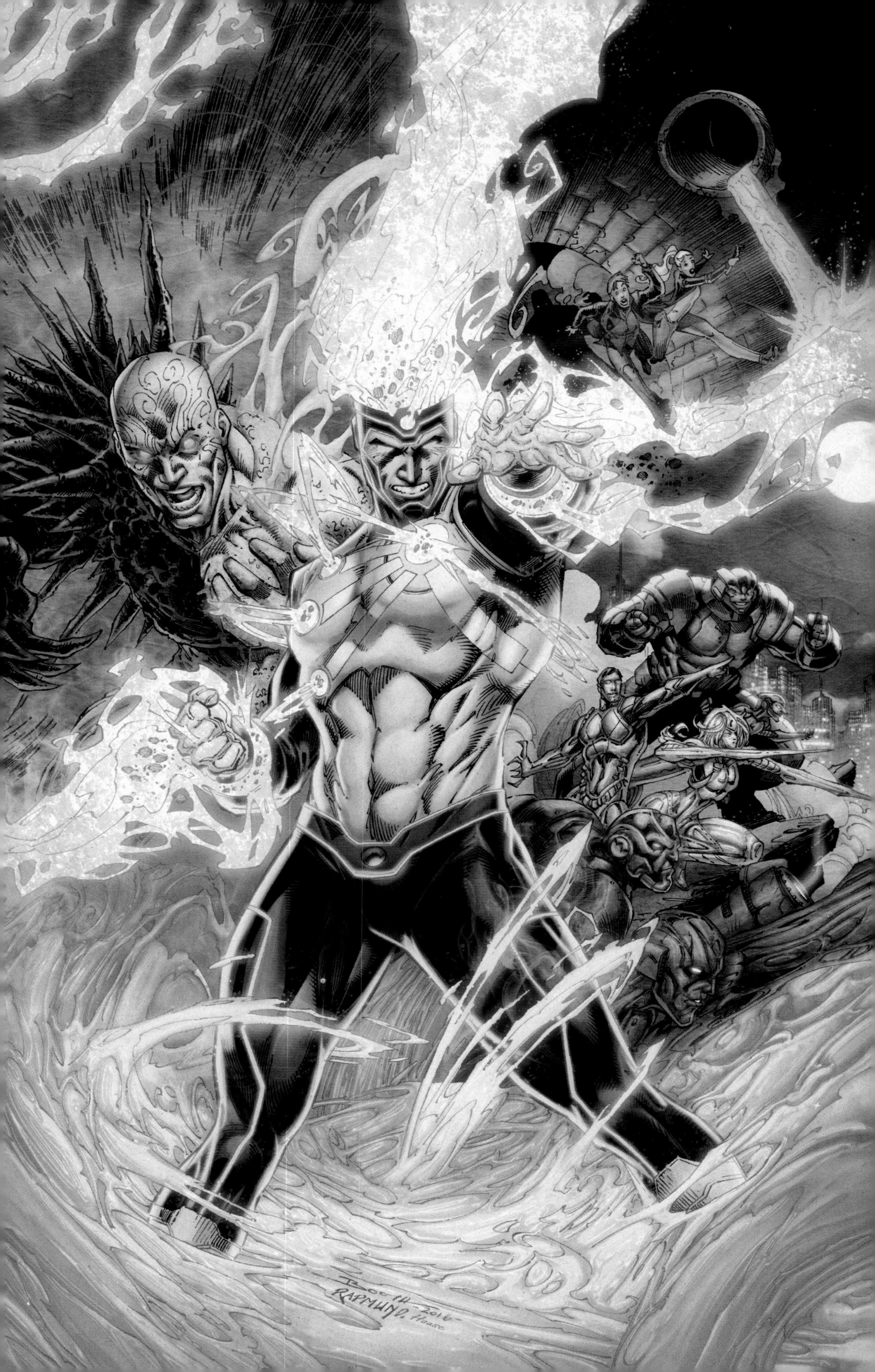

GERRY CONWAY writer EDUARDO PANSICA penciller ROB HUNTER inker ANDREW DALHOUSE colorist COREY BREEN letterer
BRETT BOOTH and NORM RAPMUND with ANDREW DALHOUSE cover

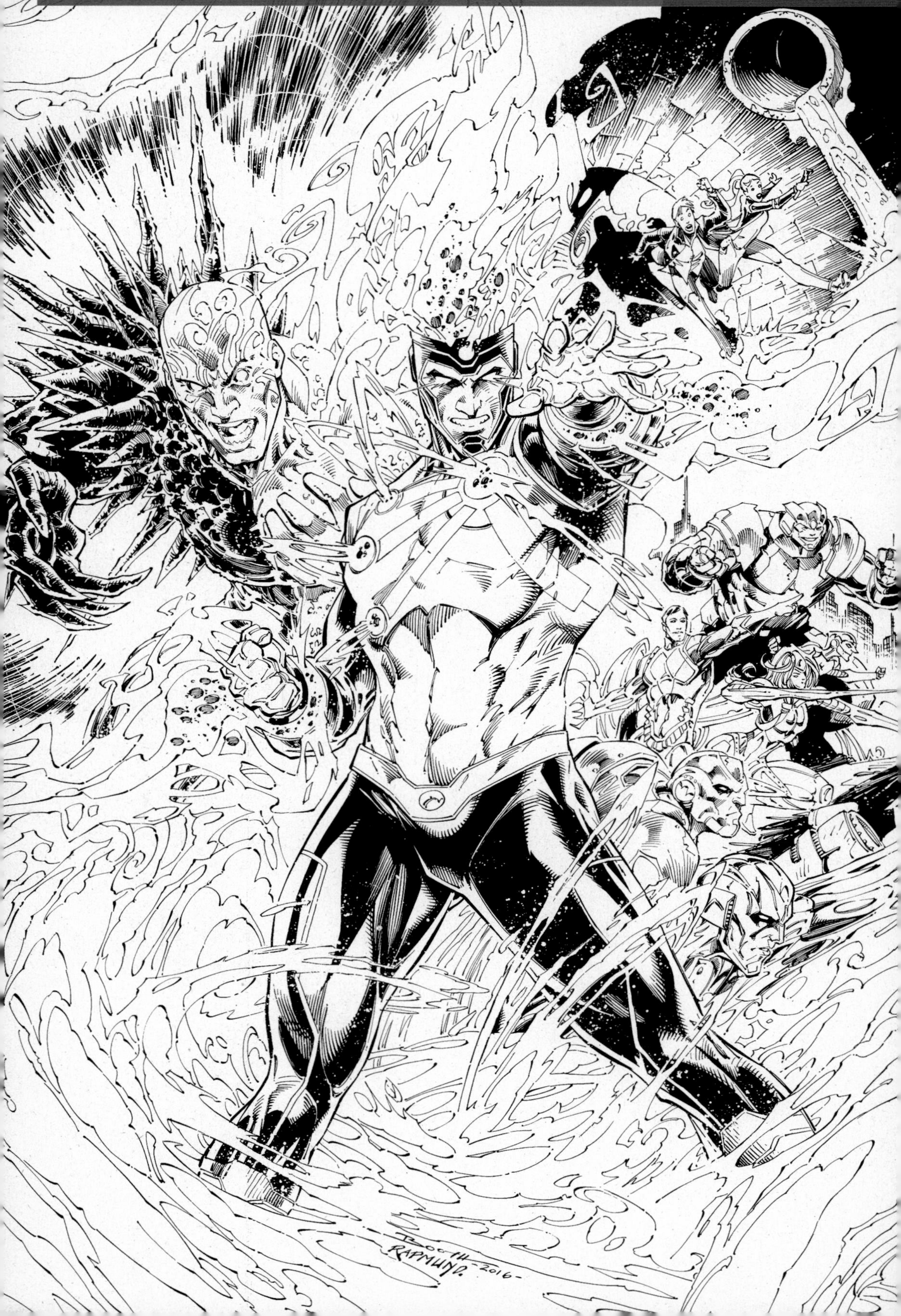
BOOTH-
RAPMUND-2016-

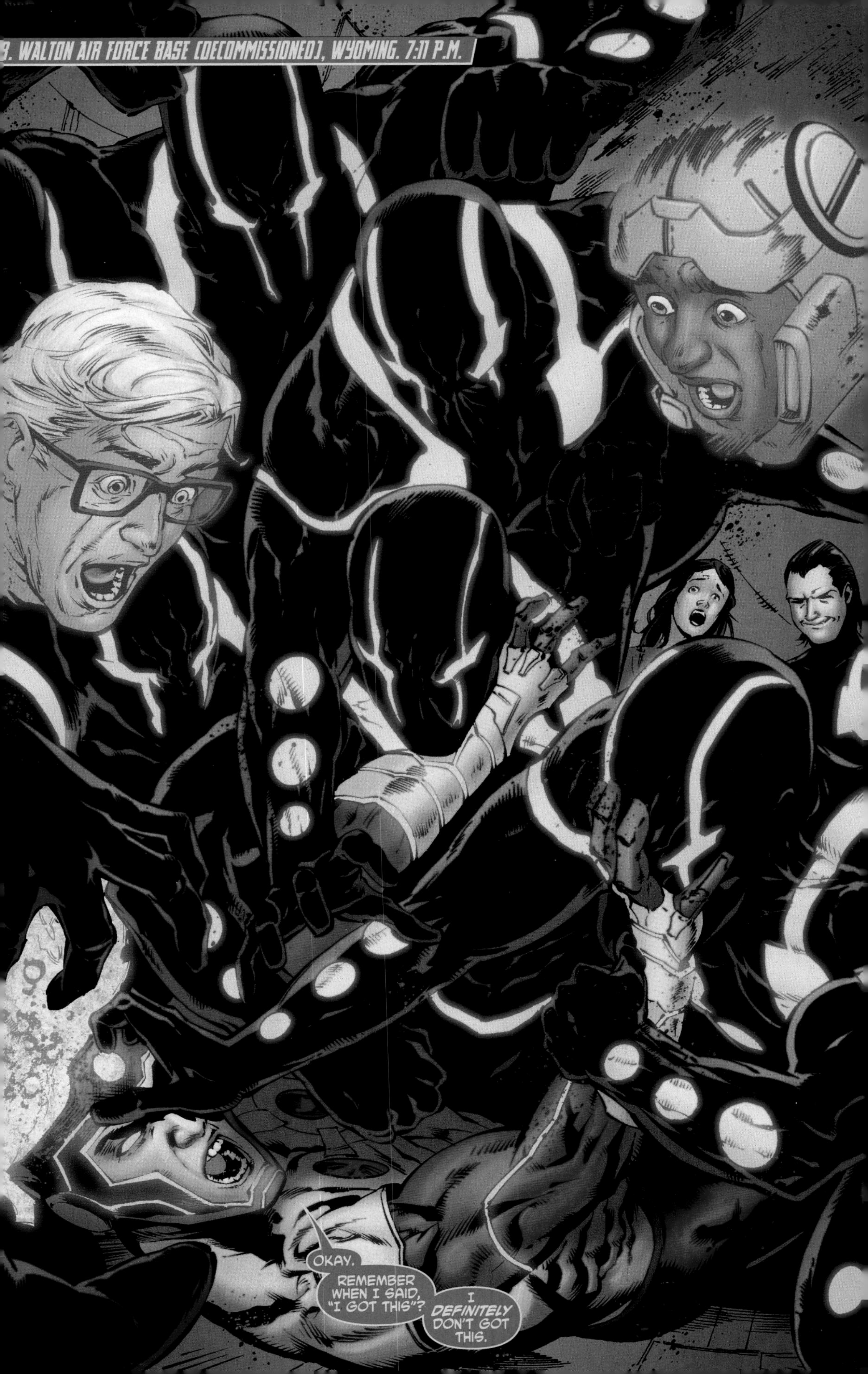
3. WALTON AIR FORCE BASE (DECOMMISSIONED), WYOMING. 7:11 P.M.
OKAY.
REMEMBER WHEN I SAID, "I GOT THIS"?
I DEFINITELY DON'T GOT THIS.

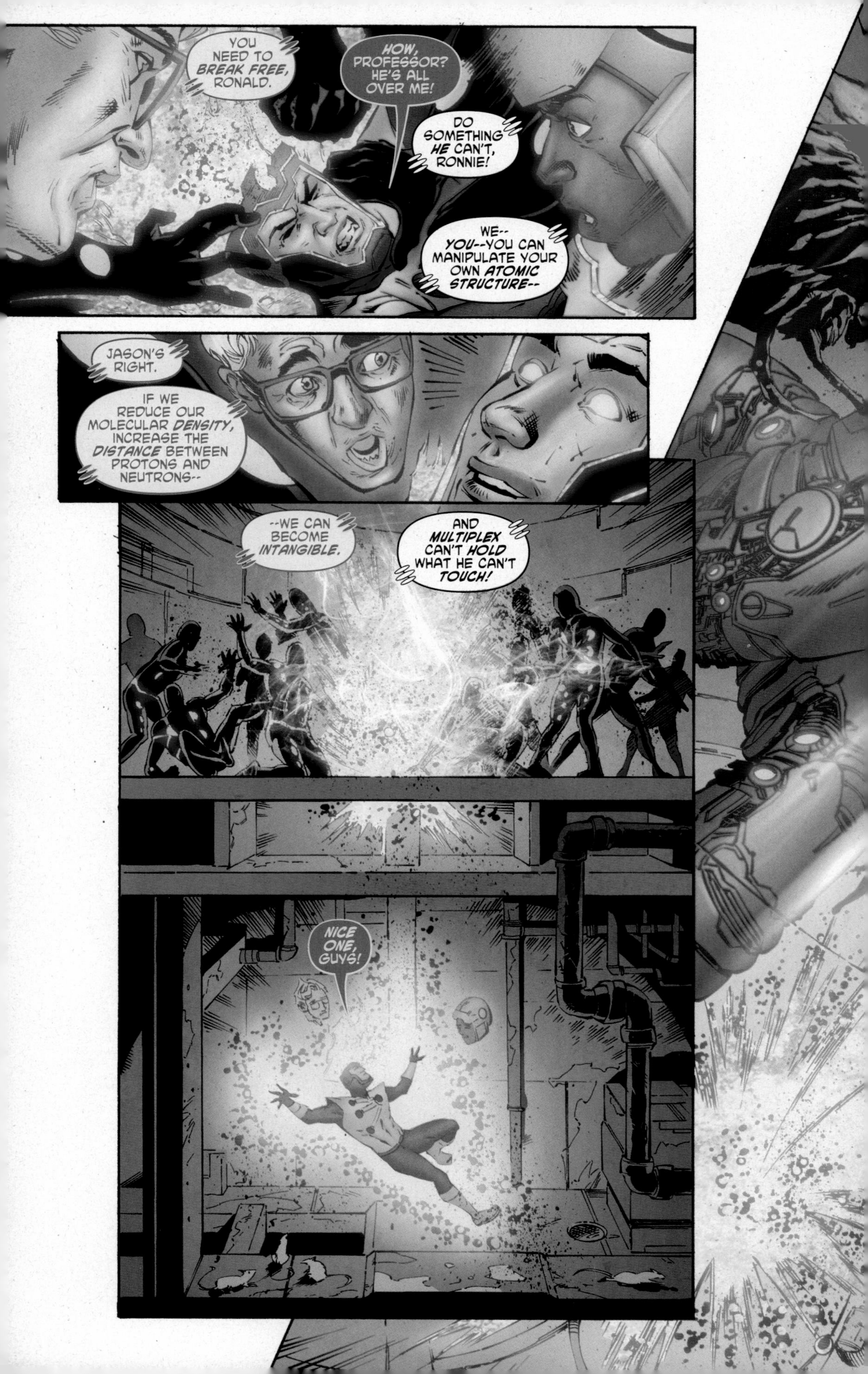
YOU NEED TO BREAK FREE, RONALD.
HOW, PROFESSOR? HE'S ALL OVER ME!
DO SOMETHING HE CAN'T, RONNIE!
WE-- YOU--YOU CAN MANIPULATE YOUR OWN ATOMIC STRUCTURE--
JASON'S RIGHT.
IF WE REDUCE OUR MOLECULAR DENSITY, INCREASE THE DISTANCE BETWEEN PROTONS AND NEUTRONS--
--WE CAN BECOME INTANGIBLE.
AND MULTIPLEX CAN'T HOLD WHAT HE CAN'T TOUCH!
NICE ONE, GUYS!

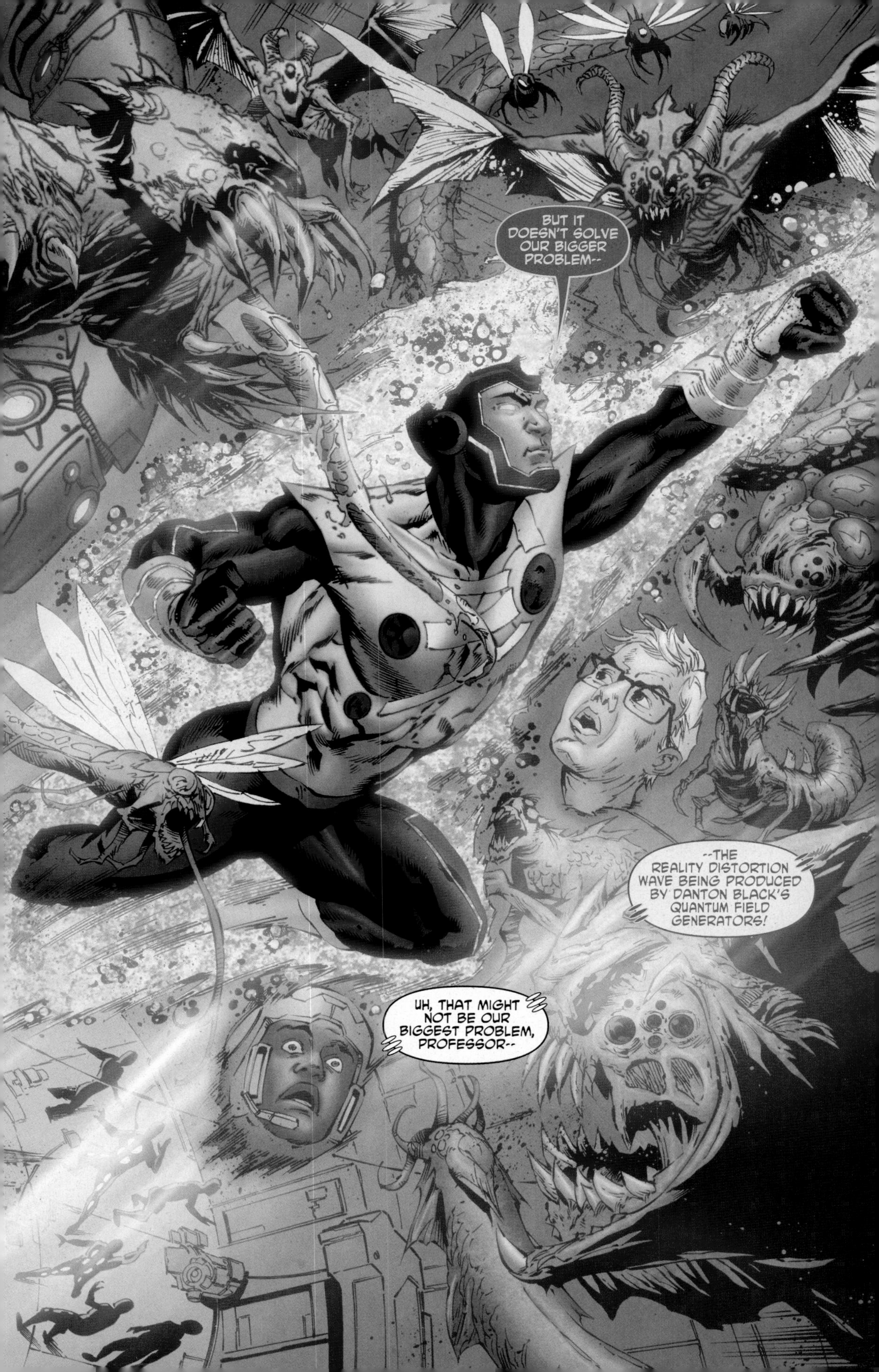
BUT IT DOESN'T SOLVE OUR BIGGER PROBLEM--
--THE REALITY DISTORTION WAVE BEING PRODUCED BY DANTON BLACK'S QUANTUM FIELD GENERATORS!
UH, THAT MIGHT NOT BE OUR BIGGEST PROBLEM, PROFESSOR--

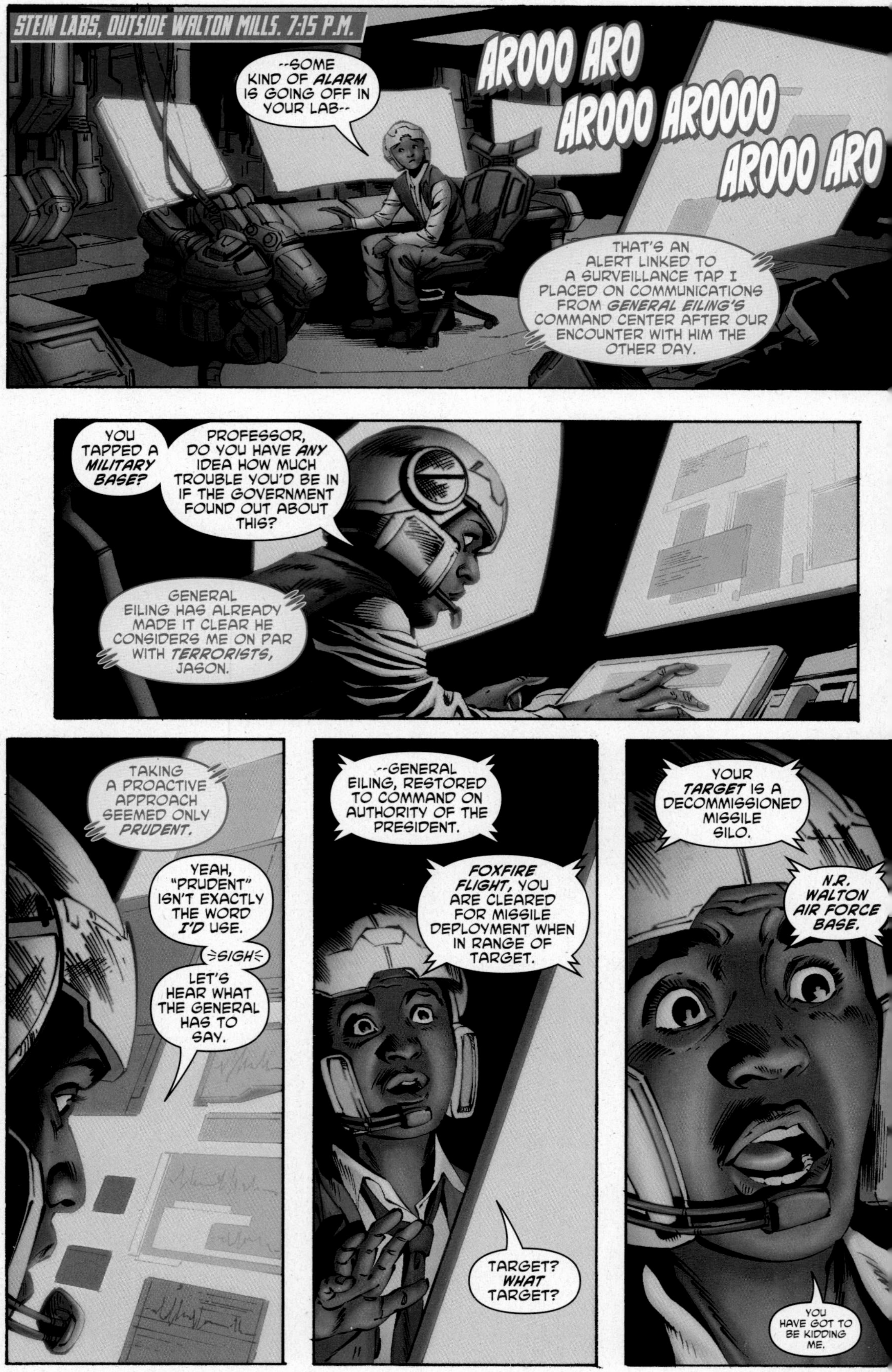
STEIN LABS, OUTSIDE WALTON MILLS. 7:15 P.M.
--SOME KIND OF ALARM IS GOING OFF IN YOUR LAB--
AROOO ARO AROOO AROOOO AROOO ARO
THAT'S AN ALERT LINKED TO A SURVEILLANCE TAP I PLACED ON COMMUNICATIONS FROM GENERAL EILING'S COMMAND CENTER AFTER OUR ENCOUNTER WITH HIM THE OTHER DAY.
YOU TAPPED A MILITARY BASE?
PROFESSOR, DO YOU HAVE ANY IDEA HOW MUCH TROUBLE YOU'D BE IN IF THE GOVERNMENT FOUND OUT ABOUT THIS?
GENERAL EILING HAS ALREADY MADE IT CLEAR HE CONSIDERS ME ON PAR WITH TERRORISTS, JASON.
TAKING A PROACTIVE APPROACH SEEMED ONLY PRUDENT.
YEAH, "PRUDENT" ISN'T EXACTLY THE WORD I'D USE.
SIGH
LET'S HEAR WHAT THE GENERAL HAS TO SAY.
--GENERAL EILING, RESTORED TO COMMAND ON AUTHORITY OF THE PRESIDENT.
FOXFIRE FLIGHT, YOU ARE CLEARED FOR MISSILE DEPLOYMENT WHEN IN RANGE OF TARGET.
TARGET? WHAT TARGET?
YOUR TARGET IS A DECOMMISSIONED MISSILE SILO.
N.R. WALTON AIR FORCE BASE.
YOU HAVE GOT TO BE KIDDING ME.

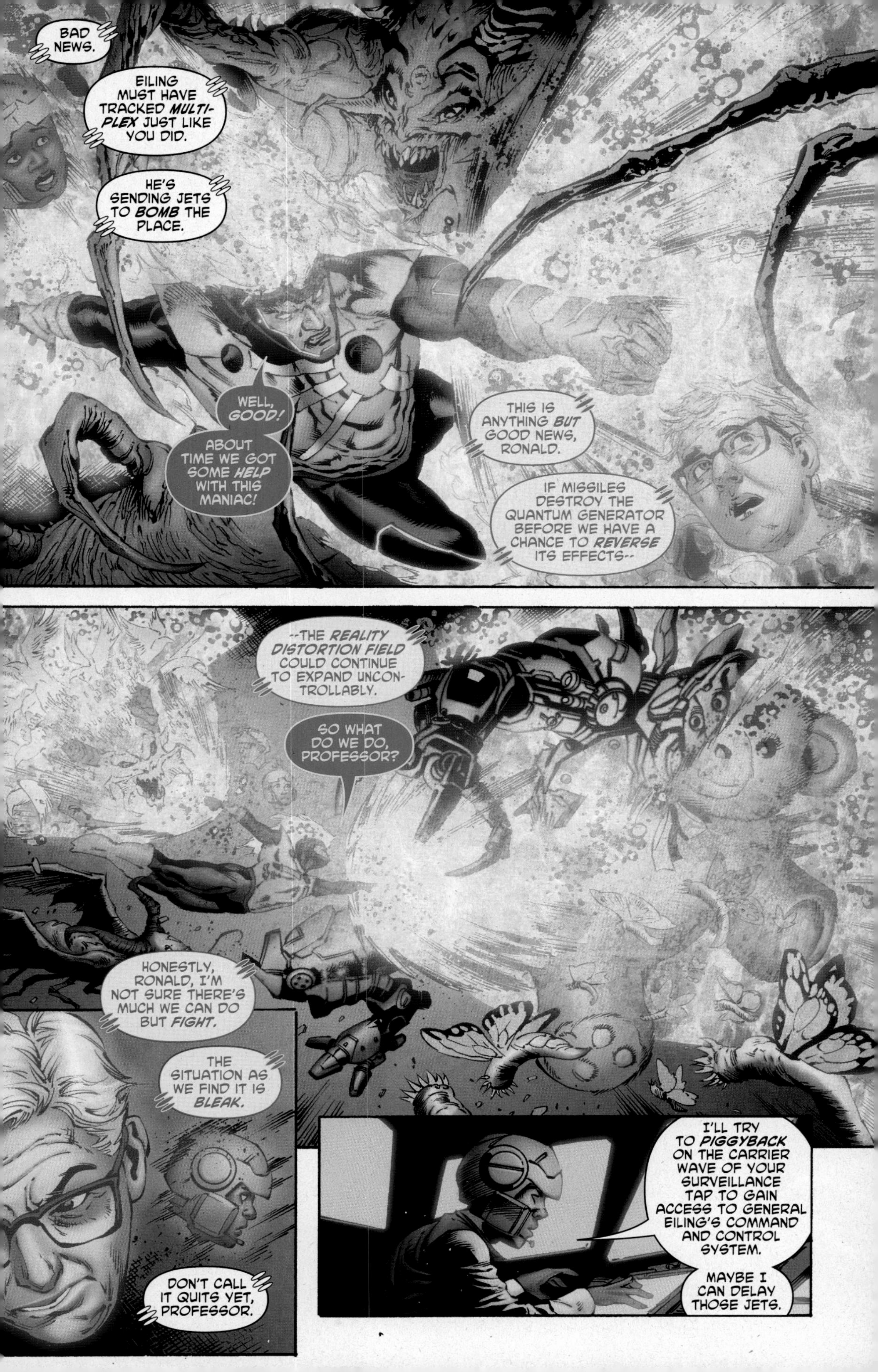

BAD NEWS.
EILING MUST HAVE TRACKED MULTIPLEX JUST LIKE YOU DID.
HE'S SENDING JETS TO BOMB THE PLACE.
WELL, GOOD!
ABOUT TIME WE GOT SOME HELP WITH THIS MANIAC!
THIS IS ANYTHING BUT GOOD NEWS, RONALD.
IF MISSILES DESTROY THE QUANTUM GENERATOR BEFORE WE HAVE A CHANCE TO REVERSE ITS EFFECTS--
--THE REALITY DISTORTION FIELD COULD CONTINUE TO EXPAND UNCONTROLLABLY.
SO WHAT DO WE DO, PROFESSOR?
HONESTLY, RONALD, I'M NOT SURE THERE'S MUCH WE CAN DO BUT FIGHT.
THE SITUATION AS WE FIND IT IS BLEAK.
DON'T CALL IT QUITS YET, PROFESSOR.
I'LL TRY TO PIGGYBACK ON THE CARRIER WAVE OF YOUR SURVEILLANCE TAP TO GAIN ACCESS TO GENERAL EILING'S COMMAND AND CONTROL SYSTEM.
MAYBE I CAN DELAY THOSE JETS.

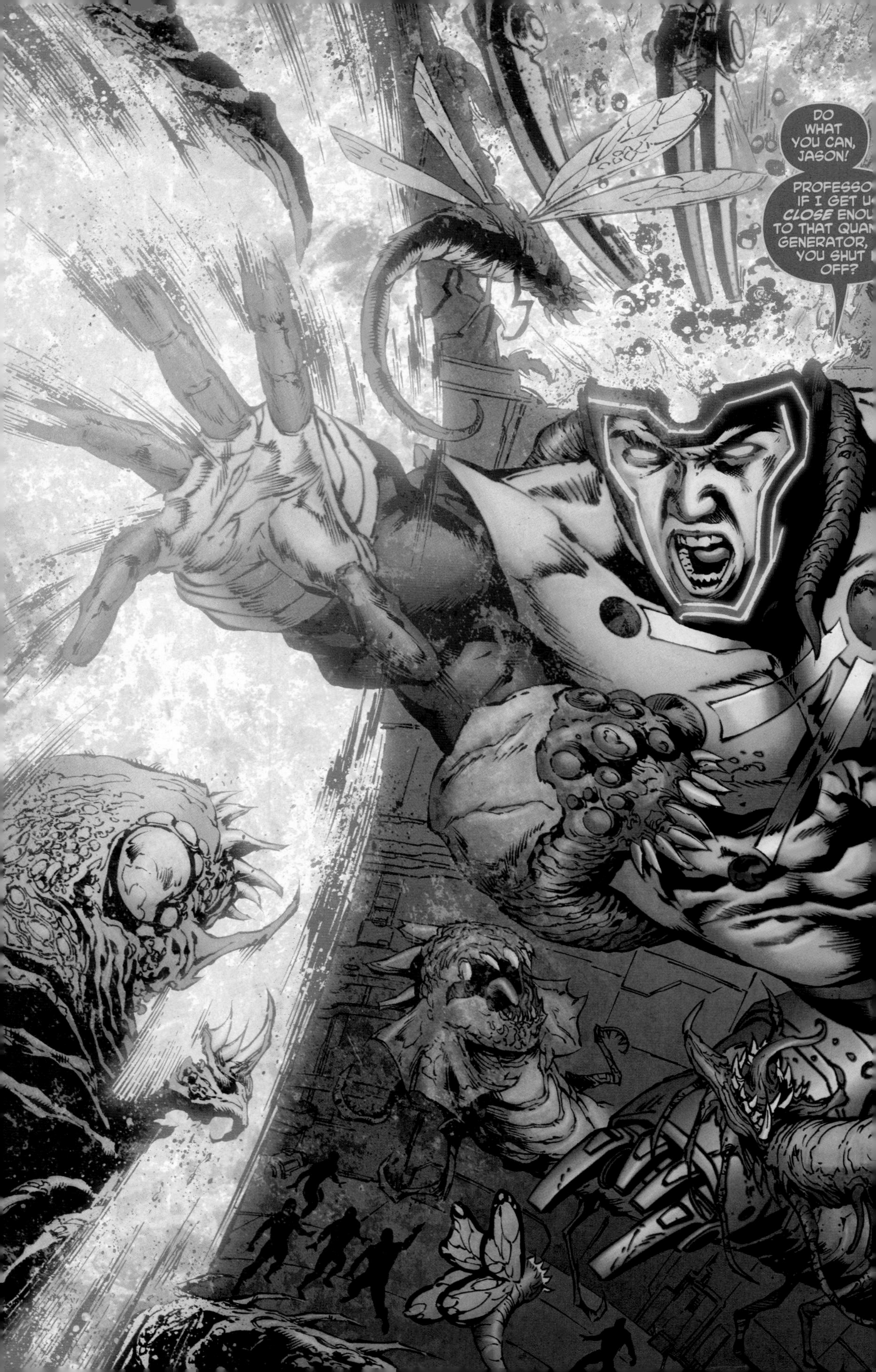
DO WHAT YOU CAN, JASON!
PROFESSO IF I GET U CLOSE ENOU TO THAT QUAN GENERATOR, YOU SHUT OFF?

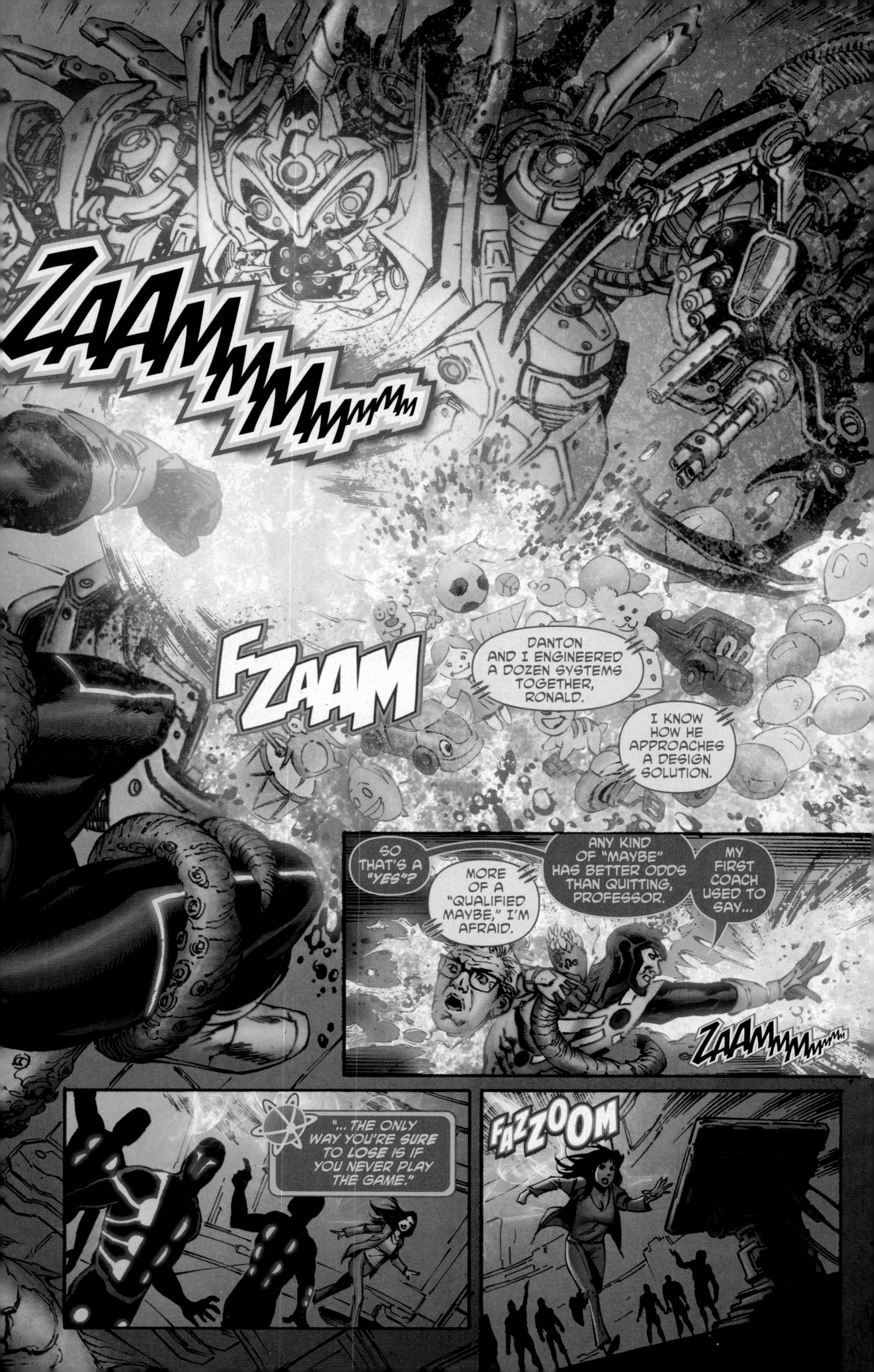
ZAAMMMMMMM
FZAAM
DANTON AND I ENGINEERED A DOZEN SYSTEMS TOGETHER, RONALD.
I KNOW HOW HE APPROACHES A DESIGN SOLUTION.
SO THAT'S A "YES"?
MORE OF A "QUALIFIED MAYBE," I'M AFRAID.
ANY KIND OF "MAYBE" HAS BETTER ODDS THAN QUITTING, PROFESSOR.
MY FIRST COACH USED TO SAY...
ZAAMMMMMM
"...THE ONLY WAY YOU'RE SURE TO LOSE IS IF YOU NEVER PLAY THE GAME."
FAZZOOM

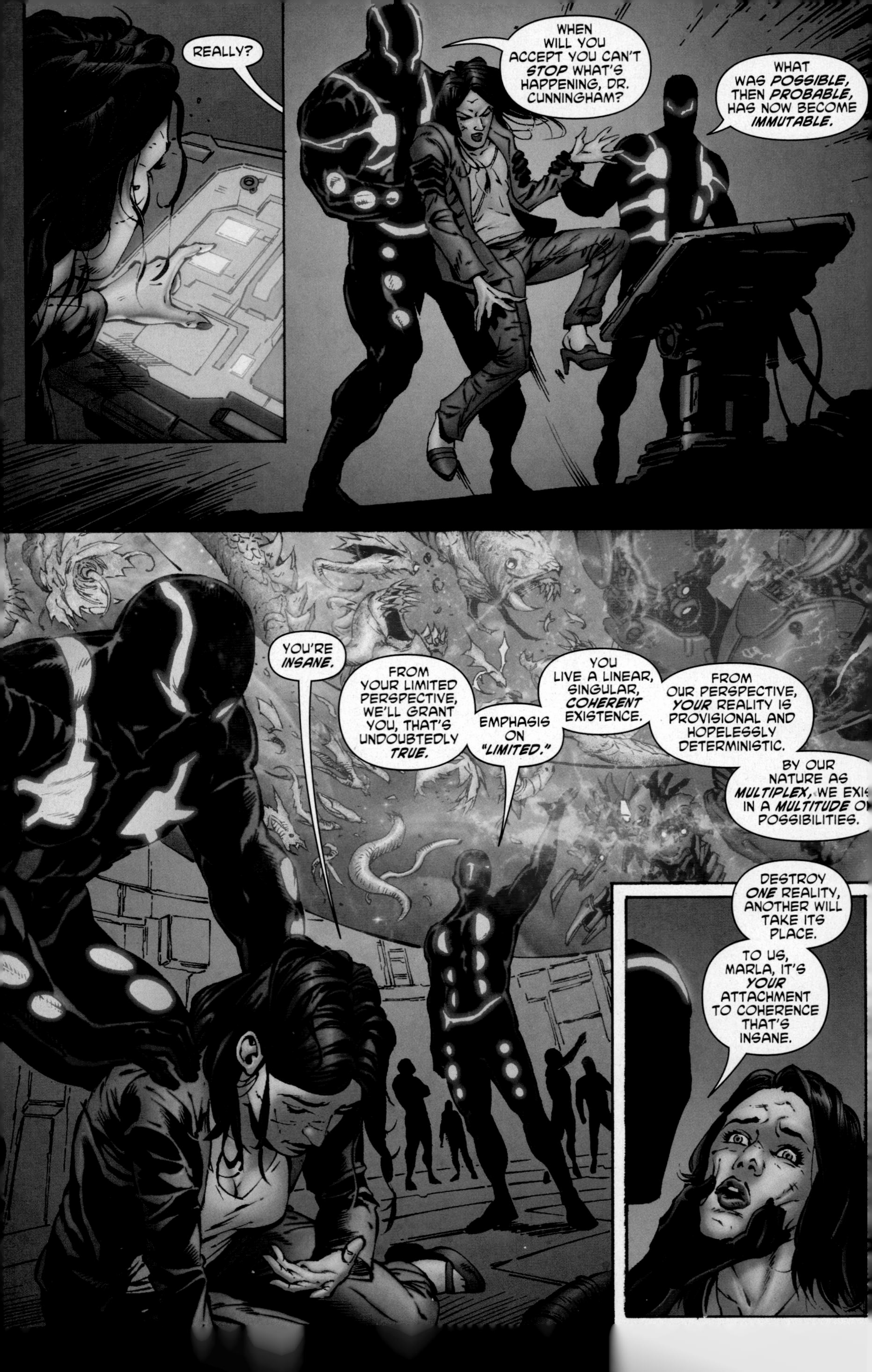

REALLY?
WHEN WILL YOU ACCEPT YOU CAN'T *STOP* WHAT'S HAPPENING, DR. CUNNINGHAM?
WHAT WAS *POSSIBLE,* THEN *PROBABLE,* HAS NOW BECOME *IMMUTABLE.*
YOU'RE *INSANE.*
FROM YOUR LIMITED PERSPECTIVE, WE'LL GRANT YOU, THAT'S UNDOUBTEDLY *TRUE.*
EMPHASIS ON *"LIMITED."*
YOU LIVE A LINEAR, SINGULAR, *COHERENT* EXISTENCE.
FROM OUR PERSPECTIVE, *YOUR* REALITY IS PROVISIONAL AND HOPELESSLY DETERMINISTIC.
BY OUR NATURE AS *MULTIPLEX,* WE EXIS IN A *MULTITUDE* O POSSIBILITIES.
DESTROY *ONE* REALITY, ANOTHER WILL TAKE ITS PLACE.
TO US, MARLA, IT'S *YOUR* ATTACHMENT TO COHERENCE THAT'S INSANE.

FOXFIRE FLIGHT APPROACHING TARGET, GENERAL.

WITHIN MISSILE RANGE IN TEN, NINE, EIGHT--

WHAT THE HELL?

DON'T "WHAT THE HELL" ME, AIRMAN.

WHAT'S WRONG?

I'M SEEING TWO SETS OF COORDINATES FOR FOXFIRE FLIGHT, SIR.

A.S.C.A. BASE, GEORGIA.

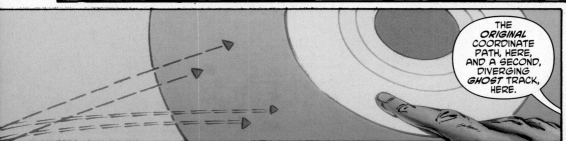

THE ORIGINAL COORDINATE PATH, HERE, AND A SECOND, DIVERGING GHOST TRACK, HERE.

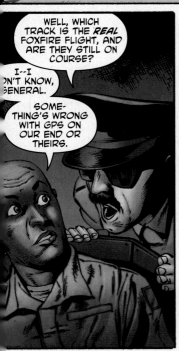

WELL, WHICH TRACK IS THE REAL FOXFIRE FLIGHT, AND ARE THEY STILL ON COURSE?

I--I DON'T KNOW, GENERAL.

SOME-THING'S WRONG WITH GPS ON OUR END OR THEIRS.

ARE YOU SAYING WE HAVE TWO MISSILE-BEARING JETS HOMING IN ON A TARGET, BUT WE DON'T KNOW WHERE THEY ARE?

UHHHHH...

...IT LOOKS THAT WAY, SIR?

UNACCEPTABLE, AIRMAN!

FIX IT. NOW.

YES, SIR, GENERAL EILING, SIR.

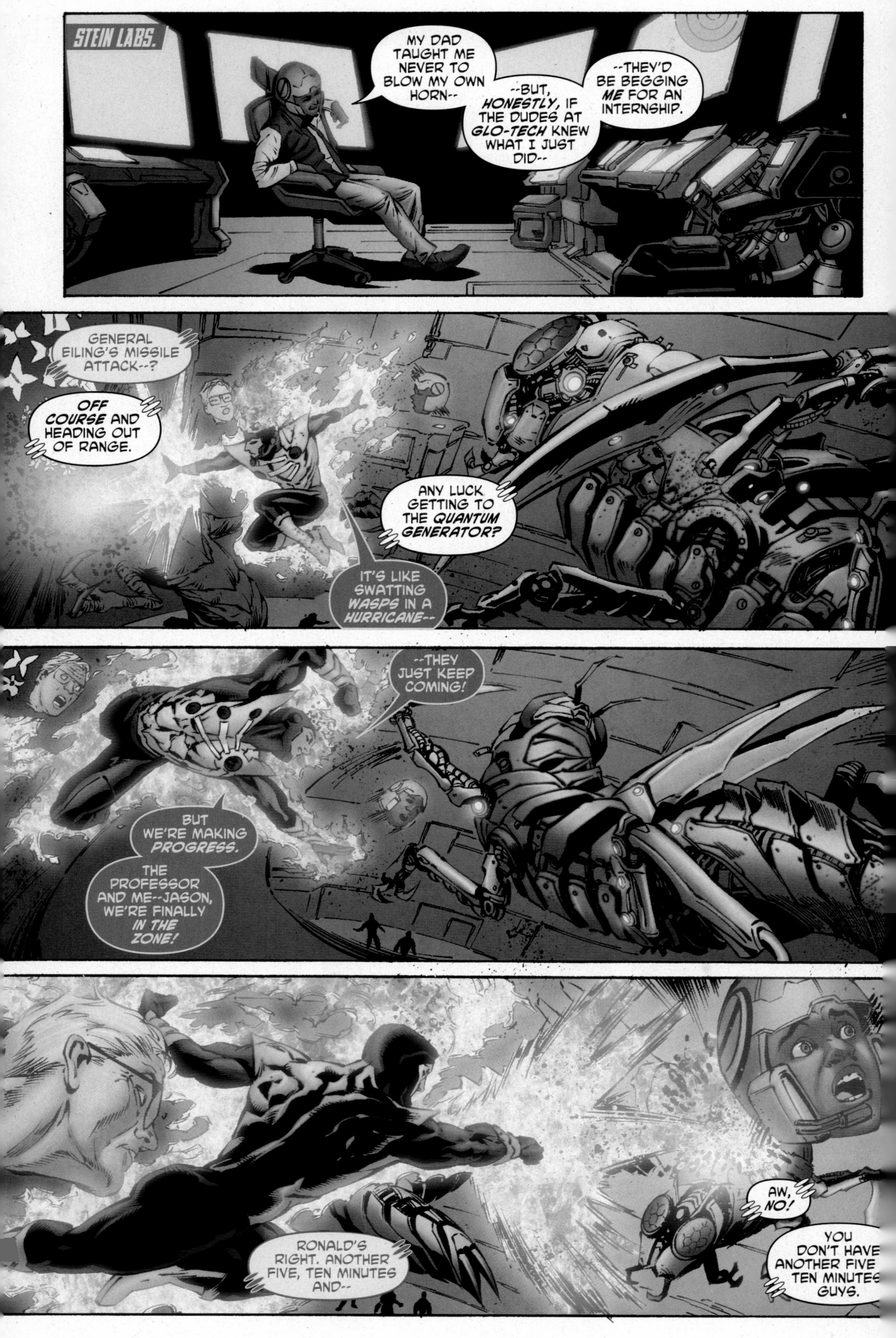
STEIN LABS.
MY DAD TAUGHT ME NEVER TO BLOW MY OWN HORN--
--BUT, HONESTLY, IF THE DUDES AT GLO-TECH KNEW WHAT I JUST DID--
--THEY'D BE BEGGING ME FOR AN INTERNSHIP.
GENERAL EILING'S MISSILE ATTACK--?
OFF COURSE AND HEADING OUT OF RANGE.
ANY LUCK GETTING TO THE QUANTUM GENERATOR?
IT'S LIKE SWATTING WASPS IN A HURRICANE--
--THEY JUST KEEP COMING!
BUT WE'RE MAKING PROGRESS.
THE PROFESSOR AND ME--JASON, WE'RE FINALLY IN THE ZONE!
RONALD'S RIGHT. ANOTHER FIVE, TEN MINUTES AND--
AW, NO!
YOU DON'T HAVE ANOTHER FIVE TEN MINUTES GUYS.

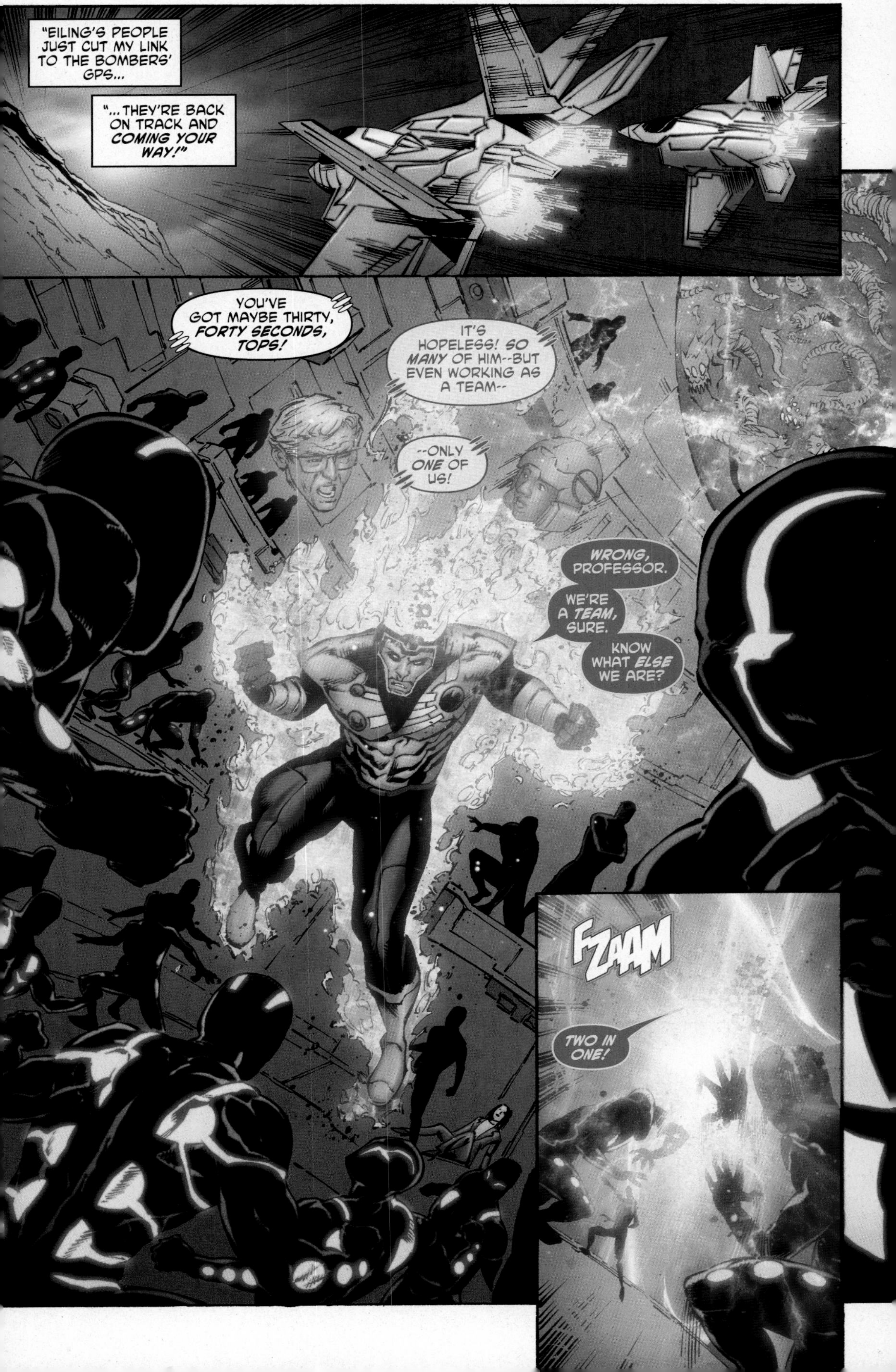
"EILING'S PEOPLE JUST CUT MY LINK TO THE BOMBERS' GPS...
"...THEY'RE BACK ON TRACK AND COMING YOUR WAY!"
YOU'VE GOT MAYBE THIRTY, FORTY SECONDS, TOPS!
IT'S HOPELESS! SO MANY OF HIM--BUT EVEN WORKING AS A TEAM--
--ONLY ONE OF US!
WRONG, PROFESSOR.
WE'RE A TEAM, SURE.
KNOW WHAT ELSE WE ARE?
FZAAM
TWO IN ONE!

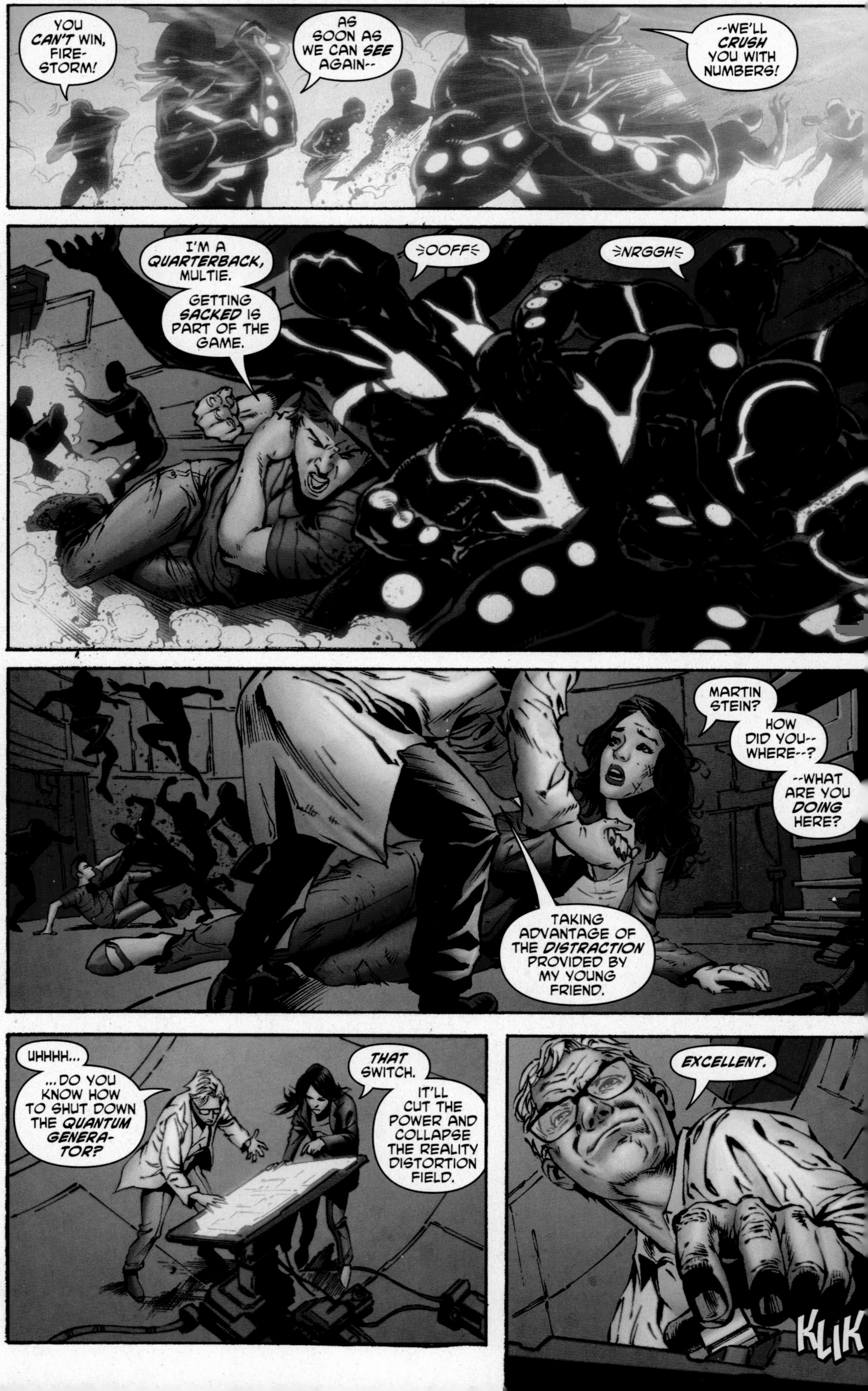
YOU CAN'T WIN, FIRE-STORM!
AS SOON AS WE CAN SEE AGAIN--
--WE'LL CRUSH YOU WITH NUMBERS!
I'M A QUARTERBACK, MULTIE.
GETTING SACKED IS PART OF THE GAME.
OOFF
NRGGH
MARTIN STEIN?
HOW DID YOU-- WHERE--?
--WHAT ARE YOU DOING HERE?
TAKING ADVANTAGE OF THE DISTRACTION PROVIDED BY MY YOUNG FRIEND.
UHHHH...
...DO YOU KNOW HOW TO SHUT DOWN THE QUANTUM GENERATOR?
THAT SWITCH.
IT'LL CUT THE POWER AND COLLAPSE THE REALITY DISTORTION FIELD.
EXCELLENT.
KLIK

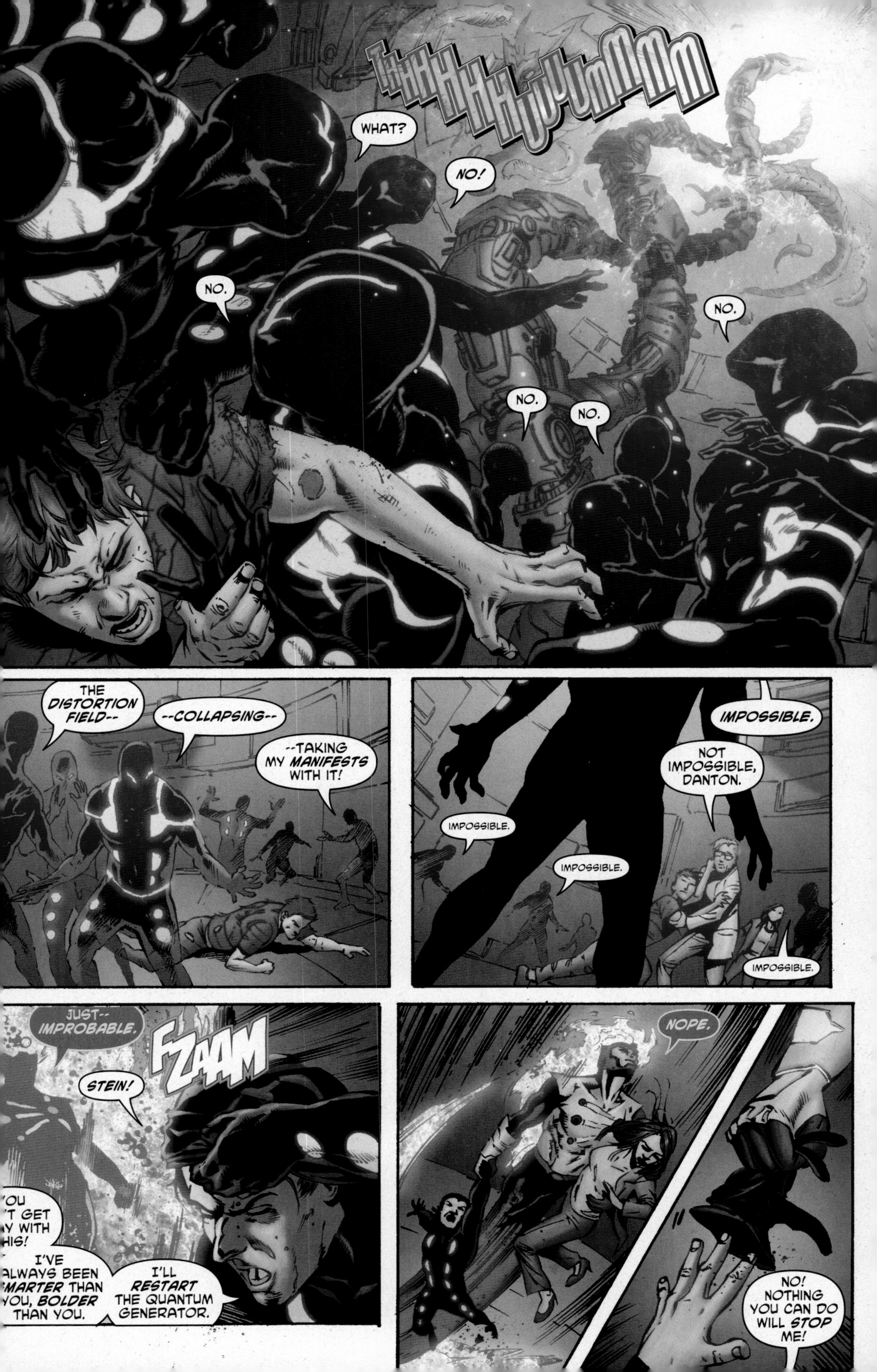
THHHHHHUUUMMMM
WHAT?
NO!
NO.
NO.
NO.
NO.
THE DISTORTION FIELD--
--COLLAPSING--
--TAKING MY MANIFESTS WITH IT!
IMPOSSIBLE.
NOT IMPOSSIBLE, DANTON.
IMPOSSIBLE.
IMPOSSIBLE.
IMPOSSIBLE.
JUST-- IMPROBABLE.
FZAAM
STEIN!
I'VE ALWAYS BEEN SMARTER THAN YOU, BOLDER THAN YOU.
I'LL RESTART THE QUANTUM GENERATOR.
NOPE.
NO! NOTHING YOU CAN DO WILL STOP ME!

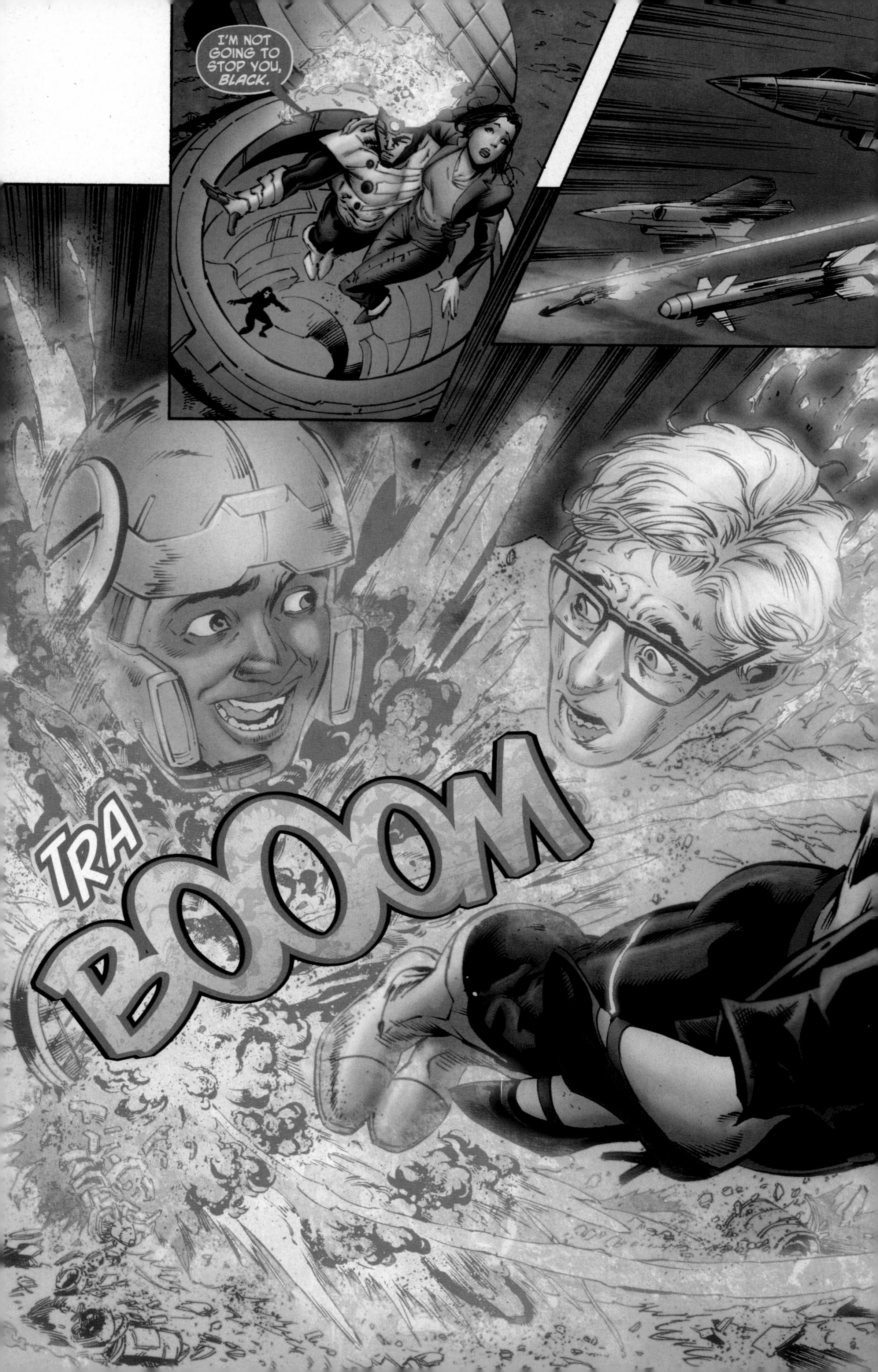
I'M NOT GOING TO STOP YOU, BLACK.
TRA
BOOOM

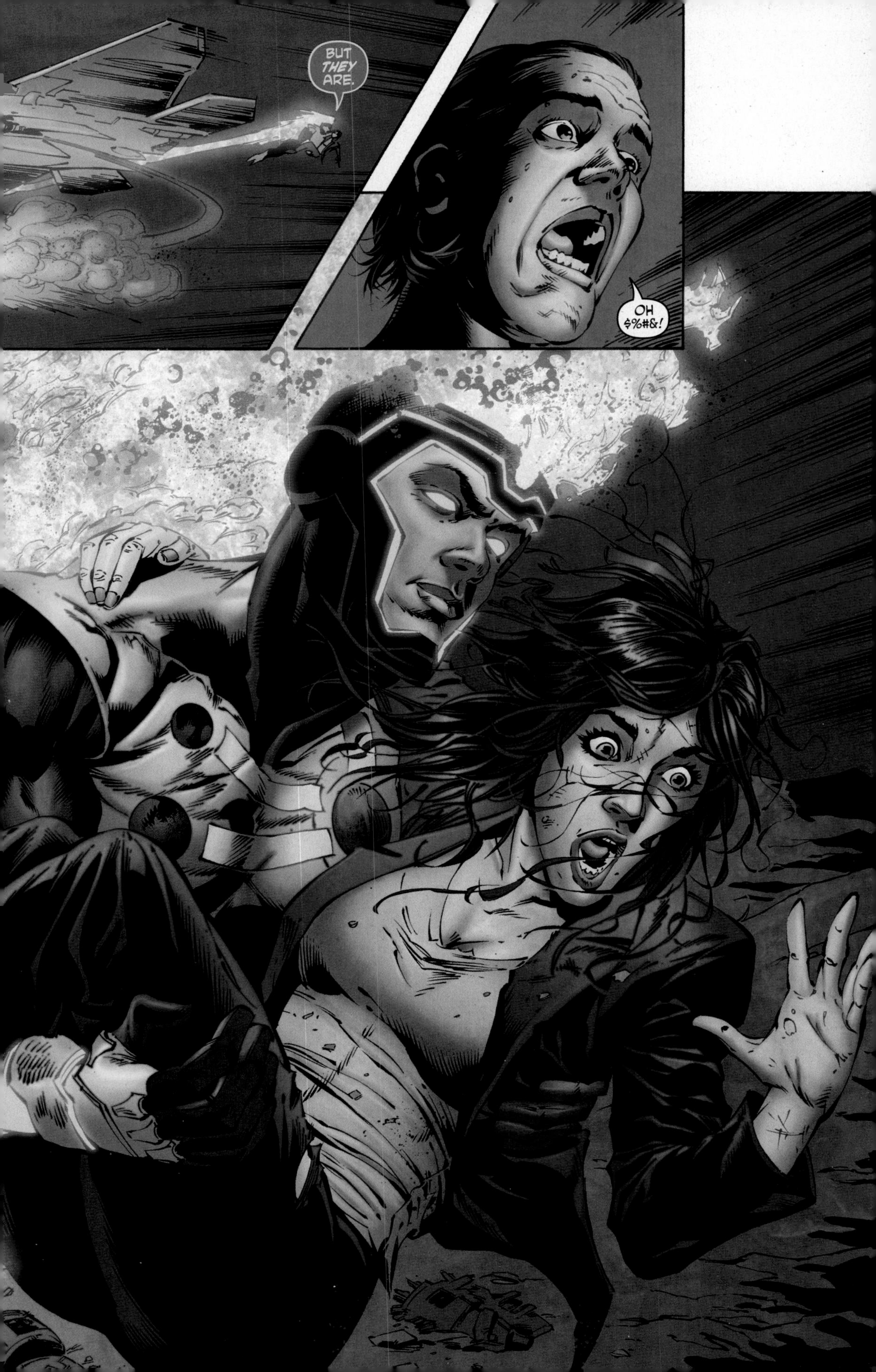
BUT THEY ARE.
OH $%#&!

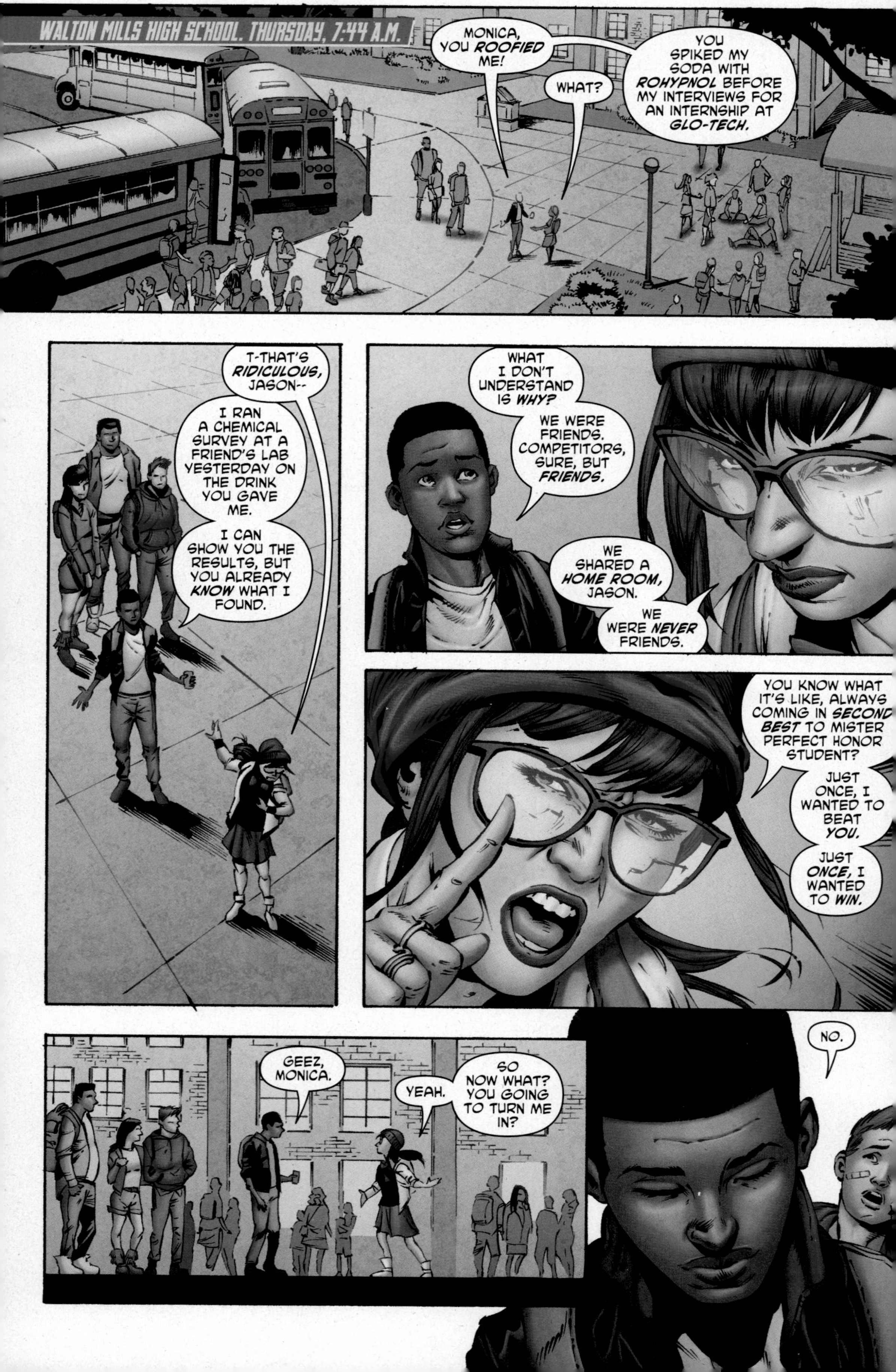
WALTON MILLS HIGH SCHOOL. THURSDAY, 7:44 A.M.
MONICA, YOU ROOFIED ME!
WHAT?
YOU SPIKED MY SODA WITH ROHYPNOL BEFORE MY INTERVIEWS FOR AN INTERNSHIP AT GLO-TECH.
T-THAT'S RIDICULOUS, JASON--
I RAN A CHEMICAL SURVEY AT A FRIEND'S LAB YESTERDAY ON THE DRINK YOU GAVE ME.
I CAN SHOW YOU THE RESULTS, BUT YOU ALREADY KNOW WHAT I FOUND.
WHAT I DON'T UNDERSTAND IS WHY?
WE WERE FRIENDS. COMPETITORS, SURE, BUT FRIENDS.
WE SHARED A HOME ROOM, JASON.
WE WERE NEVER FRIENDS.
YOU KNOW WHAT IT'S LIKE, ALWAYS COMING IN SECOND BEST TO MISTER PERFECT HONOR STUDENT?
JUST ONCE, I WANTED TO BEAT YOU.
JUST ONCE, I WANTED TO WIN.
GEEZ, MONICA.
YEAH.
SO NOW WHAT? YOU GOING TO TURN ME IN?
NO.

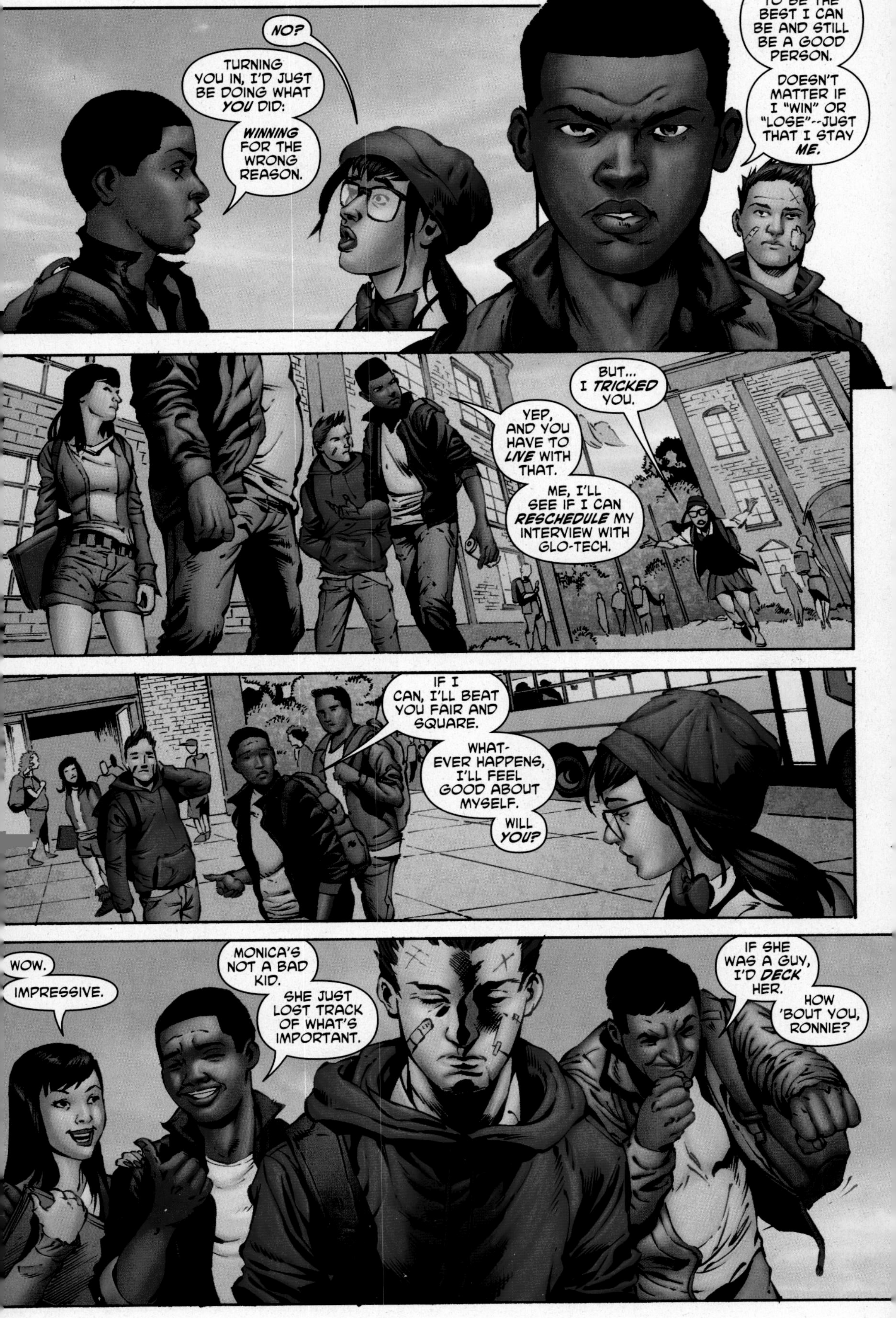
TURNING YOU IN, I'D JUST BE DOING WHAT YOU DID: WINNING FOR THE WRONG REASON.
NO?
I WANT TO BE THE BEST I CAN BE AND STILL BE A GOOD PERSON.
DOESN'T MATTER IF I "WIN" OR "LOSE"--JUST THAT I STAY ME.
YEP, AND YOU HAVE TO LIVE WITH THAT.
BUT... I TRICKED YOU.
ME, I'LL SEE IF I CAN RESCHEDULE MY INTERVIEW WITH GLO-TECH.
IF I CAN, I'LL BEAT YOU FAIR AND SQUARE.
WHAT-EVER HAPPENS, I'LL FEEL GOOD ABOUT MYSELF.
WILL YOU?
WOW.
IMPRESSIVE.
MONICA'S NOT A BAD KID.
SHE JUST LOST TRACK OF WHAT'S IMPORTANT.
IF SHE WAS A GUY, I'D DECK HER.
HOW 'BOUT YOU, RONNIE?

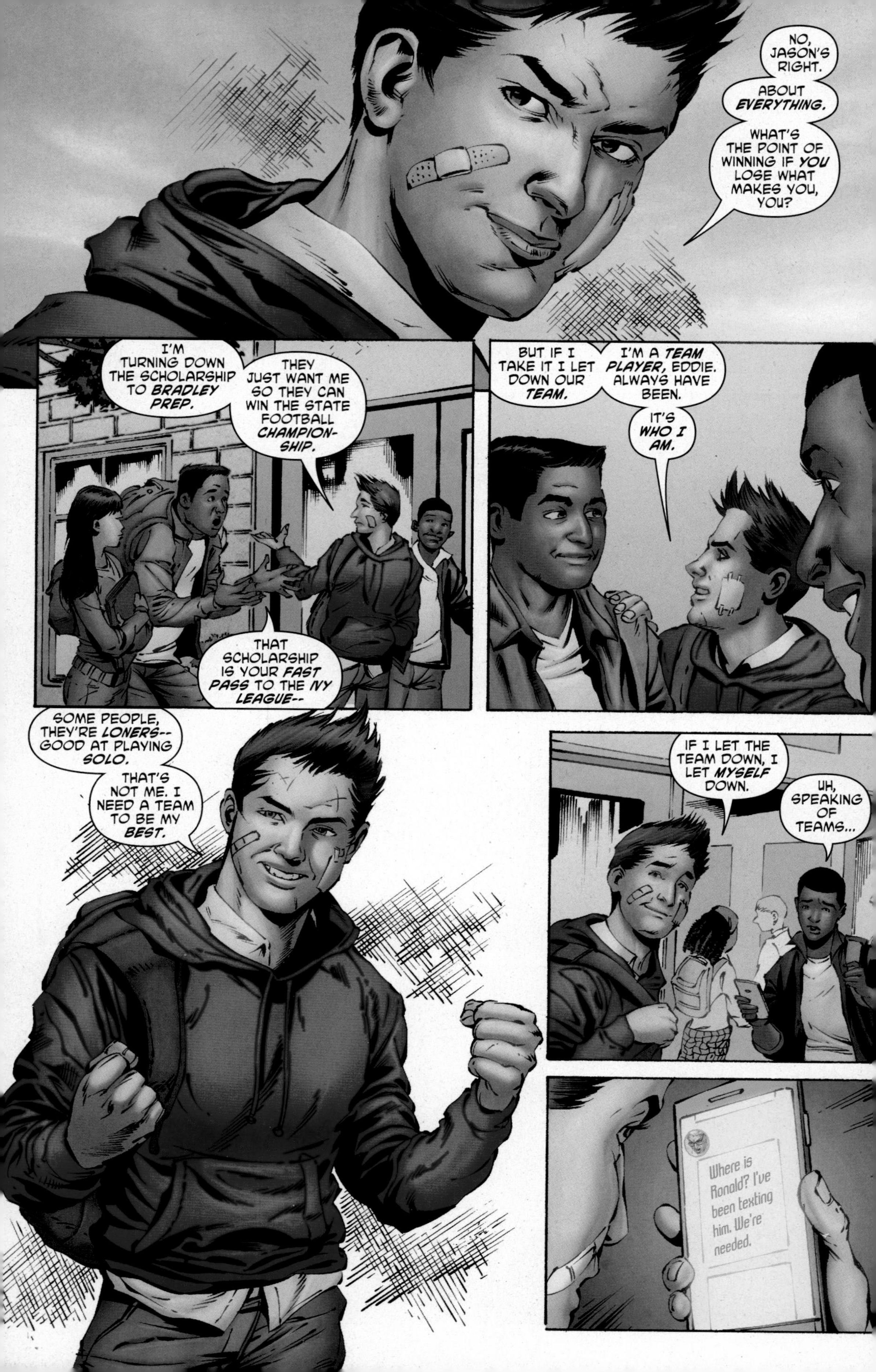
NO, JASON'S RIGHT.
ABOUT EVERYTHING.
WHAT'S THE POINT OF WINNING IF YOU LOSE WHAT MAKES YOU, YOU?
I'M TURNING DOWN THE SCHOLARSHIP TO BRADLEY PREP.
THEY JUST WANT ME SO THEY CAN WIN THE STATE FOOTBALL CHAMPIONSHIP.
THAT SCHOLARSHIP IS YOUR FAST PASS TO THE IVY LEAGUE--
BUT IF I TAKE IT I LET DOWN OUR TEAM.
I'M A TEAM PLAYER, EDDIE. ALWAYS HAVE BEEN.
IT'S WHO I AM.
SOME PEOPLE, THEY'RE LONERS--GOOD AT PLAYING SOLO.
THAT'S NOT ME. I NEED A TEAM TO BE MY BEST.
IF I LET THE TEAM DOWN, I LET MYSELF DOWN.
UH, SPEAKING OF TEAMS...
Where is Ronald? I've been texting him. We're needed.

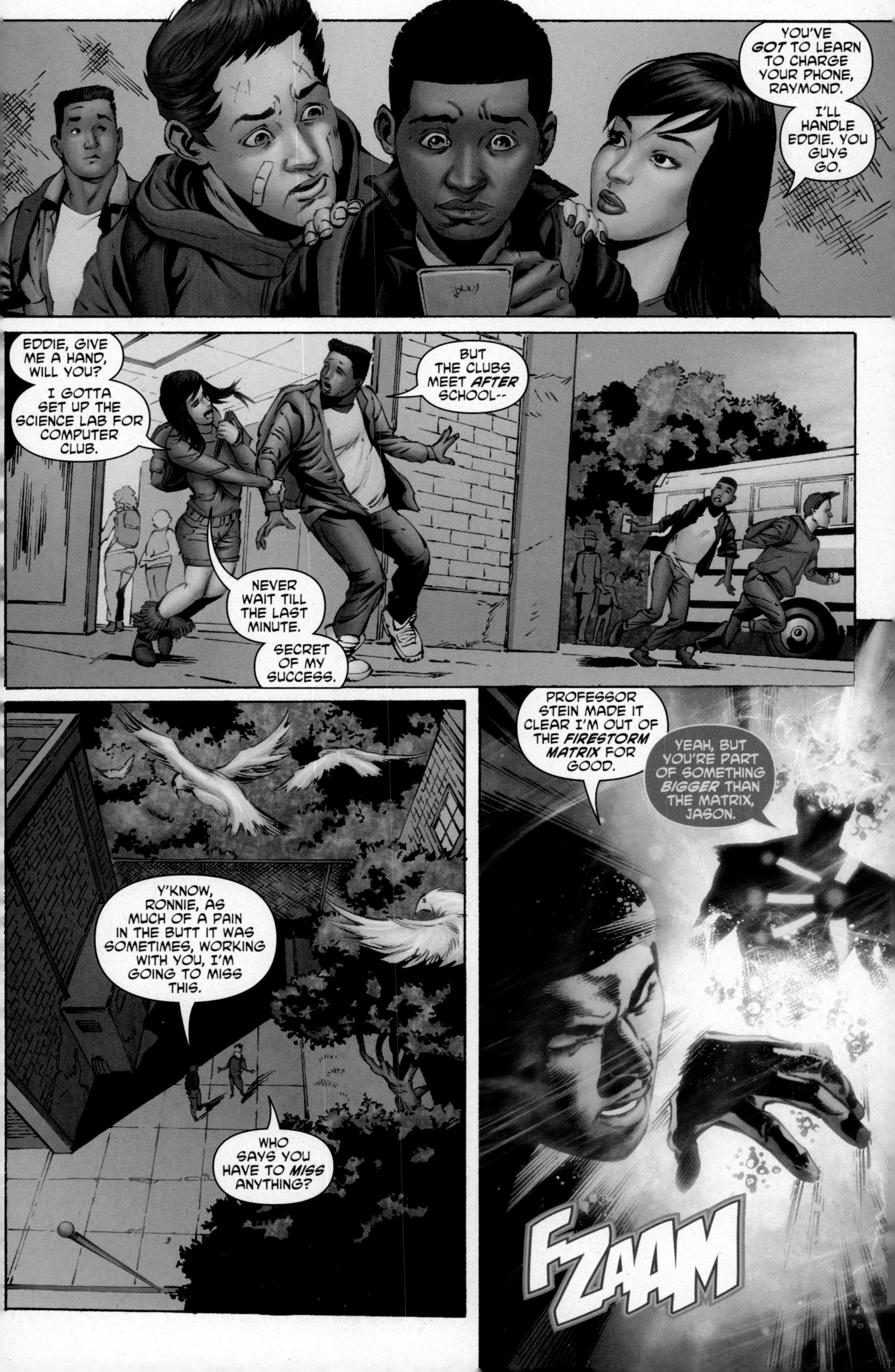
YOU'VE GOT TO LEARN TO CHARGE YOUR PHONE, RAYMOND.
I'LL HANDLE EDDIE. YOU GUYS GO.
EDDIE, GIVE ME A HAND, WILL YOU?
I GOTTA SET UP THE SCIENCE LAB FOR COMPUTER CLUB.
BUT THE CLUBS MEET AFTER SCHOOL--
NEVER WAIT TILL THE LAST MINUTE.
SECRET OF MY SUCCESS.
Y'KNOW, RONNIE, AS MUCH OF A PAIN IN THE BUTT IT WAS SOMETIMES, WORKING WITH YOU, I'M GOING TO MISS THIS.
WHO SAYS YOU HAVE TO MISS ANYTHING?
PROFESSOR STEIN MADE IT CLEAR I'M OUT OF THE FIRESTORM MATRIX FOR GOOD.
YEAH, BUT YOU'RE PART OF SOMETHING BIGGER THAN THE MATRIX, JASON.
FZAAM

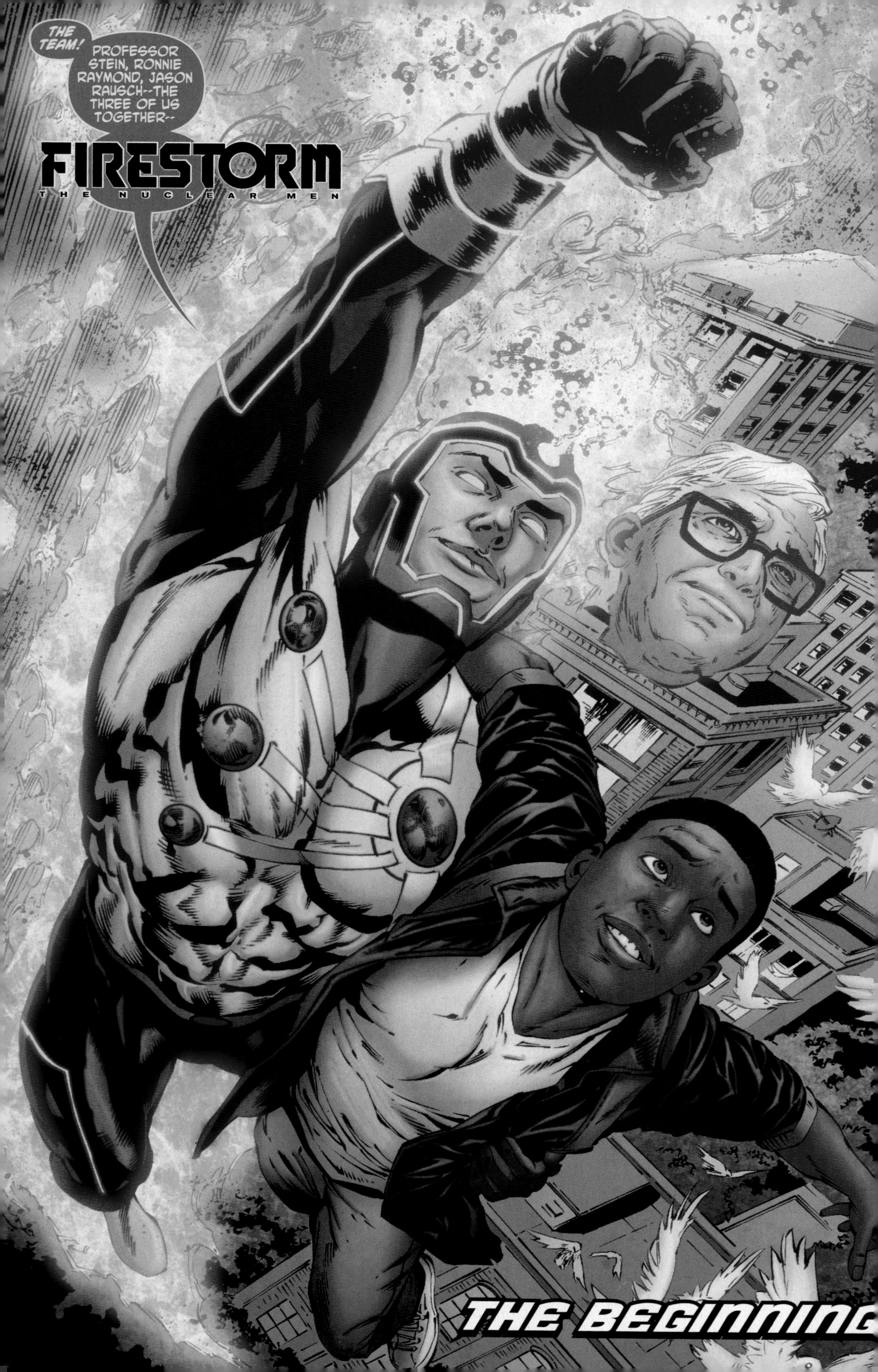
THE TEAM!
PROFESSOR STEIN, RONNIE RAYMOND, JASON RAUSCH--THE THREE OF US TOGETHER--
FIRESTORM
THE NUCLEAR MEN
THE BEGINNING

ART AND CHARACTER DESIGNS BY
EDUARDO PANSICA

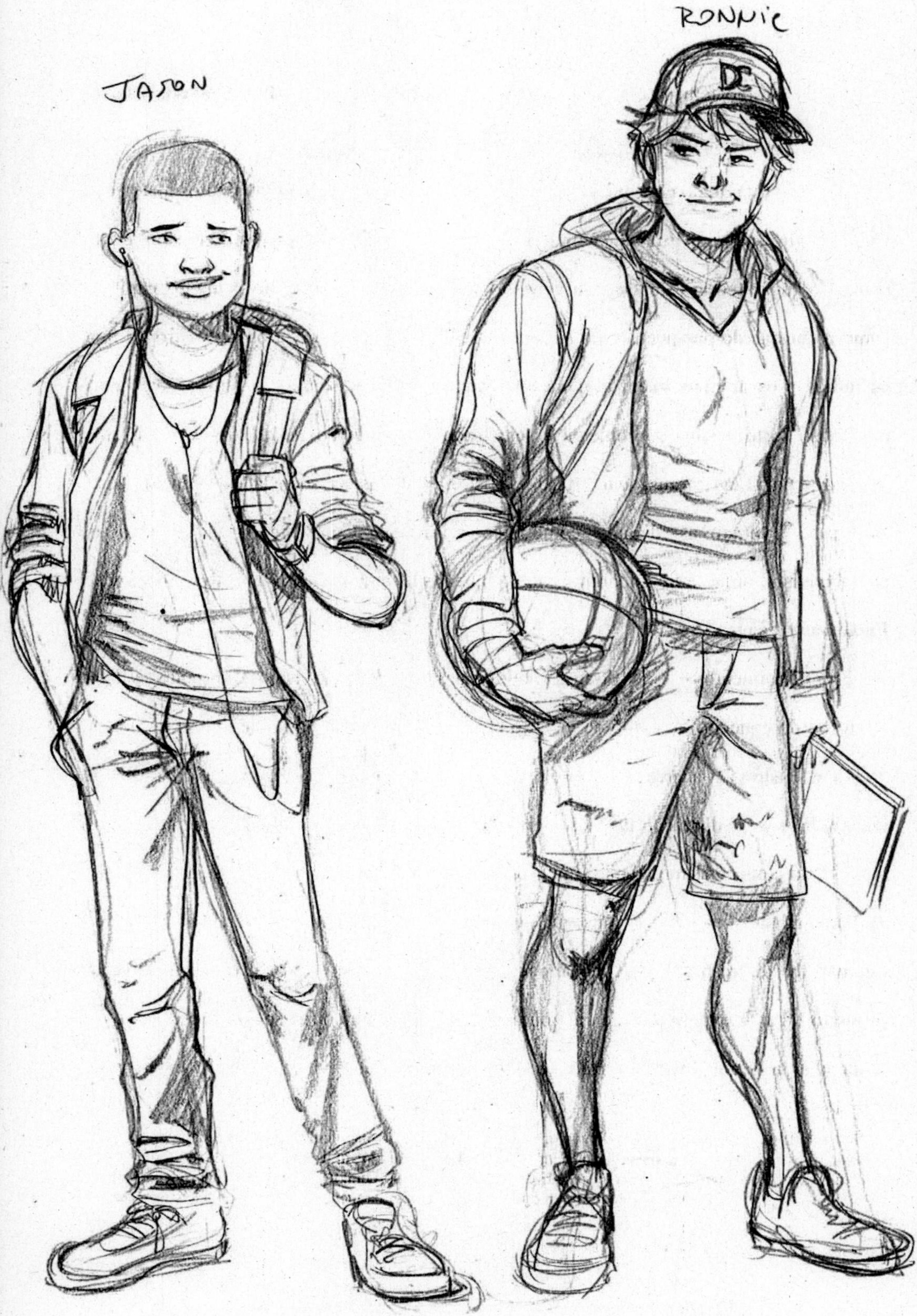
JASON
RONNIE
DC

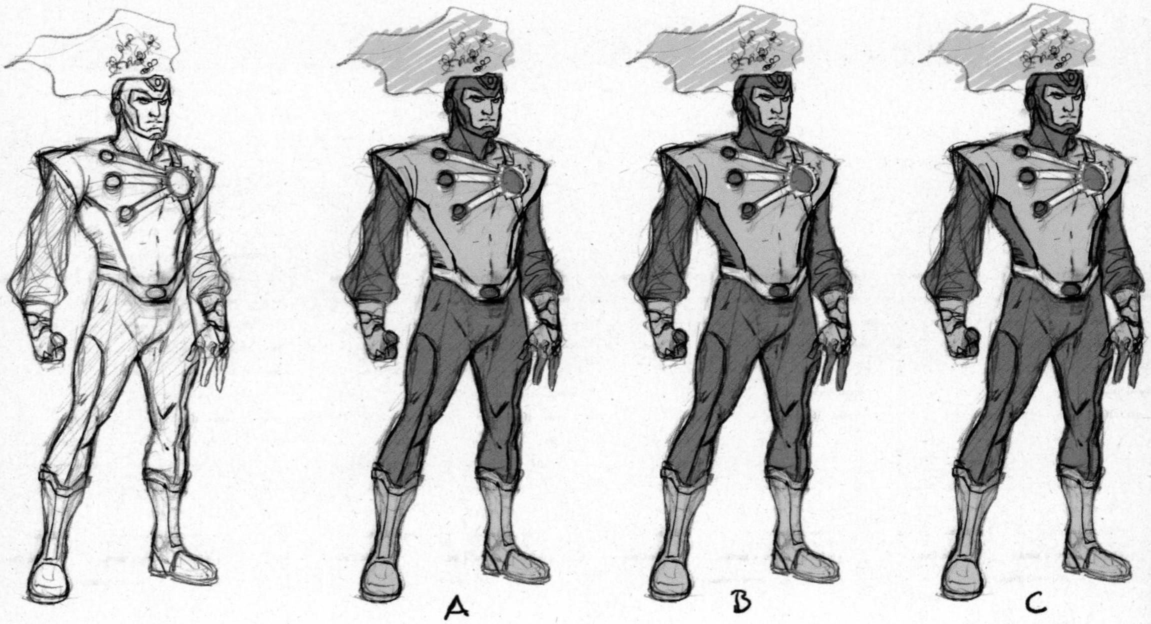
A
B
C

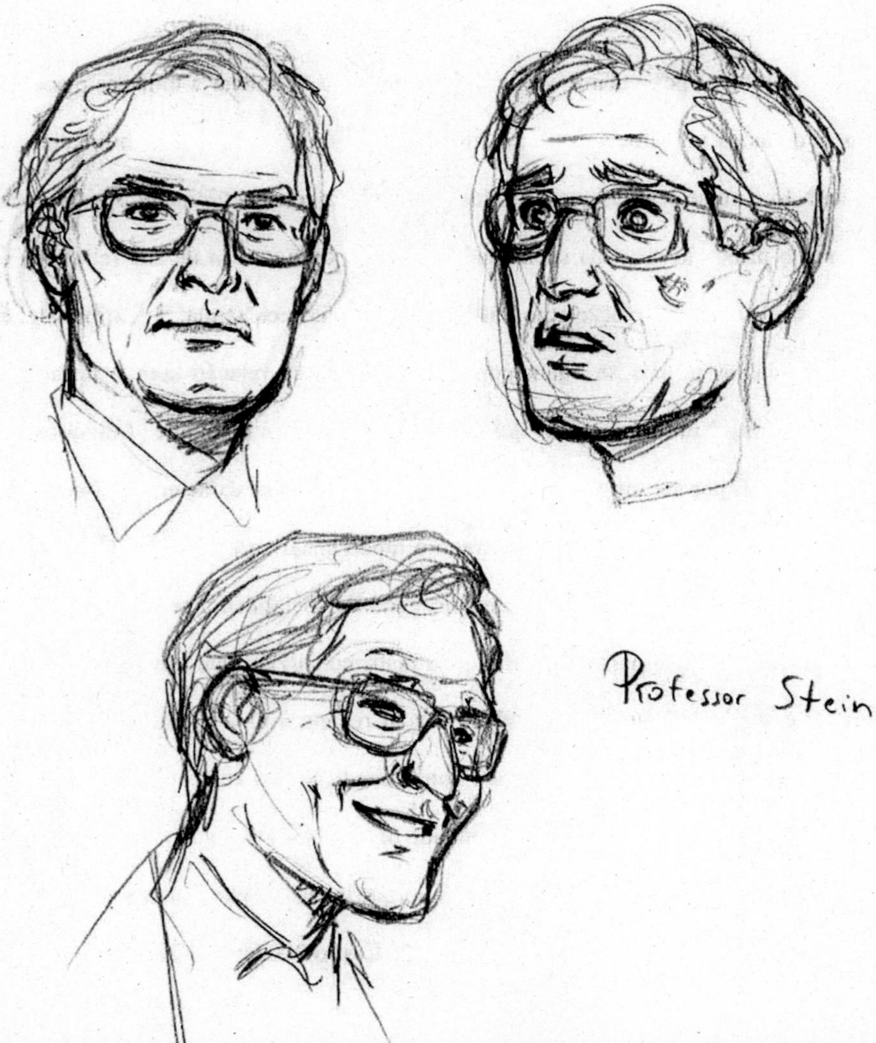
Professor Stein

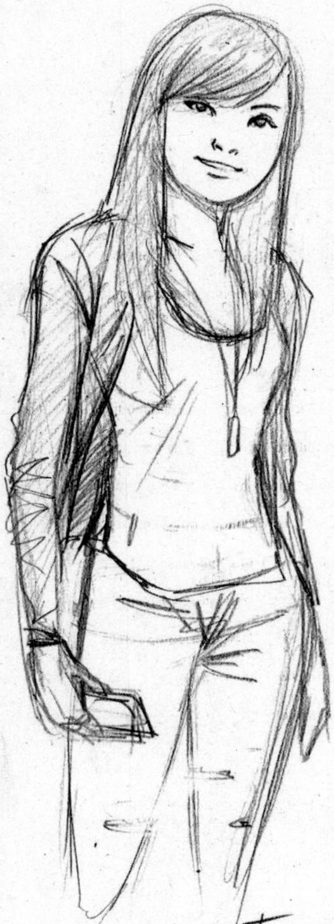

TONYA LU

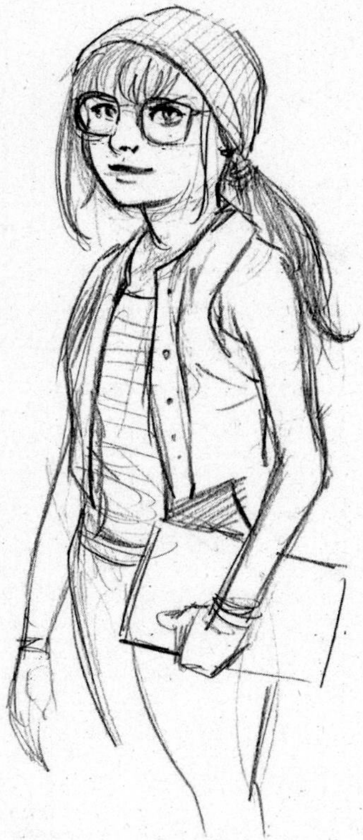

MONICA LITTMAN

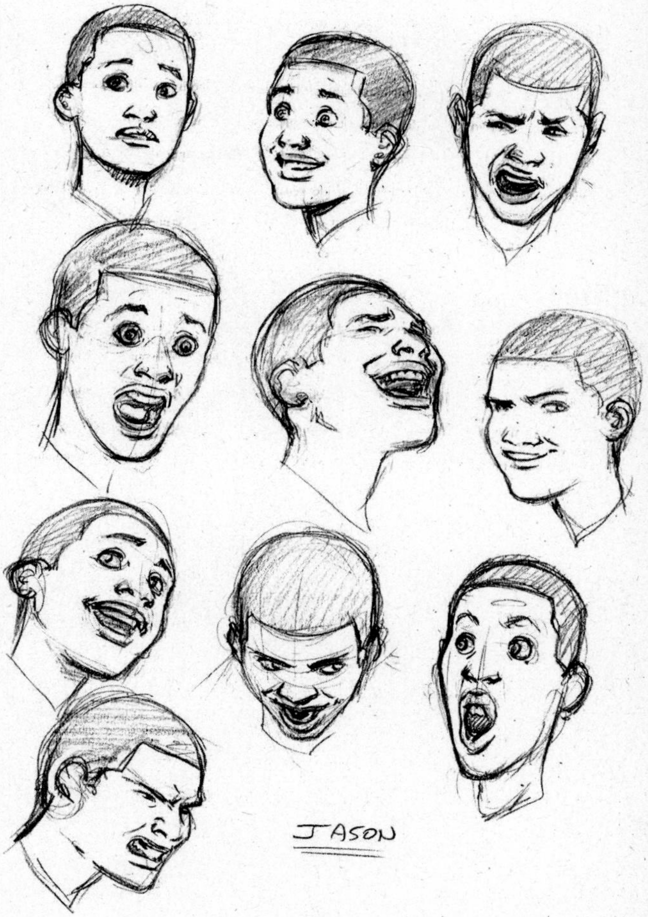

JASON

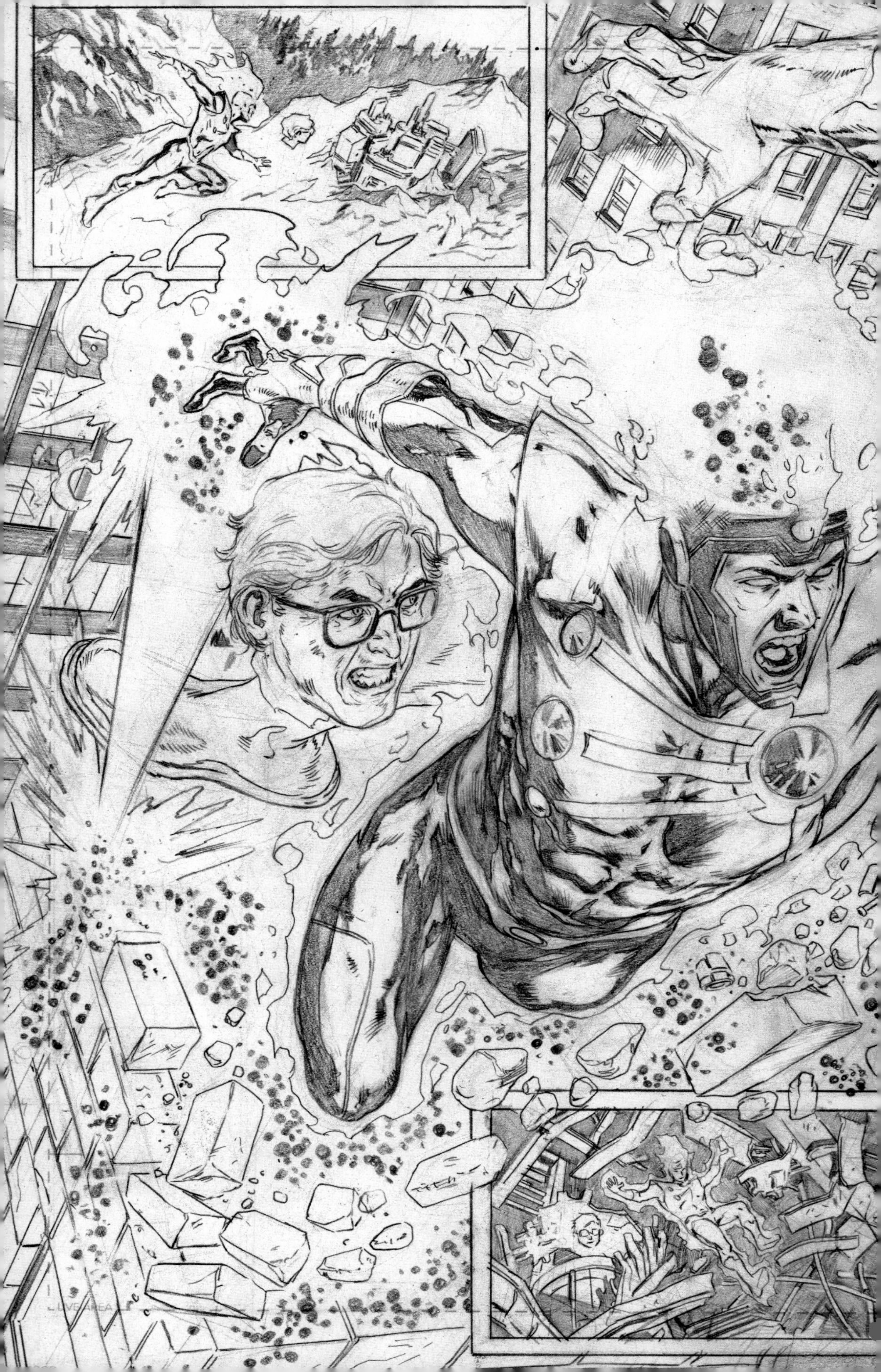

LEGENDS OF TOMORROW #3, pages 14-15   Pencils by Eduardo Pansica

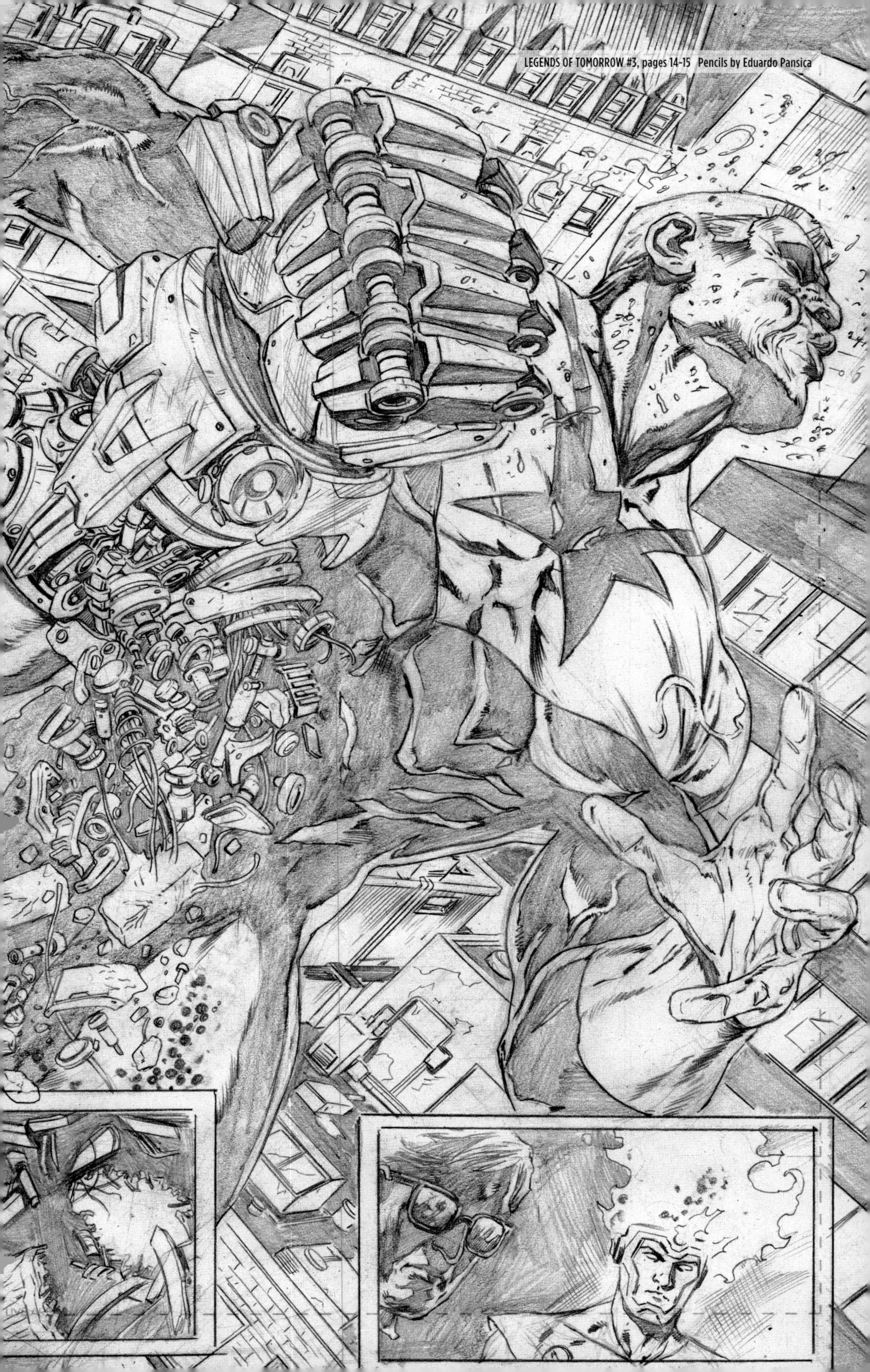

"Thrilling and shocking in equal measure."
—IGN

"Geoff Johns is a master storyteller."
—NEWSARAMA

"High energy adventure, huge stakes, great characters, a dastardly foe, and great creative talent."
—COMIC BOOK RESOURCES

FROM THE WRITER OF *JUSTICE LEAGUE* & *AQUAMAN*
GEOFF JOHNS
with IVAN REIS

BLACKEST NIGHT:
GREEN LANTERN

BLACKEST NIGHT:
GREEN LANTERN CORPS

READ THE ENTIRE
EPIC!

BLACKEST NIGHT

BLACKEST NIGHT:
GREEN LANTERN

BLACKEST NIGHT:
GREEN LANTERN
CORPS

BLACKEST NIGHT:
BLACK LANTERN
CORPS VOL. 1

BLACKEST NIGHT:
BLACK LANTERN
CORPS VOL. 2

BLACKEST NIGHT:
RISE OF THE BLACK
LANTERNS

BLACKEST NIGHT:
TALES OF THE CORPS

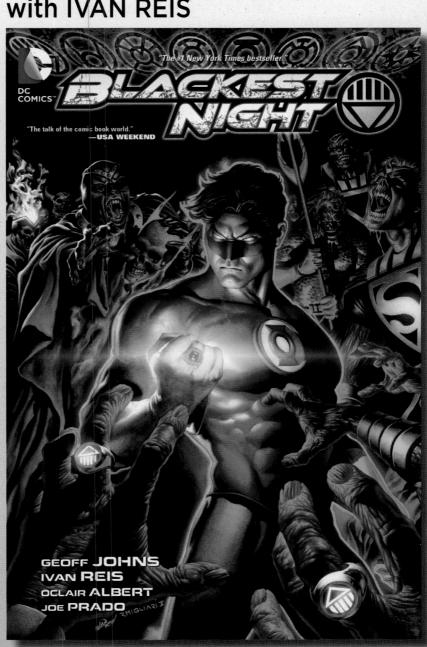

"The #1 New York Times bestseller."

DC COMICS™

BLACKEST NIGHT

"The talk of the comic book world."
—USA WEEKEND

GEOFF JOHNS
IVAN REIS
OCLAIR ALBERT
JOE PRADO

DC COMICS™

READ THE FOLLOW-UP TO THE *NEW YORK*
TIMES #1 BEST-SELLING BLACKEST NIGHT

BRIGHTEST DAY

GEOFF JOHNS and PETER J. TOMASI

BRIGHTEST DAY
VOL. 2

BRIGHTEST DAY
VOL. 3

GREEN LANTERN:
BRIGHTEST DAY

GEOFF JOHNS
PETER J. TOMASI
IVAN REIS
PATRICK GLEASON   **FERNANDO PASARIN**
ARDIAN SYAF   **SCOTT CLARK**   **JOE PRADO**

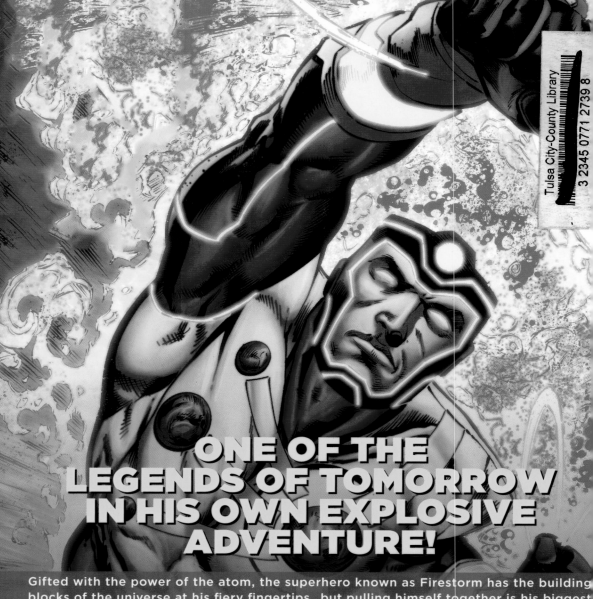

ONE OF THE LEGENDS OF TOMORROW IN HIS OWN EXPLOSIVE ADVENTURE!

Gifted with the power of the atom, the superhero known as Firestorm has the building blocks of the universe at his fiery fingertips...but pulling himself together is his biggest challenge of all.

Because Firestorm is not just one hero—he's a matrix of minds, including those of students Ronnie Raymond and Jason Rausch and the brilliant Professor Stein. Fused together, the fury of Firestorm is a force to be reckoned with. But broken apart, it's a ticking time bomb...and everyone from Firestorm's worst adversaries to the U.S. government wants to have their fingers on the button.

Now Jason, Ronnie and Professor Stein are locked in a race against time—and fearsome foes like Danton Black and Major Force—to preserve the Firestorm Protocol before it falls apart. Can they outrace their enemies and harness the power, or will the fire consume them one by one?

Find out in **FIRESTORM: THE NUCLEAR MAN**, a red-hot action-adventure saga from comics legend and co-creator **GERRY CONWAY** and artist **EDUARDO PANSICA**! Collects **FIRESTORM: THE NUCLEAR MAN** stories from LEGENDS OF TOMORROW #1-6.

$14.99 USA $19.99 CAN ISBN: 978-1-4012-6578-6

dccomics.com

51499 >

9 781401 265786